THE GRAND EXPEDITION

The Bust of the Son of the Immortal Chatham deservedly crowned with Laurels.

French Monkies in attitudes of derision.

Dutch Frogs smoking their pipes in safety.

John Bull, somewhat gloomy but for what it is difficult to guess after so glorious an achievement.

A British Seaman in the Dumps

The Immortal William Pitt, Earl of Chatham obscured in Clouds

THE MOTTO.
Great Chatham with One hundred thousand Men,
To Flushing saild — and then saild back again!!

GLORY

A FLYING VIEW, OF THE RETURN OF THE EXPEDITION.

O TEMPORA! O MORES!!

A DESIGN FOR A MONUMENT.
TO BE ERECTED
IN COMMEMORATION OF THE
GLORIOUS AND NEVER TO BE FORGOTTEN GRAND EXPIDITION.
So ABLY PLANND AND EXECUTED IN THE YEAR 1809.

London Pub.d Sept.r 14 1809 by Tho.s Tegg N.o 111 Cheapside

Price One Shilling Coloured

11. Sep. 1809

The Grand Expedition

THE BRITISH INVASION OF HOLLAND
IN 1809

Gordon C. Bond

THE UNIVERSITY OF GEORGIA PRESS
Athens

Copyright © 1979 by the University of Georgia Press
Athens, Georgia 30602

Set in 11 on 14 point Caledonia type
Printed in the United States of America

Library of Congress Cataloging in Publication Data

Bond, Gordon C
   The grand expedition.
   Bibliography.
   Includes index.
   1. Walcheren Expedition, 1809.   I. Title.
DC234.87.B66   949.2'05   78-2707
            ISBN 0-8203-0448-4

TO STEPHANIE, MICHAEL, AND ANNIE

Lord Chatham with his sword undrawn,
Kept waiting for Sir Richard Strachan;
Sir Richard, eager to be at 'em,
Kept waiting too—for whom? Lord Chatham!

Morning Chronicle (London)
26 February 1810

Contents

Maps

Preface

The work presented here is the result of an investigation conducted over many years into the British expedition to the Scheldt in 1809. My purpose has been to present for the first time a thorough examination of the reasons behind this British effort, a documented account of the campaign, and an analysis of the factors responsible for its dismal failure. Designed to form a diversion for the Austrian forces battling Napoleon in Germany, the expedition also hoped to destroy the growing menace of the French naval establishments in the Scheldt River. Not only did the expedition fail in its principal objectives, but it produced serious repercussions for Great Britain both at home and on the Continent.

It would have been impossible to complete this study without the assistance and cooperation of the staff at the National Maritime Museum, Greenwich, the Institute of Historical Research of the University of London, the National Army Museum and the British Museum, London, and the Public Record Office. I am also indebted to the Public Record Office for permission to reproduce one of the maps found in the *Chatham Papers*. In Paris I would like to acknowledge my thanks to the staff of the Service Historique de l'Armée, Vincennes, for their assistance during my research there. Financial support for much of my research has been provided by Auburn University through its Research Grant-in-Aid program. To the friendly and helpful staff of the Ralph Brown Draughon Library of Auburn University I also owe a debt of thanks.

I have benefited from the advice of friends and colleagues in preparing this work. It is with pleasure that I thank Professor Donald D. Horward, under whose guidance this research was begun; my colleagues Robert R. Rea and Robin F. A. Fabel, who read the manuscript and provided editorial advice; Donald G. Jeane of the Auburn University Geography Department, for the preparation of the maps; Mrs. Linda White, for typing the final manuscript; and Carol McDonald Fisher, for her thorough reading and conscientious editorial assistance in preparing the manuscript for publication. Finally, I am grateful to my wife, Stephanie, for her support in seeing this work to completion.

1

The Cocked Pistol

On a sunny Friday afternoon, 21 July 1809, Robert Barlow, the commissioner of the British navy, along with several members of cabinet, boarded a yacht in London and sailed down the Thames River. Their destination was the anchorage off the southeast coast of England known as the Downs. On their arrival the following morning they beheld a sight few had ever seen before. As far as the eye could see there were sails. Literally hundreds of ships of every description were rendezvousing in the Downs. Their total number exceeded six hundred, including some 266 warships—ships of the line, frigates, sloops, brigs—and transports of different types and sizes, all preparing to sail on the most extensive amphibious operation Britain had ever attempted.[1] The origins of this "Grand Expedition," as it was referred to in the contemporary British press, are to be found in preceding events at sea, in Spain, in Austria, and in the Netherlands.

In October 1805 Napoleon's dreams of invading Great Britain were dashed near the Cape of Trafalgar when Adm. Horatio Nelson destroyed the combined Spanish-French fleet. During the following two years the French emperor conquered Austria (1805), Prussia (1806), and Russia (1807) and made himself the virtual master of Europe. Only Britain remained outside his control, and until such time as the French navy were again large enough to challenge the British fleet on the sea, an invasion of the British Isles was impossible. Consequently, Napoleon was forced to devise a new tactic to deal with his perpetual enemy: the Continental System. Developed during 1806/1807, this policy called for economic warfare against the "nation of shopkeepers," whereby France, either through the cooperation of friends or by the use of force against enemies, would close the entire European continent to British trade and commerce. By weakening Britain's economy, Napoleon would destroy her ability to wage war, and also make it impossible for Great Britain to provide the huge subsidies to Continental allies, which had characterized all the previous coalitions against France.[2]

It was one thing to develop a policy and quite another to enforce it, as Napoleon soon realized. In fact, it can be argued that it was the continuing attempts to enforce this Continental System which eventually led to Napoleon's downfall. To be effective, it was necessary to apply the Continental System to the entire European continent, for without a total embargo the policy was doomed to failure. Attempting to enforce his policy eventually caused Napoleon problems throughout Europe. One of the most troublesome areas was the Iberian peninsula.

Napoleon's attempts to enforce the Continental System in the Iberian peninsula soon entangled him so thoroughly in the affairs of Portugal and Spain that he could never successfully extricate himself. Portugal had maintained its traditionally good relations with Great Britain, and in 1807, in spite of the demands of the French emperor to join the Continental System, continued to trade with the British. Spain, on the other hand, had ended hostilities with Revolutionary France in 1795 and soon after formed an alliance with its former enemy across the Pyrenees. The befuddled and occasionally insane Bourbon king of Spain, Charles IV, seldom exercised direct control over the affairs of his country. The real power in Spain rested in the hands of Manuel de Godoy, who had parlayed his close association with his queen, Maria Luisa, into political power. It was Godoy who was responsible for Spain's continuing support of Napoleon's policies. In 1806, however, anticipating Napoleon's defeat at the hands of Russia and Prussia, Godoy began to move Spain out of the French camp.[3] Napoleon's victories at Jena and Auerstädt quickly brought the Spanish back into line, but Godoy's perfidy did not escape the emperor's notice. Once the Treaty of Tilsit had settled matters in eastern Europe, Napoleon turned his attention to Iberia.

Both Spain and Portugal were badly ruled and economically, politically, and socially very backward by Napoleon's standards. Neither had governments capable of effectively enforcing the Continental System, even if they had been inclined to try. Napoleon needed no excuse to seize the recalcitrant Portugal, long a friend of Britain. As for Spain, Godoy could no longer be trusted, and besides, the Spanish people would be well rid of their weak and corrupt Bourbon ruler. In October 1807 Napoleon negotiated the Treaty of Fontainebleau with Godoy, whereby, in return for a kingdom in southern Portugal, the Spanish leader would allow passage of some twenty-eight thousand troops through Spain for the conquest of Portugal.[4] By the time the treaty was officially ratified, Gen. Jean-Andoche Junot had led his French army into Portugal and had captured Lisbon on November 29. The ruling Braganza family escaped the country aboard a British ship.[5] Soon additional troops were filtering into Spain and by March 1808 Marshal Joachim Murat, Napoleon's brother-in-law, had been designated "Lieutenant of the Emperor in Spain," and placed at the head of one hundred thousand French soldiers now in Spain. The occupation of Portugal and the increased presence of French forces soon caused widespread Spanish unrest in the spring of 1808 which played into the hands of Charles IV's scheming son, who deposed his father and proclaimed himself ruler of Spain as Ferdinand VII. Napoleon was not entirely displeased with this political development and the resulting confusion in Madrid. He directed Murat to "invite" the ruling Bourbon family to Bayonne, in southern France, for consultation with the French emperor. There on May 10 Napoleon forced both father and son to renounce their throne and, along with Godoy, to accept exile in France. The former rulers of Spain watched helplessly as Napoleon appointed his oldest brother, Joseph Bonaparte, king of Spain.[6]

Meanwhile, the Spanish people, kept in the dark concerning the fate of their government, rose in revolt on May 2 against Murat's occupation of Madrid. The French marshal quickly crushed the uprising following some bloody street fighting and executed numerous rebel leaders. However, the inspiration of the *Dos de Mayo*, later immortalized in the paintings of Goya, spread rapidly throughout the countryside and soon most of Spain was in open revolt against French rule.[7] By June 1808 Spanish army units were joining local militia in guerrilla activity against the French army of occupation and after minor successes astounded Europe with a remarkable achievement. On July 19 in southern Spain, Gen. Don Francisco Castaños surrounded and defeated Gen. Pierre Dupont de l'Etang's twenty-thousand-man corps at Baylen and forced their surrender. This shattering blow to French prestige caused reverberations throughout Europe and gave renewed hope to the growing resistance in both Spain and Portugal. By the end of the month, King Joseph had evacuated Madrid and withdrawn his French forces to northern Spain. Meanwhile, rebel juntas were springing up throughout Spain and, bolstered by British arms and money, organized opposition to French rule continued to grow.[8]

Resistance to Napoleon's domination was also developing in Portugal. Spanish military forces had occupied the northern and southern portions of the country when Junot invaded in late 1807. However, by the summer of 1808, as Spain's resistance to French rule increased, the Spanish forces in Portugal retired. The vacuum created was quickly filled by rebel Portuguese bands who refused to accept the French occupation. In Oporto, north of Lisbon, the junta appealed to London for assistance. Seizing this opportunity, the cabinet immediately dispatched a force of fifteen thousand men under the command of Sir Arthur Wellesley (the future duke of Wellington) to the Peninsula. Landing at the mouth of the Mondego River, Wellesley moved south toward Lisbon and on August 21 defeated Junot's forces at the Battle of Vimiero. The controversial Convention of Cintra, signed a few days later, freed Portugal from French rule by providing for the evacuation of Junot's troops by British ships to France.[9] Britain had now secured a friendly base of operations on the Continent.

Realizing that matters were getting out of hand in the Peninsula, Napoleon decided to go to Spain himself late in 1808 and restore order. The emperor planned to quickly smash Spanish and Portuguese opposition with over three hundred thousand of his imperial soldiers. On November 10 Napoleon was on the move from Vitoria toward Madrid and by December 4 had retaken the capital. Spanish resistance was quickly being broken. Meanwhile, Sir John Moore, the new British commander in Portugal, had been instructed by London to invade Spain and join forces with the Spanish armies operating in the northern part of the country. However, by the time Moore reached Salamanca in late November, the Spanish forces in northern Spain had been routed, and the best the British general could hope for was to form a diversion to prevent Napoleon's immediate conquest of southern Spain. Just as Moore had expected, the emperor, on learning of the British movement into Spain, set out to crush the invader. Due to Spanish fumbling and incompetence, Moore's position in northern Spain quickly became untenable. There followed one of the most famous retreats in military history. Marching through rugged mountainous terrain in the dead of winter, his soldiers suffering terrible deprivations, Moore was able to win the race to Corunna in northern Spain where his forces were to be evacuated by British transports. At Corunna, Moore was forced to fight a battle on 16 January 1809 to protect the embarkation of his army. The conflict resulted in the general's death, but most of his exhausted and battered troops escaped by sea.[10] Napoleon was not at Corunna. Realizing that it would be impossible to catch the fleeing British and concerned over rumors of an Austrian mobilization and a conspiracy against him in Paris, he turned the pursuit over to Marshal Nicolas Soult and quickly returned to France.[11] Soult, after suffering heavy casualties during the rapid pursuit and at the Battle of Corunna, turned to the south to occupy Oporto.

The fighting in the Peninsula in 1808 and early 1809 had resulted in the first serious defeats for Napoleon's armies. French prestige was severely damaged; rebel forces in Spain and Portugal took heart; and elsewhere in Europe, those who longed for Napoleon's downfall began to reevaluate their position. Such was the case in Austria.

Since its crushing defeat at Austerlitz in 1805, the Hapsburg Empire had gradually begun to show signs of revival. Under the capable leadership of Count Philippe de Stadion and the archduke Charles, numerous administrative and military reforms had been introduced, many of these copied after the French model.[12] The Austrian infantry and cavalry were reorganized along French lines, a revised drillbook was provided for improved tactics, and the artillery branch was increased in ordnance and in the number of gunners. In addition, Stadion had determined to transform the Austrian army into a truly national as opposed to a purely professional fighting force. Regiments of volunteers were organized in Vienna and other large cities of the Austrian German provinces; patriotic literature was circulated and parades and festivals were encouraged to arouse maximum enthusiasm.

By late 1808 a "war party" had developed in Vienna, spurred on by developments in the Iberian peninsula. Led by the emperor Francis I's wife, Ludovica, and supported by Stadion and Prince von Metternich, the Austrian ambassador to France, the group soon had the ear of the Hapsburg emperor. In his memorandum of 4 December 1808 to Francis I, Metternich estimated that because of the "bleeding sore" in Spain, Napoleon would have fewer than two hundred thousand men at his disposal should hostilities break out in central Europe.[13] At the same time Stadion argued that action should be taken immediately because the financial drain on Austria's resources occasioned by full mobilization would only allow the army to be maintained at its full complement until the spring. British subsidies might be forthcoming, but only once actual warfare had erupted. All these factors weighed heavily in the discussions in Vienna during the early months of 1809. Finally, in April, Francis I gained secret assurances from Czar Alexander I of Russian neutrality in the event of a Franco-Austrian war (April 15), while in London a general treaty alliance with Great Britain was being concluded (April 24).[14] Meanwhile, anticipating the results of the Russian and British negotiations, the archduke Charles commenced hostilities without a declaration of war when he led his Austrian army against surprised French forces in southern Germany.

Following some initial Austrian successes, French military superiority became evident as Napoleon's Grand Army swept into southern Germany and occupied Vienna in May. Austria, meanwhile, turned to her ally and requested not only subsidies for her armies but also British military operations on the Continent in order to divert French troops which might be used to reinforce Napoleon's army on the Danube. Vienna suggested three theaters of operations as being particularly significant to the overall war effort. The first would be an English landing in southern Italy designed to cooperate with the archduke John and his Austrian army moving from the north. Second, the British operations in the Iberian peninsula should be expanded as extensively as possible. Finally, Austria urged that an expedition be dispatched to northern Germany to take advantage of the growing anti-French sentiment there and to support the various insurgent bands.[15] Such action might even persuade the pusillanimous Frederick William III of Prussia to join the coalition and free Germany from French dominance.

In May Prince Louis Starhemberg, the Austrian minister to Great Britain throughout most of the Napoleonic period, arrived in London to press further these points. Meeting with George Canning, the British secretary of state for foreign affairs, he stressed the importance of a diversionary attack in northern Germany and urged immediate action.[16]

The British government had already decided to act, in part at least, upon these proposals. In April Sir Arthur Wellesley had returned to Portugal at the head of a British army. During the last week of June another British force commanded by Gen. Sir John Stuart seized several islands in the Bay of Naples, ultimately intending to land on the Italian mainland and join forces with the archduke John.[17] Neither of these operations afforded the Hapsburg army confronting Napoleon the desired diversion, however. Starhemberg's government believed this could be best achieved by sending an expedition to northern Germany. Establishing such a theater of operations raised several questions for Canning and his fellow cabinet members. Starhemberg argued that a British landing in the Elbe or Weser rivers might incite a general outbreak against the French in Germany. While Canning conceded that an expedition to northern Germany might produce a significant diversion for Austria, success necessarily depended on popular support; and little had been demonstrated recently for either Frederick von Schill or the duke of Brunswick.[18] Could the British expect more? There were other important considerations also. The problems of logistics for such an operation, especially the difficulties involved in effecting a retreat if the expedition failed, weighed heavily. However, the overriding factor was the question of money. Napoleon's Continental System was hurting the British economy. Also, the cabinet had pumped money and arms valued at more than £2.5 million into the Peninsula during the last half of 1808 and was now hard pressed to finance Wellesley's operation in Portugal.[19] Consequently, there simply was not enough specie available to cover the cost of another regular campaign on the Continent or even to support sizable reinforcements to the Peninsula.[20] After carefully considering these factors, the cabinet abandoned the proposed German expedition.

Another scheme, long considered by various British governments, was now thrust into prominent consideration. The admiralty, entrusted with the defense of the homeland from invasion, advocated a plan for attacking the French shipping, arsenals, and dockyards in the Scheldt River across the North Sea in the Netherlands. In 1797 the merits of seizing the Scheldt estuary and the island of Walcheren had been outlined to William Pitt, then prime minister, in the following manner.

The island of Walcheren, in Zealand, recommends itself for the destination of a conjunct expedition. . . . The situation of this island, with regard to the mouths of the Scheldt, is such that, in the event of obtaining it, we could completely command the navigation of that river, and render the possession of the other Zealand islands, and the countries bordering on them of no value, because we could control the former Dutch and Austrian Netherlands. Flushing, situated on the southern extremity of the island, is the best naval port on the north coast of the Netherlands, and the place from which attempts to attack Britain could be best made.[21]

Pitt's government eventually shelved the proposed attack and it was not seriously considered again until April 1807, when Robert Stewart, Viscount Castlereagh, joined the British cabinet as the secretary of state for war and colonies. Cognizant of the growing danger of the Scheldt's naval complex and of the importance of destroying these ships and facilities before their defenses became impregnable, Castlereagh proposed an immediate military expedition to the Scheldt.[22] However, Napoleon's victory at Friedland (June 1807) and the subsequent Treaty of Tilsit (July 1807) cancelled the British secretary's immediate designs. During the next two years Castlereagh drafted numerous proposals for a Scheldt expedition.[23] But other military demands and the general situation on the Continent prevented their execution.

By 1809 the Scheldt had become the second largest naval arsenal of France (after Toulon) and was often referred to by Napoleon as "a cocked pistol pointed at the head of England." The admiralty considered it such a threat that it maintained two British squadrons off the coast of the Netherlands at all times to meet a surprise attack and to prevent newly built French ships from escaping to other ports. Here Napoleon was rebuilding his navy and perhaps would one day launch his effort to invade the British Isles.[24] A French invasion force sailing from this stronghold could land in the Thames in less than twenty-four hours. The Scheldt possessed fine harbors for accumulating such a force and good shelter from ocean winds. As many as ninety sail of the line could be housed at one time in the ports of Flushing, near the entrance of the West Scheldt, and farther up the winding river at

Terneuse and at the medieval commercial city of Antwerp. The Scheldt was fed by an extensive river system and an intricate maze of canals which facilitated the transport of naval supplies from all areas of Europe, especially from the Black Forest via the Rhine and its tributaries.[25]

For many years the Scheldt had formed part of the boundary between the Austrian Netherlands (Belgium) and the United Provinces (Holland). When the French revolutionary wars broke out in 1792, Belgium quickly became a battleground and was overrun and annexed to France in early 1793. By 1795 Holland had become a French satellite labeled the Batavian Republic. In order to bring the latter more fully under French control, Napoleon had revised the Dutch constitution in 1806 and had transformed the republic into the Kingdom of Holland under his brother, Louis Bonaparte. To be sure, Napoleon probably never envisioned the Dutch kingdom as a permanent creation. Its establishment was a temporary measure, a situation to be tolerated until it was more feasible to incorporate it into the French empire.[26] In the meanwhile, Holland, though nominally independent, was expected to serve Napoleon's interests. Perhaps Louis never fully understood this, or, more likely, he was incapable of administering the necessary policies, especially the execution of the terms of the Continental System. Regardless, his brief reign witnessed numerous clashes between the two Bonaparte brothers which led not only to Louis's eventual abdication, but to his permanent break with Napoleon.[27]

Louis was a sincere and kindhearted individual who, during his brief reign, succeeded in winning the affections of his Dutch subjects. Indeed, no king ever tried harder to please his people nor loved his subjects more, and as a result he fell completely under Dutch influence. And herein lay the seeds of his demise. Napoleon had expected Louis to be a pliable agent readily accepting and executing directives from Paris; but the king of Holland had ideas of his own.[28] As a result, relations between Louis and Napoleon were continually strained. In November 1807 the emperor, unhappy with Louis's weak coastal defenses, annexed the port and environs of Flushing, on the island of Walcheren, to France; this gave him direct control over the growing naval establishment in the Scheldt River.[29] Napoleon's emphasis on the Continental System and Louis's failure to enforce it; Holland's resistance to implementing the Napoleonic codes; Louis's refusal to either cancel the public debt or lower the interest rate in order to make his government solvent; his inability to raise the requisite number of troops for the Grand Army or Holland's defense; and his refusal to introduce conscription, all combined by 1809 to strain severely relations between Louis and his brother.[30]

The situation in Holland and especially the kingdom's weak coastal defenses were well known to the British authorities. The admiralty kept especially close surveillance of the activities in and around the Scheldt, relying upon spies and naval vessels patrolling off the coast of Flanders and Holland. Intelligence reports received in early 1809 indicated that British apprehension was justified. The French naval strength in the Scheldt was rapidly increasing. Capt. James Boxer, in the cutter *Idas*, reconnoitered Flushing on January 2 and reported sighting seven ships of the line in port. Other reports described in detail the port facilities of Flushing and suggested that the entire island of Walcheren might be taken without great difficulty.[31] Further intelligence indicated that there were nine ships of war on the stocks at Antwerp and three at Flushing under construction. The building of these ships followed a prescribed system. The large sail of the line were constructed on the slips and docks of Antwerp and then sailed down river to Flushing to be outfitted with gun carriages and other necessary equipment. However, the shallow entrance to the Flushing basin made it necessary to mount the guns outside the port.[32] In view of this, when the admiralty learned in March 1809 that ten unarmed French sail of the line had entered Flushing, the prospect of destroying the ships and the Scheldt's facilities influenced the war minister, Castlereagh, to urge an immediate attack.

On March 24 Sir David Dundas, newly appointed commander

in chief of the army, was called to a cabinet meeting at Burlington House and asked to supply fifteen thousand men for an immediate attack upon the French positions in the Scheldt. Dundas advised that such a force could not be raised at that time because of the decimated state of the army which had only recently returned from Corunna. Many of the troops were ill, all were poorly clothed and equipped, and considerable time would be required to prepare them for further duty.[33] Although immediate action was impossible, Castlereagh began to lay the groundwork for an expedition to the Scheldt.

Consequently, by the time Prince Starhemberg arrived in London in May to press for a British landing in northern Germany, the cabinet had not only discarded plans for the German venture, but it was practically committed to Castlereagh's plan to attack the French naval complex in the Scheldt.[34] The situation on the Continent now seemed propitious to destroy this threat to British security as well as to form a significant diversion for the Austrian forces confronting Napoleon on the Danube. Intelligence reports continued to confirm rumors that Antwerp, and in fact the entire northern coast of France and Holland, had been stripped of troops in order to reinforce Napoleon's army in Austria.[35] Moreover, only enough specie was available for a limited campaign. An attack upon the Scheldt naval center would serve as a diversion for Austria by threatening an area which was near the French capital and of vital importance to Napoleon. Forces destined for Austrian service might be diverted to meet the British challenge. The expedition would also fulfill a purely selfish purpose for Great Britain by eliminating this menace to their shipping and security. With these objectives in mind, preparations were soon underway.

Such were the circumstances and converging events which made it possible for Robert Barlow to view the British armada poised to sail from the Downs in July 1809.

2

Castlereagh's Expedition

On May 8 Castlereagh wrote Sir David Dundas, commander in chief of the army, asking for information concerning the state of the army and the earliest date the troops would be fit for service. Two weeks later he was soliciting plans for organizing two corps: the main body composed of 25,000 infantry and 5,000 cavalry; the other, a reserve of 10,000 infantry and 2,000 cavalry.[1] Dundas responded the following day with a proposal providing for the initial corps but reported that not enough soldiers were yet available to compose the reserve Castlereagh had requested. However, the troops were recuperating quickly from their service in Spain and were being reinforced by men added to the regular army as a result of the latest militia act.[2] Consequently, by June 18, when Castlereagh requested that 35,000 infantry and 1,800 cavalry be prepared for immediate embarkation, Dundas had the necessary troops available.

During the last week of May, Castlereagh solicited information from some of the leading military figures in the country who had been with the British army in Holland in 1793/94. He requested their opinions on the best means of implementing an attack on the French navy and naval complex in the Scheldt and the feasibility of such an operation. Lt. Col. J. H. Gordon, secretary to the commander in chief of the army, submitted his statement on May 31 in which he outlined two possible avenues of attack. The first involved an amphibious operation whereby the army would be landed on the coast and would protect the navy's ascent of the Scheldt to a joint attack on Antwerp. His second proposal called for a primarily maritime operation with troops being landed on the banks of the Scheldt only when needed to facilitate the attack on Antwerp. If the first plan were adopted, Gordon suggested that the army could be landed in the vicinity of Ostend or Blankenburg. In order for this plan to be successful, both of these cities would have to be captured immediately before moving inland. Delay here would spell disaster for the expedition, for Antwerp was an additional sixty miles inland by the most direct route. The army's march would be a difficult one through a marshy countryside intersected by ditches and canals and spotted with numerous fortified villages. Even overcoming these obstacles, the troops would arrive on the left bank of the Scheldt river opposite Antwerp and would likely experience great difficulty in crossing. The only alternate course from the coast to Antwerp overland was a circuitous route, equally hazardous, of some one hundred miles. Gordon therefore recommended adopting his second proposal. Troops could be landed on Walcheren and South Beveland or Cadsand in the Scheldt estuary to provide cover for the fleet's advance upriver to Sandvliet. Here the main military force could disembark and march on Antwerp (some twenty miles away) "at the same time that a corps endeavored to take possession of the fort and batteries upon the river, and that the boats of the fleet, well manned, armed and towing launches with troops, proceeded with the tide direct to the city."[3]

This is the basic plan, with minor alterations, which was eventually adopted. Gordon cautioned in closing, however, that this would be a very "desperate enterprise" and one which would expose the entire army and navy to great risk.

Other opinions were solicited from three prominent officers at the Horse Guards. Gen. Sir John Alexander Hope, who had served as second in command to Moore in the Peninsula, was currently deputy quartermaster general. In basic agreement with Gordon, Hope recommended that Walcheren and South Beveland be taken simultaneously, thereby ensuring control of both branches of the Scheldt. Then, "it might be investigated how far it was practicable to take advantage of a flowing tide, and, by an embarkation from the point of South Beveland highest up the river, to attempt Antwerp by a coup de main. . . ."[4] The overall operation would be one of great risk, Hope observed, but if attempted soon after the occupation of Walcheren and South Beveland, it had a "fair chance of success."

If an approach to Antwerp via the West Scheldt were not feasible, Hope suggested the possibility of proceeding up the East Scheldt, landing between Bergen-op-Zoom and Sandvliet, and marching the twenty-odd miles to Antwerp. Even if all the objectives were not achieved, the capture of the arsenal at Flushing and occupation of the island of Walcheren would offset to some degree failure to take Antwerp. In concluding his report, Hope observed that this campaign would not only serve as a significant diversion for Austria, but also would end the threat to English security and perhaps ultimately lead to an even larger operation on the Continent.

The opinions of Lt. Gen. Robert Brownrigg, quartermaster general of the army, and the adjutant general, Maj. Gen. Harry Calvert, were similar to the preceding reports.[5] Both agreed that the expedition should proceed up the West Scheldt to attack Antwerp after having first gained possession of Walcheren and South Beveland. The two officers were also quick to point out the dangers involved. Calvert cautioned that the attack would have to be conducted with celerity to be successful.

From the moment our fleet and army appeared off Walcheren, the enemy must necessarily be apprised of the object of the enterprise . . . and he would be at liberty to concentrate all his means of defense, which would be facilitated by the canals of the country and the general course of the rivers. . . . He would not hesitate immediately to draw all his troops from the fortresses in Holland, the Netherlands, and French Flanders, and from more remote quarters, if he had sufficient time for the purpose.[6]

Finally, Sir David Dundas presented Castlereagh his opinion of the projected expedition. Dundas had been in command at Antwerp for a short time in 1794 and was acquainted with the problems the expedition might encounter. Dundas shared Castlereagh's concern over the growing naval establishment in the

Scheldt and realized the importance of destroying it. His proposals paralleled those submitted by his fellow officers, concluding that "in what ever way Antwerp is to be approached or taken, the service is one of very great risk, and in which the safe return of the Army so employed may be very precarious."[7]

Seemingly, these pessimistic opinions by the military, the most optimistic of which gave the expedition only a "fair prospect of success," should have raised serious doubts in Castlereagh's mind about the propriety of dispatching the expedition to the Scheldt. However, two factors combined to negate the impact of these reports. First, during the first week of June, the cabinet learned of the Austrian victory over Napoleon at the Battle of Aspern-Essling (May 21–22). This exciting news persuaded Castlereagh and his colleagues to take prompt action to aid their ally. In fact, as Castlereagh later stated, it "had a preponderating influence with His Majesty's Government in the consideration of that question."[8] The Scheldt expedition, already under consideration, was immediately at hand.

Second, Castlereagh had been receiving for several months favorable intelligence from the Continent which Gordon and the other military men did not possess. On March 15, for example, Castlereagh had learned that most of the French troops garrisoning the islands of Zealand, the Dutch province through which the Scheldt debouched into the North Sea, had been ordered to join the Grand Army immediately. Three weeks later the admiralty acquired through a secret agent a sketch of Flushing indicating the layout of its basin and docks. Later in April Capt. John Martin Hanchett, reconnoitering the Scheldt estuary in His Majesty's sloop *Raven*, reported that he had access to detailed information concerning the fortifications and number of troops stationed in Walcheren. Hanchett urged an attack on Flushing, suggesting that "a line of battleships may run alongside the walls of the town so close that men may land from the yard arm; and I volunteer to be the first man that lands from them."[9]

Additional intelligence in May further emphasized the weakened defenses in the Scheldt area. On May 8 a report placed the number of troops at Flushing at just four battalions, composed for the most part of Germans, Dutch, Spanish, and Irish. It was learned that Gen. Louis-Claude Monnet de Lorbeau, the French commandant of Flushing, was dangerously ill and subject to replacement.[10] Further reports declared the disposition of the population to be strongly pro-English. Rumors of the impending expedition were circulating on the Continent and the inhabitants of the Scheldt reportedly lived in constant fear of an English attack. Dissension also existed between the French and Dutch forces, and as a result a large number of Dutch ships used in the naval service in the Scheldt had withdrawn from the flotilla and had returned to other parts of Holland. The French attempted to replace these with some forty ships belonging to English and Dutch smugglers anchored at the town of Ter Veere on the island of Walcheren. Here they established a naval arsenal, fortified the town, and placed an embargo on all shipping in hopes of recruiting men and ships to serve in their flotilla.[11]

Finally, Castlereagh received news that a French courier had arrived at Antwerp on June 22 bearing orders for all troops and carpenters to march at once to join the Grand Army, leaving only a small force to guard the city. Additional reports placed the strength of the Dutch forces in Holland at only 3,000 with an additional French corps of about 2,400 near Antwerp and some 3,000 on the island of Walcheren. These 8,400 men were reported to be the largest force that could be thrown against an English attack for some five or six days.[12]

It was, therefore, intelligence reports such as these, as well as the desire to take advantage of Napoleon's defeat in Austria, which caused the cabinet to disregard the military opinions and pursue the expedition to the Scheldt.[13]

With the expedition definitely decided upon, Castlereagh now turned to his most important decision: the appointment of the commander. Had Sir John Moore not fallen at Corunna, the leadership of the expedition most likely would have been his. But since he had passed from the scene and Sir Arthur Wellesley had returned to the Peninsula, the problem was to find another capable and energetic commander. The choice was John Pitt, second earl of Chatham, the older brother of William Pitt. Now fifty-three, Chatham had served in the American Revolution and in 1799 had commanded a brigade under the duke of York during the Anglo-Russian expedition to the Helder in northern Holland. For the past seven years he had been a member of the cabinet as master general of the ordnance.

Much speculation has arisen concerning the appointment of Chatham, who, though generally respected and admired, was well known for his lackadaisical habits, for which he acquired the title, the "late" Lord Chatham.[14] Some have contended that it was because of Chatham's personal friendship with George III that he received the command, which carried with it an attractive income.[15] Another explanation, less plausible, has been suggested by those who believe that George Canning, the foreign secretary, was masterminding a reshuffle of the cabinet. With Chatham, whom Canning felt he could manipulate, as commander of the expedition, Canning was hopeful of forming a new cabinet with Chatham as prime minister, once the successful campaign against the French was completed.[16] Others have speculated that Chatham, a cabinet member, was given the appointment in a desperate effort to prop up the faltering Portland ministry. On the other hand, Sir David Dundas considered this choice of army commander a very good one.[17] Regardless of the reasons behind his appointment, Chatham's reputation and credentials hardly recommended him for command of an operation where celerity was the sine qua non. He seems best described by Lt. Col. C. Greenhill Gardyne who once wrote, "he was a veteran accustomed to the routine of official duty, but without experience as a leader, and without the qualities necessary to the success of an enterprise which demanded decision of character and activity of mind and body."[18] Although Castlereagh must have been aware of Chatham's limited abilities, he was, for whatever reasons, fully committed to the earl as his commander in chief of the expedition.

Castlereagh first approached Chatham with the offer on May 18. Recovering at home from a recent illness, Chatham was initially reluctant to accept the command, requesting more information before making a decision. During the following weeks Chatham and Castlereagh were engaged in numerous conferences with military and naval officials in which aspects of the expedition were discussed. On June 9 the admiralty presented a memorandum outlining its views on attacking the Scheldt installations. It suggested that once Walcheren was secured, the navy could then assist the army in ascending the river and attacking Antwerp. Specific details were to be left to the discretion of the naval and military commanders. A few days later Capt. Sir Home Popham of the Royal Navy, presented Castlereagh with a memorandum which he had originally prepared for Pitt in 1798.[19] Popham supported the joint operation concept which Castlereagh and Chatham were considering. One problem plagued the expedition's planners, however. Could the army be landed in the upper Scheldt at Sandvliet? Most of the plans under consideration called for the divisions of the army intended to attack Antwerp to be ferried up the West Scheldt and landed on the mainland near the small village of Sandvliet. But little information was available concerning the beach in that vicinity and whether a landing there was possible. Chatham was convinced that if this plan were feasible the expedition could succeed and indicated he would be willing to lead it. Consequently, on June 14, a week after London had received news of Aspern-Essling, Castlereagh wrote George III:

Lord Castlereagh begs to acquaint your Majesty that your Majesty's confidential servants, having considered the information which has been collected relative to an operation against the enemy's naval resources in the Scheldt, are humbly of the opinion that, by employing an adequate force of not less than 35,000 men, the attempt may be made with every prospect of success, provided the practicability of a landing at Sandvliet can be assured. Till this point can be further investigated, they are desirous to postpone receiving your Majesty's final commands upon the measure, requesting in the mean time, your Majesty's permission to proceed, with as much secrecy and expedition as possible, with all the preliminary arrangements which, when completed, will contribute to render the troops equally applicable to any other service.

Your majesty's servants are desirous of humbly submitting to your Majesty that the conduct of the proposed expedition be entrusted to the Earl of Chatham.[20]

Following the king's favorable response, the admiralty, on June 19, reported that it had investigated the possibility of landing the army at or near Sandvliet. If Walcheren and South Beveland were occupied by the army, then the navy could convey the landing force safely to the mainland and disembark them near Sandvliet.[21] On June 22 Castlereagh informed the king of this latest information and requested that the troops be ordered to the Scheldt. George III agreed to the proposition, but wryly commented that it would have been desirable to have had more detailed information concerning the strength of the enemy in the area. On the same day Castlereagh received from Dundas a detailed list of troops prepared to embark on the expedition, including 35,000 infantry and 1,900 cavalry. Additional troops were added thereafter until the actual force under orders to sail on the expedition exceeded 44,000.[22]

Meanwhile, on June 9, the admiralty had given the naval command to Rear Adm. Sir Richard Strachan. Strachan had been in command of a squadron watching the Dutch coast when ordered into port to assume his new responsibilities. His personality seems to have been in sharp contrast with that of Chatham's. Strachan is described by Capt. Graham Moore, Sir John's brother, in the following manner: "I know him to be extremely brave and full of zeal and ardour, at the same time that he is an excellent seaman, and, tho' an irregular, impetuous fellow, possessing very quick parts and an uncommon share of sagacity and strong sense." Strachan was evidently popular with his men who nicknamed him

"Mad Dick" because of his violent temper and wild cursing. It was said that "when he swore he meant no harm, and when he prayed he meant no good."[23] A lethargic general and an impetuous admiral make strange bedfellows. Relatively unknown, at least in comparison with Chatham, Strachan appears to have been a capable naval officer, although perhaps given to involvement in detailed minutiae to the neglect of overall operations. The naval command under Strachan included several excellent officers, the most outstanding of whom was Rear Adm. Sir Richard Keats. Others appointed to command squadrons included Rear Adm. Edward A. Otway; Rear Adm. Amelius Lord Beauclerk; Rear Adm. Allan Hyde, Lord Gardner; and Commo. Edward C. R. Owen. Sir Home Popham, considered by many to be the best pilot in the British navy, was appointed captain of the fleet.[24]

The lieutenant generals serving under Chatham comprised a distinguished and qualified command. Sir Eyre Coote, who had served with distinction in Egypt, was designated second in command. The quartermaster general of the British army, Robert Brownrigg, accompanied the expedition as Chatham's chief of staff. Others included George Gordon, the marquis of Huntley; Sir Alexander John Hope; Henry William, Lord Paget; Thomas Grosvenor; Alexander Mackenzie Fraser; and Sir James St. Clair Erskine, the earl of Rosslyn, who at one time had served as commander in chief of the British forces in the Mediterranean.[25]

By the end of June preparations for the expedition were well under way. Between June 24 and July 9 troops in cantonments scattered throughout the British Isles began marching to the principal ports of embarkation—Deal, Dover, Chatham, Harwich, Ramsgate, and Portsmouth. Almost half of the forces embarked at this latter port in an effort to make it appear that the expedition was being oufitted for Portugal, thereby preserving perhaps some element of surprise.[26] Meanwhile, Castlereagh was experiencing difficulty in obtaining enough transports for the expedition. The rate for ships rented to the British government as troop transports was twenty-one shillings per ton monthly; however, as early as

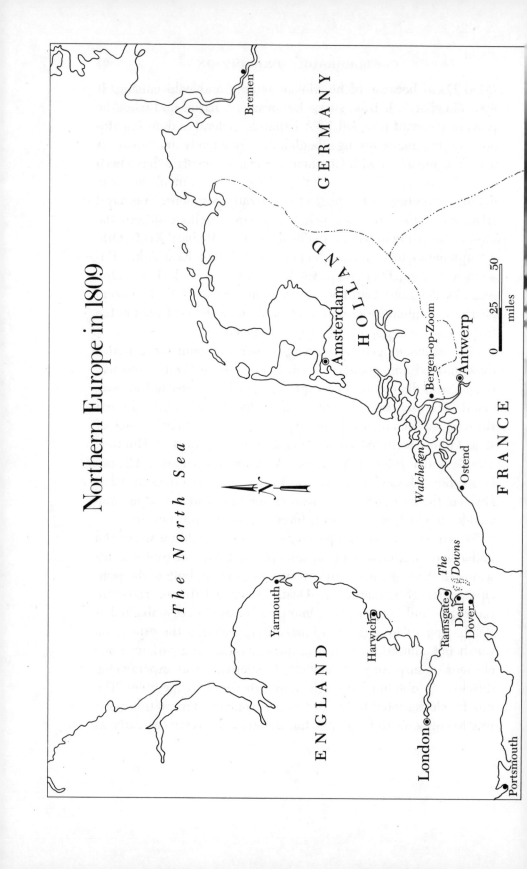

Northern Europe in 1809

April, due to the extreme shortage of available vessels, Castle-reagh was forced to increase the rate to twenty-five shillings. This increase succeeded in attracting additional ships operating in the coastal trade, but the problem remained critical. It was rumored in July that the government might have to resort to hiring neutral ships in British ports in order to furnish enough transports for the expedition.[27] Fears increased that delay might arise because of overdue cavalry transports from Portugal; but by July 15 most of the vessels had arrived and were proceeding to Ramsgate.[28]

There was also concern that the troop transports, which were not so maneuverable as ships of war, would cause an unnecessary hazard in navigating the narrow, shifting channels of the Scheldt. Sir Home Popham suggested that the troops destined to sail up the river to attack Antwerp should be embarked on smaller ships of war and the troops instructed to land on either Walcheren, South Beveland, or Cadsand be embarked on the large sail of the line and transports.[29] In order to do so and to accommodate more troops, many of the ships of war had their lower deck guns removed. In all, some twenty-five thousand men were to be embarked on warships, the remainder on transports and smaller vessels. The naval force which sailed on the expedition was awesome for that day. "The number of sail, when the whole is assembled, will amount, as nearly as can be calculated, to 616, of which 352 will be transports, and 264 ships of war."[30]

On July 12 a general embargo was ordered on all ships in British ports to preserve as much secrecy concerning the expedition as possible.[31] Four days later Chatham received his orders from the king.

You will consider that this conjoint Expedition has for its object the capture or destruction of the enemy's ships, either building at Antwerp and Flushing or afloat in the Scheldt; the destruction of the Arsenals and Dockyards at Antwerp, Terneuse, and Flushing, the reduction of the island of Walcheren, and the rendering, if possible, the Scheldt no longer navigable for ships of war.[32]

Chatham was instructed to cooperate with the naval commander to secure as many of these objectives as possible. Should the enemy oppose the expedition with an overwhelming force, he was to evacuate his army and immediately return to England, leaving behind a sufficient force to maintain possession of the island of Walcheren until the government decided upon further action.

In order to further clarify the objectives of the expedition, Castlereagh wrote Chatham a week later. After first emphasizing the importance of checking the French naval power in the Scheldt river and the significance of such an operation as a major diversion for Austria, Castlereagh advised that no general operation on the Continent was anticipated and that the expedition was to be "more immediately against the fleet and arsenals of France in the Scheldt." Castlereagh also attempted to impress upon Chatham the importance of rapid movement in the campaign, cautioning that any delay in operations might prove fatal to the success of the expedition. Finally, Chatham was instructed that if the question arose whether to retain a foothold on the Continent or to evacuate, he was to be guided by the situation on the Continent, which

does not, at the present moment, permit his Majesty's Government to contemplate the possibility of commencing operations with a British army from a point so much in advance towards the frontier of France as Antwerp; neither is there any allied force as yet in the field in the north of Germany, of sufficient magnitude, with whom an advance from thence could be combined; nor has it been deemed consistent with the celerity of movement on which the success of the intended attack may depend, to send the army equipped upon a scale which would qualify it to enter immediately upon a campaign.

The expedition must therefore be considered as not, in the first instance, assuming any other character than that of a coup de main. While the operation is in progress other prospects may open themselves, and events occur which may induce his Majesty's Government to extend their views.[33]

Perhaps foreseeing the friction which would soon develop between the commanders of the army and navy, Castlereagh closed his lengthy correspondence by stating that His Majesty "feels

sure that his army and navy will vie with each other" in conducting this important campaign and trusts "the utmost spirit of con-
cert and harmony will prevail, throughout the whole of their
operations."[34]

Sir Richard Strachan, commander of the naval force, received
his orders from the admiralty the following day. In them the lords
of the admiralty emphasized the importance of occupying South
Beveland and Cadsand while Walcheren was being invaded in
order to assure prompt, safe passage up the West Scheldt. Strachan was further ordered to hold his ships ready to evacuate the
troops at a moment's notice, if that should become necessary. Finally, the admiral was instructed to keep a "perfect understanding" with the army and its commander, "the cordial cooperation
of the two services being essential to the happy and successful
issue of this enterprise."[35]

It was feared that stormy weather prevalent in late summer
might present a problem if the expedition were not launched
soon. Sir Home Popham had expressed his concern in June. "I see
the season advancing fast; and, if we are imperceptibly led on til
the midsummer fine weather is past, we shall have the most dread-
ful of all difficulties, the elements, to encounter." Chatham agreed.
"We must get on faster."[36] Dundas and Castlereagh attempted to
expedite the embarkation, but the sheer immensity of the project
—some seventy thousand military and naval personnel, over six
thousand horses, the field and battering train numbering more
than two hundred pieces of ordnance, ten million rounds of ammunition, and several hundred wagons and carts and other stores
—made delay inevitable.[37] Gradually, however, the last week in
July saw final preparations completed.

The British people were both optimistic and apprehensive about
the expedition. Daily, the newspapers carried the latest details
concerning the "grand expedition," as they often termed it, and
editorialized on the significance of the forthcoming campaign.
Nothing seemed too much for the force to accomplish. One paper
reported that Napoleon had returned to Paris and that "we should

not be at all surprised to hear of his appearing as the opponent of Lord Chatham." Another editorialized that the expedition might form the nucleus of an army of liberation to free Europe from the dreaded "Tyrant!" Perhaps France could be invaded after the Scheldt complex was destroyed. "What the ulterior progress of the armament may be, will probably depend on the course of events; but with such a force as at least 50,000 men, a subsequent attack on Boulogne by traversing the Netherlands and entering France . . . may be in the scale of probability."[38]

Along the southeast coast of England, crowds gathered as the expedition prepared to sail. At Deal, where troops were being embarked, it was reported that the boatmen volunteered their services to carry the men to the ships in the harbor "at no expense to the government." Some well-wishers took to their boats or hired yachts to sail out to where the ships were anchored to offer encouragement to the departing troops. One of these, Sir William Curtis, sailed out among the ships of the fleet in a yacht "beautifully painted, adorned with a streamer bearing devices prognosticating victory and glory, and carrying delicate refreshments of all kinds to the military and naval commanders, and the principal officers."[39]

Meanwhile, on July 19, the roar of cannon from across the Channel confirmed reports received in London the previous day. Napoleon had won another victory. On July 5–6, just north of Vienna, the French army had defeated the Hapsburg forces under the command of the archduke Charles at the battle of Wagram. Subsequent reports indicated that although the Austrians had retired from the field in good order, further resistance had been considered useless, and that on July 12 an armistice had been signed at Znaim. Clearly, the news of Wagram was disappointing to the British government. But since the primary objective of the expedition was the destruction of the French naval complex in the Scheldt, it appears that no consideration was ever given to canceling the expedition. In spite of this disheartening news from Austria, the British still expected their expedition to achieve meaningful results. A signed armistice did not necessarily mean that a peace would follow; but if it did, a significant diversion could still be accomplished by a successful operation in the Scheldt, thereby weakening Napoleon's negotiating position.[40] And now, with the Hapsburg defeat, the destruction of the Scheldt complex seemed even more important to British security.

On July 19 both Chatham and Castlereagh left London for the coast, followed two days later by several other members of the cabinet who wanted to witness the final preparations of the Grand Expedition.[41] Here, along the southeast coast of England, the most impressive combined naval and military force Britain had ever assembled against France was finally launched at dawn on Friday, July 28.[42]

3

King Louis's Complaint

Although the British cabinet had hoped to preserve some degree of secrecy in preparing the expedition, the extensive arrangements and unusual activity in the principal ports of Great Britain had indicated to the authorities on the Continent that a major operation was forthcoming.[1] Holland and more particularly the Scheldt had been long suspected as the objective of an English attack. The correspondence of both Napoleon and his brother Louis contain frequent references to such a possibility.

Since becoming king of Holland in 1806, Louis had attempted to placate the Dutch people while trying to execute the policies formulated by Napoleon, a course which gradually led to strained relations between the brothers.[2] The strategic importance of Holland and the naval establishments in the Scheldt was obvious to both rulers. It was only natural, therefore, that the French emperor should show particular interest in the defensive measures taken by Louis. In 1807, as the installations in the Scheldt River became more extensive and the size of the French fleet increased, Napoleon decided to exercise more direct control over the defense of this area. By the Treaty of Fontainebleau on November 11, Louis was forced to cede to France the port and city of Flushing, enabling Napoleon to strengthen that city's defenses and garrison it with French troops.[3] The remainder of the island of Walcheren continued to be Dutch territory, defended solely by Louis's troops and National Guard.

Early in 1809 both Louis and Napoleon began to anticipate a British attack on the naval bases in either northern France or Holland. The establishments in the Scheldt attracted particular concern. In January the French emperor confessed that he held reservations about the ability of his commandant at Flushing. "I

have received some serious complaints concerning General Monnet, who commands at Flushing. My intention is to replace him."[4]

In February Napoleon wrote Louis, inquiring about the state of
the Dutch troops and the means of defending Holland should the
English attempt an invasion: "I request that you send me the
state of all your troops, in order that, in the general arrangements
which I am going to make, I see what you have to fear from an
English landing this summer, and your means to oppose it."[5]
Louis's response was not encouraging; his brother's earlier requests for Dutch forces for Germany and Spain had left Holland
almost defenseless. Of the sixteen battalions of the Dutch army,
eight were stationed in Germany and two in Spain. The remaining
six battalions were in Holland, several of these encamped along
the coast. Over one-half of these troops were reported to be ill
and in the hospital. Louis complained, therefore, that he simply
did not have sufficient military strength to provide adequate defensive measures: "If Your Majesty never wishes to lose Holland,
I ask that you return my troops; otherwise, I am continually exposed to unexpected attack, and perhaps at a time when your
Majesty is occupied elsewhere and cannot come to my aid."[6]

Napoleon would not consider withdrawing these troops from
Germany at this critical time. Reports indicated that Austria was
mobilizing its forces, and Napoleon believed war imminent. In
response to Louis's plea for more troops to defend Holland, Napoleon could only instruct his brother to recruit an additional
twenty thousand men and provide for the security of his kingdom. "All my troops are employed, and you will surely be attacked by June or September."[7] Two days later, however, on
March 13, Napoleon did include among his military projections
for the coming year almost one million francs for the defenses in
Zealand and North Brabant. These included 110,000 francs for
additional fortifications at Antwerp, 300,000 for the construction
"by July" of some lunettes to protect the approaches to Flushing,
and 500,000 francs to construct batteries on the island of Cadsand.[8]

Later in March Napoleon again inquired about the defensive measures taken in Holland. He cautioned Louis to ready his troops for action since war on the Continent was expected at any moment.[9] Napoleon was now directing his attention to the east, and Louis was expected to stand on his own and defend his coasts.

By early April the king of Holland was receiving disquieting reports of unusual activity in English ports. Rumors had it that a large military force was preparing to embark, but its objective was unknown. Apprehensive that the coast of Holland would be the destination of the expedition, Louis was relieved in mid-April when the British force sailed for Portugal.[10] He was still uneasy, however, and on April 4 he had penned a letter to the emperor describing once again the poor state of defenses which continued in Holland. An English attack was certain, he wrote, and if it came he would be unable to offer serious resistance. Louis concluded with another plea for the return of his troops.

I request from Your Majesty the division that I have in Germany and the one I have in Spain; I venture to represent that Holland is as essential to conserve as Hamburg, and that with the incomplete military force that I have, I can neither protect the Helder, nor Helvoet, nor Walcheren, nor Amsterdam from a coup de main; a serious attack will be certain success. I know that Your Majesty directed me to furnish 20,000 more men; but, believe me, I have done all that was humanly possible to do, and whatever may happen, I have nothing to blame myself for.[11]

Growing increasingly apprehensive over the defenseless condition of his country, Louis experienced an additional fright the second week in April. On April 8 an English squadron commanded by Adm. James Gambier attacked a French fleet in the Basque Roads off the Isle of Aix. By using fire ships, the English were successful in destroying three ships of the line and damaging several others.[12] This operation made Louis even more aware of the danger to the fleet in the Scheldt. Consequently, on April 26 he wrote his brother again, complaining of the insufficient force under his command, but stating his willingness to sacrifice his coastal areas in order to protect the French establishments in the Scheldt: "Comte d'Hunebourg and Admiral Decrès have written me relative to the squadron at Flushing. I am arming and reinforcing the flotilla which is in Zealand, and, if the enemy actually attacks, I will send the few troops that I have to General Monnet and only keep what is absolutely necessary to protect Amsterdam."[13]

Although Napoleon was occupied during the spring of 1809 with affairs in Spain and Austria, he had not neglected entirely the defenses of northern France. On March 23 he had set in motion arrangements to establish seventeen provisional demibrigades as a reserve for his army on the Rhine and for the defense of the coast. Most of the troops in the north were concentrated in camps at Boulogne, St. Omer, and Ghent. Gen. Gilles-Joseph-Martin Bruneteaux, comte de Sainte-Suzanne, was given the command at Boulogne; Gen. Jacques-Antoine, baron de Chambarlhac de Laubespin, Ghent; and Gen. Antoine-Alexander Rousseau, St. Omer.[14] The camps of Boulogne and St. Omer were but three and two days' marching time from Antwerp, respectively. On April 15 two more demibrigades under Gen. Antoine-Guillaume Rampon were added to the camp at St. Omer.[15] The strengths of these fluctuated during the spring and early summer, since many of the troops were ordered to join the Grand Army and replacements were usually difficult to obtain. Precautions were taken below Antwerp to block any enemy advance up the Scheldt. A boom, made of chain with large logs attached and secured by ten anchors, was constructed across the river above the village of Sandvliet. A gap large enough for one ship at a time to pass was left in the center of the boom, thereby permitting the small craft to sail up the river but preventing large ships from passing without first breaking the boom. Two forts, Lillo and Liefkenshoek, situated on either bank of the river, gave protection to the boom.[16]

Resigned to meeting the impending British attack with the forces at hand, Louis left Amsterdam the first week in May to inspect his defenses and bolster the morale of the troops. On May 6 he informed Napoleon that he was examining the fortifications on the island of Schouwen and was proceeding to Walcheren the following day. He had already established some camps and armed his flotilla, but he still considered Holland inadequately defended because of the paucity of troops and equipment.[17]

Louis's tour of Walcheren was well received. Cheering throngs greeted him at the provincial capital of Middelburg, where he reviewed the troops. Continuing his inspection of the defenses on Walcheren, Louis visited General Monnet, the French commandant of Flushing. Although Flushing was now French territory, the Dutch king wished to view its defenses and report his personal findings to Napoleon. His tour did nothing to relieve his anxiety over the Scheldt's security.

Sire, I have just finished my visit to Zealand and the Brabant. I did not wish to pass so close to Flushing and the fleet without visiting them in order to render an account to Your Majesty. Flushing appears to be in a state of weakness of which I had no idea, and the general who commands there does not hold good order; there is no firmness or unity in the command, and the troops do not have the harmony or spirit which they should have.[18]

Louis's visit with Adm. Edouard-Thomas de Burgues, comte de Missiessy, commander of the French fleet in the Scheldt, was equally disquieting. After being received with a twenty-one-gun salute, the king of Holland took time to observe the fleet executing routine maneuvers. Later he discussed with the admiral the possibility of an English attack upon the fleet. Louis learned to his horror that Missiessy had taken no definite precautions to resist the English, preferring to await the actual onslaught, "for fear of announcing to them [the English] that the French feared them."[19] Louis suggested that the fleet should ascend the river above the boom at the forks of Lillo and Liefkenshoek for added protection. When Missiessy declared that such a measure would require authorization from the ministers in Paris, Louis deemed the entire situation inexcusable and promptly dispatched a letter to Napoleon asking him to take some positive action: "I request that Your Majesty give some orders concerning your squadron and Flushing. I have rearmed a great part of my flotilla. But it is said that the English are preparing five to 600 flat boats; and it worries me to see so much time lost in making preparations. The season is perfect for an attack; the fleet ought to have been at Antwerp long ago."[20]

Louis returned to Amsterdam on May 31, his fears not allayed by what he had witnessed on his inspection tour. Even more depressing was Napoleon's reaction to his reports. Perhaps feeling that Louis's letters were inspired by his jealousy over the cession of Flushing, the French emperor paid them scant attention.[21]

Wishing to build confidence in the Dutch people and perhaps also to intimidate the English, who were certain to read it, Louis ordered an Amsterdam paper to publish a report detailing the "elaborate" defensive measures taken in Holland.

The most effective measures have been taken in Holland to repel any attack on the part of the English, if they dare make a descent on this country, in order to keep their agreement, which it is said they have made with Austria, to make a powerful diversion in her favor. It is nevertheless doubtful that after the disasters which have befallen the Austrian armies, the English will feel still obliged to keep their promises. . . . But whether they keep their word or not, we have established at different points on our coast some detached corps, which, in case of necessity, can be promptly brought together. A numerous reserve is equally disposed, if needed, to be transported to these same points.[22]

June brought more problems for the king of Holland. An insurgence led by Frederick von Schill in northern Germany prompted an anti-French reaction in Holland.[23] Straining Dutch-French relations even further was a diatribe against the Dutch appearing in the French journal Le publiciste, which accused the Dutch of originating rumors detrimental to the empire. One such rumor reportedly stated that "the French Army is encircled and lost; the emperor Napoleon, so ignorant in the art of war, at the head of a cowardly and pusillanimous army, has already laid down his arms."[24] Louis complained to his brother, but to no avail.

Relations between the two brothers steadily deteriorated during the month of July, prompted in part by a dispute over Dutch execution of the terms of the Continental System. Learning of two decrees issued by Louis allowing American ships to trade in Dutch ports, Napoleon notified his brother that France was closing its frontiers to Holland and recalling its ambassador.[25] Anti-French sentiment was revived in Holland and Belgium, where at Antwerp the French officials feared serious trouble. Napoleon's criticism of Louis's regime became more direct:

If you want me to cite to you all the Dutch houses which are trumpets of the English, that will be easy. Your regulations of the customs are so poorly executed, that all the correspondence of England with the continent are made through Holland. This is so true, that M. de Starhemberg, Austrian envoy, has passed through Holland on his return to London. It is possible that this is not your fault; it is not less true that Holland is an English province.[26]

While these exchanges were being made between the two brothers, the people of northern France and the Low Countries were becoming aware than an English attack was imminent.[27] By mid-July most of the newspapers on the Continent were publishing extracts from English newspapers which described the extensive preparations being made for the expedition, often quoting editorials from London which suggested the Scheldt as the probable destination. By July 20 continental papers could not only reveal the commanders for the British army and naval force, but could also announce that a large number of the new Congreve rockets invented by Gen. William Congreve were being included on the expedition. On the twenty-first the Amsterdam papers told of troops sent to the Dutch coast for defensive purposes.[28]

In spite of the rumors and intelligence reports of an impending English attack, more and more troops were being ordered from the coastal areas of Holland and northern France to reinforce the

French armies in Germany. The British intelligence received in London during June and July had been essentially correct. Most of the troops stationed at Antwerp had been transferred to the Grand Army.[29] In July Napoleon asked his minister of war for the last companies of artillery remaining in France. The few remaining regular troops in the north were thinly spread, and agitation against the French was increasing daily in the Low Countries.[30]

On July 15 General Henri Clarke, French minister of war, was forced to employ refractory conscripts to fill the depleted ranks of some of the regular regiments stationed in the Scheldt area. Clarke also alerted the military commanders at Boulogne, St. Omer, and Ghent, as well as King Louis, that the English attack could occur at any point.[31] Under these circumstances, Napoleon agreed to reduce his original demand for twenty-six artillery companies to ten or twelve, instructing three of the remaining companies to stay in the north "in order to be able to transport a few pieces of ordnance promptly in case the enemy should make an attempt upon our coast."[32] On July 21 he ordered that the National Guard not be changed again until October 15, when he hoped they could go home for the winter.

The size of the English expeditionary force was estimated at forty thousand by two French prisoners who escaped to the Continent on July 22. Troops and material were being loaded when they crossed the Channel, but the destination of the expedition was still a mystery.[33] General Sainte-Suzanne, commander of the Boulogne camp, and the other military commanders at Ghent and St. Omer suspected that the Scheldt was the objective of the British force and made preparations accordingly. On July 25, as the first elements of the British expedition prepared to sail, General Rousseau, commanding the French forces on the island of Cadsand, bemoaned that if the English landed ten thousand men on that island, they could turn his batteries and sail up the Scheldt unhindered by the guns of Flushing.[34] By the time Rousseau's request for additional troops to defend the coast was approved, however, the British had been sighted offshore.[35] Meanwhile, King

Louis, chagrined over his relations with Napoleon, and exhausted from preparing for the British attack, decided to take a brief vacation and visit his mother and sister at Aix-la-Chapelle. The crisis, he believed, had been passed, for the armistice signed on July 12 at Znaim had ended the fighting in Germany. The long awaited British expedition could no longer provide the diversion Austria so desperately needed the month before.[36] Consequently, as fate would have it, Louis departed Amsterdam just as the first British ships sailed from the Downs.[37]

4

The Expedition Sails

The Scheldt is a large, winding river flowing into the North Sea via the Dutch province of Zealand. In 1809 Zealand consisted of the islands of Walcheren, North and South Beveland, Schouwen, and several other smaller islands.[1] In the province there were some 121 towns and villages, the largest being on Walcheren, which was heavily populated for its size. Middelburg, the provincial capital, had a population of about sixteen thousand, which made it slightly larger than the port city of Flushing. Zealand occupied a position of some prominence among the other Dutch provinces; its inhabitants were among the most wealthy in the Netherlands, "owing to their traffic by the sea."[2]

Most of the islands of Zealand were below sea level and were protected from the sea by an extensive network of dykes. These vast dykes, some measuring more than fifty feet at their base and often wide enough on top "so that two carriages may pass abreast,"[3] not only encircled the islands but also the individual villages and farms, giving "a singular and fortified appearance to the whole."[4] The islanders were forced to wage a constant battle with the sea and were subjected to frequent floods. Much stagnant water, resulting from the low terrain which never allowed the drainage ditches and canals to be completely emptied, contributed a general unhealthfulness to the islands. The British were aware of these conditions from past experience but did not consider extra health precautions necessary for their troops.[5]

The Scheldt river was divided at its estuary by the island of Walcheren, and its course for approximately forty miles was in two separate channels, the East Scheldt and the Honte or West Scheldt. Becoming a single channel at Batz, on the southeastern tip of South Beveland, the Scheldt remained navigable for large ships as far upriver as Antwerp and even a few miles beyond. The West Scheldt separated, by two miles, Walcheren on the north and the island of Cadsand on the south and was accessible from the sea only by the two narrow channels which threaded between the treacherous sandbars at the river's estuary: the Deurloo channel, for ships entering from the north, and the Wielingen, for those sailing from the south.

The upper branch or East Scheldt flowed past Walcheren on the north and formed a difficult passage between North and South Beveland on the south and Schouwen, Toleland, and North Brabant on the north and east. A rather shallow river replete with sandbars and shoals, the East Scheldt posed serious navigational problems, even to those familiar with its mysteries. The West Scheldt possessed fewer of these navigational hazards and therefore was selected for the main theater of operations. The East Scheldt was regarded as an alternate route.[6]

No matter which branch of the Scheldt was to be used, the occupation of the islands of Walcheren and South Beveland was imperative because of their strategic locations. Since the West Scheldt had been selected as the primary route of the army to Antwerp, the island of Cadsand was also thrust into prominent consideration. Its batteries at Breskens on the coast opposite Flushing could sweep the entrance to the West Scheldt. By occupying Cadsand and destroying the guns at Breskens, the British could pass upriver unmolested via the Wielingen channel. Such a procedure would eliminate any delay which might occur if a protracted siege of Flushing became necessary.[7]

The British campaign was viewed as a *coup de main*. While forces were landed upon Walcheren to occupy that island and besiege Flushing, the remainder of the expedition would move up the West Scheldt to attack Antwerp and the fleet. Timing was critical, since any delay in advancing to these objectives would provide the French and Dutch with an opportunity to collect their forces.

The "Grand Division" of the expedition, as the Left Wing of the army was designated, was commanded by Sir Eyre Coote and was

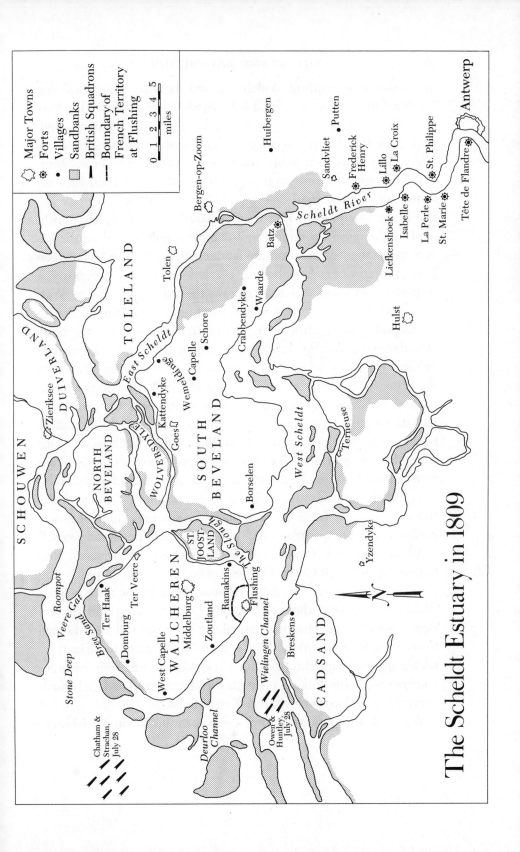

The Scheldt Estuary in 1809

Legend:
- Major Towns
- Forts
- Villages
- Sandbanks
- British Squadrons
- Boundary of French Territory at Flushing

0 1 2 3 4 5 miles

SCHOUWEN

Zieriksee

DUIVELAND

TOLELAND

Stone Deep

Veere Gat

Roompot

Bree Sand

Ter Haak

NORTH BEVELAND

Domburg

Ter Veere

West Capelle

WALCHEREN

Zoutland

Middelburg

ST. JOOST LAND

Ramakins

Flushing

The Slough

Wielingen Channel

Deurloo Channel

Breskens

CADSAND

Owen & Huntley, July 28

Chatham & Strachan, July 28

WOLVERSDYKE

Goes

Kattendyke

Wemeldinge

Capelle

Schore

SOUTH BEVELAND

Borselen

Crabbendyke

Waarde

Batz

East Scheldt

Tolen

Bergen-op-Zoom

Scheldt River

Sandvliet

Putten

Huibergen

Frederick Henry

Lillo

La Croix

St. Philippe

Liefkenshoek

Isabelle

La Perle

St. Marie

Tête de Flandre

Antwerp

West Scheldt

Temeuse

Hulst

Yzendyke

under orders to capture Walcheren and its chief port, Flushing. Coote's forces included the First Division commanded by Maj. Gen. Thomas Graham, Lt. Gen. Mackenzie Fraser's Fourth Division, and the Light Infantry under Lieutenant General Lord Paget. The entire Left Wing numbered 12,668 rank and file.[8] Zoutland Bay, on the southwest side of the island, was initially selected for the principal landing site because of its good beaches and close proximity to Flushing. Seasonal winds from the southwest might cause Zoutland Bay to be too rough for a disembarkation; consequently, an alternate landing site farther north between Domburg and East Capelle was also selected.[9] Simultaneously, a secondary invasion was to occur on the northeast side of Walcheren near Fort Ter Haak which would place that fort in British hands and enable gunboats to move into the Veere Gat, the body of water separating Walcheren and North Beveland. The control of the Veere Gat by the navy would give valuable assistance to the army in its attack upon the town of Ter Veere. This accomplished, the army and navy could move south along the Veere Gat and its continuation, the Slough passage, and thereby complete the encirclement of Walcheren at Flushing.[10] While the troops which landed near Fort Ter Haak were advancing south, the main invading force, already ashore at either Zoutland or near Domburg, would march on Flushing in three columns. To ensure the success of these landings, a demonstration near Flushing was planned with troops from the Right Wing landing if necessary.[11]

Adm. Edward A. Otway was given command of the naval contingent acting with Coote's forces against Walcheren, numbering thirty-seven ships of war. Adm. Amelius Lord Beauclerk's responsibility was to land the troops safely on Walcheren and protect them with fire from the gunboats under his command. Sir Michael Seymour was to complete the naval encirclement of the island by taking his gunbrigs through the Veere Gat and Slough passages and by eventually linking up with the ships of either Lord Gardner or Commodore Owen in the West Scheldt.[12]

While these operations were being conducted on Walcheren,

Sir John Hope, with the Reserve of the Army, was expected to free the navigation of the East Scheldt in order to land troops upon South Beveland.[13] His first mission was to destroy any batteries on the island of Schouwen which might endanger the Roompot, a protected anchorage at the mouth of the East Scheldt. Upon accomplishing this, Hope, conducted by the squadron commanded by Sir Richard Keats, was to land his troops on the northern shore of South Beveland in the vicinity of its principal town, Goes. He was then to transverse the island and protect the British forces coming up the West Scheldt. These combined forces, accompanied by the fleet, then were to advance to a landing point near Sandvliet, some fifteen miles from Antwerp.[14]

A third theater of operations centered around the island of Cadsand, the capture of which was considered necessary for the rapid advance up the West Scheldt. The Second Division of the army, commanded by George Gordon, the marquis of Huntley, was given this assignment. It included the two brigades under Maj. Gen. William Dyott and Brig. Gen. Henry T. Montresor, totaling 4,891 troops.[15] One brigade was to land upon Cadsand while the other formed a diversion near Flushing to facilitate the landing on Walcheren. Commo. Edward C. R. Owen, the naval commander of the Second Division, was well chosen for his task because of his extensive knowledge of the waters off the Dutch coast.[16]

The remaining two divisions of the army, the earl of Rosslyn's Light Division and Lt. Gen. Thomas Grosvenor's Third Division, were to wait in the Downs during these initial operations.[17] These forces, numbering some nine thousand men along with the cavalry, ordnance, and store ships, were to sail aboard vessels under the command of Capt. Robert Barton. Barton initially was ordered to be prepared to sail on signal from one of the ships forming the line of communication between the Downs and the Scheldt, but these orders were changed in consequence of several developments which took place on July 24, and his squadron was instructed to put to sea twenty-four hours after Admiral Otway had sailed.[18]

Developed in early July, these basic plans for operations were changed to some degree as a result of a July 24 conference involving Sir Richard Strachan, Sir Home Popham, Sir John Hope, and Gen. Robert Brownrigg. Following the meeting a memorandum was issued which outlined two significant alterations. Strachan contended that his naval forces did not have sufficient landing craft to accommodate two separate landings upon Walcheren. Furthermore, not more than three thousand men could be landed at one time at Zoutland and only about eleven hundred at the secondary site near Fort Ter Haak. And since at least one and a half hours would elapse before a second wave of troops could be landed, the admiral suggested that the entire Left Wing of the army destined to occupy Walcheren be landed in a single operation, thereby enabling some four thousand men to be put ashore at one time.[19]

The second major change in the original arrangements concerned Sir John Hope's division. Rather than proceeding to South Beveland via the East Scheldt, Strachan recommended that Hope's troops hesitate until Ter Veere had fallen and then use the Veere Gat, a more direct route, to approach the west shore of South Beveland. Although Lord Chatham did not attend the conference, he did approve the alterations suggested in the memorandum.[20]

Additional changes in the original plans of operations were necessitated as a result of information Strachan received on the evening of July 24. Capt. William Bolton of the *Fisgard,* a frigate stationed in the East Capelle Roads off the southern coast of Walcheren, dispatched a cutter to Strachan with news of a significant development. "It is with great satisfaction I have the pleasure to inform you the enemy's fleet, amounting to eleven sail of the line, has this instant dropped down the Scheldt, and are anchored close off the town of Flushing."[21] Upon receiving Captain Bolton's letter, Strachan decided to reinforce Lord Gardner's squadron— six sail of the line and accompanying flotilla, stationed off Walcheren to observe Flushing and the activities of the French fleet—

with four additional ships of the line under Sir Richard Keats. Strachan even considered sailing to the estuary of the West Scheldt to lead the attack upon the French fleet if it attempted to escape from the river, but after reflecting upon the problems which might arise if he and Chatham were separated, he dispatched Keats instead. Strachan then transferred his flag from the *Amethyst* to the *Venerable,* on which Chatham and his staff were embarked.[22]

The presence of the French fleet near Flushing persuaded Chatham and Strachan to abandon the idea of landing the Left Wing in Zoutland Bay or anywhere else near Flushing and to confine operations to the northern side of the island instead. These new orders were dispatched to Admiral Otway as he arrived in the Downs on July 27 to take command of the naval force convoying Coote's Left Wing.[23] This change of plans is rather significant: now the British army would be landed on the island at the point most distant from Flushing, although the problems arising from this do not seem to have occurred to Chatham. It would, however, play a significant role in the outcome of the expedition. The British leaders were excited with the prospect of capturing the French fleet (if it remained in its present position) by landing Sir John Hope's troops on South Beveland so that the fleet's retreat upriver might be effectively impeded or even prevented. However, the fleet began to retreat upriver on July 29.[24]

The earl of Chatham and his staff had boarded the flagship *Venerable* on the afternoon of July 26. Orders had been delivered to the commanders of the naval and military forces, and in the ten days since the troops had begun embarking (July 16), most of the vessels had arrived in the Downs. This roadstead along the southeastern coast of Kent was the rendezvous point for the entire expedition and proved an excellent one, close to the embarkation points of Deal and Ramsgate and midway between Harwich on the north and Portsmouth on the south. From the Downs the divisions of the expedition would sail on their particular missions.[25]

At dawn on July 28, the *Venerable* led the ships of the expedition from the anchorage in the Downs eastward toward the Dutch coast. That evening the vanguard, including the flagship, anchored in the Stone Deep, a waterway some ten miles off the northwestern coast of Walcheren. Capt. William Bolton had previously marked out the anchorage to prevent the ships from grounding on one of the many shoals.[26] After dark, several small vessels were sent to sound and buoy the anchorage of the Roompot, at the entrance of the East Scheldt, and to chart a route into it. Early on the morning of the twenty-ninth, Sir John Hope's division arrived in the Stone Deep and was soon joined by Sir Richard Keats. Admiral Keats, after learning that his former division had arrived in the Stone Deep according to plan, had relinquished command of the blockading squadron to Lord Gardner and rejoined Hope. Keats, assisted by Sir Home Popham, then conducted Hope's troops into the Roompot to begin operations upon Schouwen and South Beveland.

Admiral Otway's squadron, conducting the Left Wing of the army, arrived during the evening of the twenty-ninth and early morning of the thirtieth. Since the morning of the twenty-ninth, the weather had been cloudy and windy, and in the evening the rain began.[27] On the following morning, Sir Home Popham returned from the Roompot with a letter from Keats which reported that Hope's division was safely in the Roompot and was anchored off Zieriksee on the island of Schouwen. Keats indicated that the anchorage was extensive enough for the ships of the Left Wing, and with the winds growing stronger, Strachan ordered Otway's ships into the Roompot. An attempt to land Coote's army on the exposed beach near Domburg therefore was abandoned because of the high seas. However, by entering the Roompot and anchoring near the entrance of the Veere Gat, a landing upon the more protected beach near Fort Ter Haak could be attempted. Following this decision, the *Venerable* was led into the anchorage, trailed by Otway's ships.[28] Immediate preparations were made to land upon Walcheren.

Meanwhile, the two divisions which had been delaying in the

Downs arrived off Walcheren and because of the severe weather also were directed into the Roompot. This represented a significant change in the original plans since the Antwerp divisions were now in the East Scheldt rather than the West Scheldt. This development necessitated another route for the advance upon Antwerp with the least possible delay.[29]

Another problem developed some twenty-five miles south of the Roompot which also would have a significant effect upon the eventual results of the expedition. Commo. Edward Owen had been given the responsibility of transporting the marquis of Huntley's division to Cadsand. The capture of Cadsand, as previously noted, was considered essential for the rapid advance up the West Scheldt. The island's occupation was important also because it would likely be the chief source of reinforcement for Flushing. Although troops and supplies could be prevented from reaching Flushing by naval blockade, a strong south-southwest wind could reduce the effectiveness of such a measure. Heretofore, Cadsand's conquest had been considered absolutely necessary for the expedition to move immediately up the West Scheldt to Antwerp without waiting for the reduction of Flushing. However, it was only a few weeks prior to the sailing that the full importance of the island was realized. It was then that the British force assigned to take Cadsand was increased to a full brigade.[30] Capt. William Bolton, when reconnoitering the coast of the island, reported that there were only two small batteries there, "one apparently of five, the other of thirteen guns, the landing is good on any part of the shore." [31]

Commodore Owen's orders of July 21 further emphasized the importance of capturing Cadsand. Owen was given thirteen ships of war to conduct and supervise Lord Huntley's landing on the island. Although both Strachan and Chatham considered one brigade sufficient for the operation, Huntley's entire division was available if needed. Owen was directed to precede the other divisions by a few hours in order to gain possession of the island prior to the landing on Walcheren. Even if difficulties developed in landing upon Cadsand, Owen was ordered to sever all communications between Flushing and Cadsand.

It will be very desirable to prevent the Enemy as much as possible from relieving the Island of Walcheren by Supplies or Reinforcements; you will therefore station Vessels so as to cut off the Communication from Cadsand, and if . . . sinking Vessels in the Ghent Passage, . . . will raise difficult Impediments, I desire you will sink such Vessels.[32]

Owen's operations on Cadsand were to be facilitated by Lord Gardner's squadron blockading the entrance to the West Scheldt. Sir Richard Strachan, in his original instructions to Lord Gardner on July 16, had informed Gardner of the general plan for the attack upon Walcheren and Cadsand but had said nothing about his giving assistance to Owen. On July 20 Strachan did instruct Gardner to have the boats of his squadron prepared to supplement Owen's squadron on Cadsand.[33] More extensive assistance was ordered on July 24:

As it will be necessary that the Launches of the Squadron under your Lordship's command should be held in constant readiness with their carronades, to support the Division under Captain Owen's Orders in landing at Cadsand, I wish that every preparation should be made accordingly, and that the Sloops of War with your Lordship should also be directed to assist in securing the Beach.[34]

This order, for some inexplicable reason, was never received by Gardner.[35] Consequently, the only orders Gardner had when Owen's ships appeared off Cadsand were that the boats of his squadron might be needed, and since he undoubtedly was preoccupied with the recent movements of the French fleet near Flushing, he thought little more about it.

The Cadsand operation was plagued by still more confusion. Lord Huntley had received his orders on July 25 detailing the landing his troops were to make on that island. These instructions stated that "it would appear that 2,000 men . . . will be a sufficient force." The preceding day Huntley had discussed the forthcoming operation with Commodore Owen and had learned that six hundred men was the maximum number which could be landed from their available landing craft in one trip. Later the same day, Huntley questioned General Brownrigg concerning the landing and was assured that there would be "ample means for landing a great part of the division."[36] Upon receiving his official orders the following day, Huntley interpreted them to mean that two thousand men were to be landed on Cadsand in one landing. In another discussion with Owen, Huntley learned that the commodore had received no other information concerning the landing. Neither Lord Chatham nor General Brownrigg was available on the twenty-sixth, and on the twenty-seventh Huntley embarked at Ramsgate.[37]

Huntley, in an effort to clarify his instructions with Lord Chatham aboard the *Venerable*, took a brig at four o'clock on the foggy morning of the twenty-eighth and approached the flagship as it was getting underway. His brig was instructed to follow the *Venerable* through the Narrows into the open sea where communication could be made. The fog thickened, and Owen, fearing that the brig might have difficulty returning to its division, recalled it. Consequently, Huntley's division continued to Cadsand with this vital question unanswered.

The question of landing upon Cadsand was further complicated by Strachan's letters to Owen on July 26 and 27. After informing the commodore that the landing upon Walcheren had been shifted to the northeast coast of the island because of the appearance of the French fleet near Flushing, Strachan cautioned Owen to use his own discretion about landing on Cadsand. "I mean if a great naval opposition is offered, and you and the Marquis of Huntley think it running too much risk to land, you are not to do it till a convenient and safe opportunity should offer, keeping it always in your recollection that it is of the greatest importance to obtain possession of Cadsand, when it can be done without that risk to which I have alluded."[38] This dispatch appeared to relieve to some degree the urgency in capturing Cadsand and perhaps suggests that Strachan failed to grasp the military consequences of not gaining possession of the island during the first hours of the invasion.

Owen's division had some difficulty maneuvering into the Wielingen Channel but anchored safely off Cadsand on the morning of the twenty-ninth. Strong winds made an immediate landing impossible, and preparations were made for an attempt on the following day. While riding out the rough weather on the twenty-ninth, Huntley dispatched a swift cutter to headquarters to inform General Brownrigg that he considered the landing facilities of Commodore Owen's ships inadequate. Huntley received a reply the following morning indicating that Lord Gardner's boats were coming to assist them.[39] Commodore Owen also had written Sir Richard Strachan on the twenty-ninth that Huntley expected to be able to land an entire brigade in one landing. It was not until the following afternoon that Owen received a reply from Strachan ordering him to suspend all operations against Cadsand until Lord Gardner arrived to assist him. Although the winds subsided slightly on the thirtieth so that a landing could have been attempted, Lord Huntley deferred such an attempt. He reasoned that it was not militarily sound to land six hundred men on the coast when it would be at least another hour before they could be reinforced. Two thousand men would have to be landed in one operation in order to hold the beach against what appeared to be a constantly increasing French force. Huntley could only estimate the actual number of French troops on Cadsand since the high dykes hid from his view the activities occurring inland.[40]

On the morning of the thirty-first Owen, thinking that he had sighted Lord Gardner's squadron coming to his assistance, moved his ships farther up the Wielingen to a point only four miles from Flushing. When it became apparent that Gardner was not approaching their position, Owen and Huntley considered several methods of running the boats on shore, but the winds increased and once again operations were abandoned.[41] Even had additional boats arrived, the strong winds and swift currents along shore would have made landing a hazardous exercise.

Throughout this confusing state of affairs, Lord Gardner's squadron was less than fifteen miles away awaiting definite orders. On July 29 Sir Richard Strachan, anchored in the Stone Deep, had ordered Gardner to join him "and anchor to the westward of the Fleet, to be ready to cover the operations under Commodore Owen and the marquis of Huntley on Cadsand." Later the same day Gardner received another order instructing him to anchor in a new position off West Capelle, "keeping the Deurloo open, by which means you will be ready to assist Commodore Owen agreeable to your orders, if the Pilots will take charge and carry you in through the Weilings [Wielingen]."[42] This maneuver, Strachan added, would lead the French to believe that an attack was being prepared near Zoutland, thus forming a diversion for the main assault being prepared near Domburg.

On July 30 Gardner received yet another dispatch from Strachan that pilots were being sent to direct his squadron into the Wielingen. Strachan also enclosed Owen's letter of the twenty-ninth requesting Lord Gardner's boats, but he did not order Gardner to send his boats or join Owen in the Wielingen. On the thirty-first, as Huntley and Owen waited for assistance off Cadsand, Gardner's squadron was anchored near West Capelle expecting momentarily to receive pilots and orders for action. The same evening Gardner learned that Strachan would be joining him the following day with pilots, and Gardner inferred that his squadron would then assist Owen on Cadsand and thereafter sail into the West Scheldt. Also on the evening of the thirty-first Gardner received Owen's letter of that afternoon stating his disappointment in not receiving the boats needed for a landing upon Cadsand and urging that they be sent immediately. Gardner refused, advising that his orders were for him to retain his present position.[43] Even had Gardner been inclined to send his boats without specific orders, the task would have been almost impossible. The winds were strong from the southwest, thereby placing Gardner some twelve miles to the leeward of Owen.[44]

Strachan did not join Gardner on August 1 but wrote Lord

Gardner a rather curious note on the second as follows: "I have at last got some Pilots, which I hope you will have tomorrow. Owen is right in not attacking Cadsand; I never approved it, and Lord Chatham will be glad."[45] Owen also received a letter on the second from Strachan advising that he was coming to lead the line of battleships up the West Scheldt past Flushing, which action was to occur as soon as Sir John Hope announced that Fort Batz was captured and the French fleet's retreat cut off. The plan was necessarily abandoned, however, when Strachan learned that the French had passed Batz before Hope's troops could take the fort.

Meanwhile, the marquis of Huntley was growing restless with inaction. On Wednesday, August 2, he was informed through Gardner that a landing upon Cadsand was not to be attempted unless it could be accomplished "without risk of loss." On the same day, Huntley learned from Owen that the troops were to be taken past Flushing and landed near Borselen on South Beveland. On August 3 Lord Huntley finally received orders for action, but not against Cadsand. "I advise Lord Huntley's division to be hastened to the Room Pot and Veere Gat; the Enemy are throwing in reinforcements fast, and Lord Chatham wishes for Lord Huntley's division."[46] These orders evidenced the abandonment of operations against Cadsand. It is interesting to note that throughout the intense days of waiting off Cadsand from July 29 to August 3, Huntley never received an order from either Brownrigg or Lord Chatham; all his instructions were issued by the navy.[47]

Sir Richard Strachan's orders to Gardner and Owen regarding the landing upon Cadsand can be partially explained by reviewing the events which took place immediately after the expedition anchored in the Stone Deep. Strachan did not learn that the number of boats was insufficient for landing, in Huntley's opinion, until the evening of July 29. Strachan immediately relayed the information to Gardner, but he did not order Gardner to assist Owen by sending his boats or by joining him with his squadron since the distance was too great for the boats. Also, no pilots were available to lead the large ships of war into the Wielingen.[48] While

Strachan attempted to recruit pilots for Gardner's squadron, the two divisions scheduled to sail up the West Scheldt arrived in the Stone Deep on the thirty-first. Due to the high winds on that day, the only course of action was to send the Antwerp-bound divisions into the protected anchorage of the Roompot to prevent their foundering.[49] Furthermore, since the winds continued from the south-southwest, there seemed little likelihood that ships could be removed from the East to the West Scheldt and passed before Flushing without great delay. Consequently, by the thirty-first the possession of Cadsand for the purpose of moving ships up the West Scheldt had ceased to be of major importance.[50] Occupying Cadsand in such adverse weather would accomplish very little. It would prevent reinforcements from being sent to Flushing, but this could be achieved by simply completing the naval blockade of Walcheren.[51] Moreover, occupation of Cadsand at such a late date would unnecessarily divide the British troops and also expose them to possible heavy casualties in reembarking, since the island offered no covered beaches suitable for such purpose.[52]

It would appear that Huntley used good judgment in refusing to land fewer than two thousand men in one landing upon Cadsand. By the morning of the thirtieth, which was the first opportunity for landing, the French had had more than twenty-four hours to reinforce their normal garrison of over one thousand men on the island.[53] Even had Gardner's boats been available, it is likely that Huntley would not have risked an invasion; the added boats would have increased the total number available to land to only eleven or twelve hundred men.[54] Had this number of men attempted to land on the thirtieth, it is questionable whether they could have succeeded; and even if they did succeed, the position of the troops would have become critical almost immediately. Four trips by the landing boats could have disembarked Huntley's entire division of approximately five thousand in about eight hours, with all troops ashore by early evening on the thirtieth. On that date the French had only between three and four thousand men to oppose a landing. However, according to General Rousseau, commandant of the island, such a force would have been sufficient to prevent a landing of up to twelve thousand British troops because of the exposed beaches of Cadsand.[55] Assuming that Huntley had been successful in destroying the batteries at Breskens, the high winds on the thirtieth and thirty-first would have denied that route to the divisions assigned to sail up the West Scheldt. In fact, on the latter date these divisions had sought refuge in the Roompot. There was no apparent advantage in reinforcing Huntley on Cadsand, and Huntley's division was certain to have suffered heavy casualties in reembarking.[56] In summary, the same unfavorable weather which forced Rosslyn's and Grosvenor's divisions into the Roompot also played a significant role in preventing Huntley from landing upon Cadsand. In view of the above circumstances, it appears fortunate that Huntley did not succeed in occupying Cadsand.[57]

Thus far, several factors had influenced the progress of the expedition. The movement of the French fleet down the Scheldt near Flushing and the inclement weather had necessarily shifted the landing site on Walcheren to the furthermost point from Flushing. Likewise the unusually strong winds had forced Grosvenor's and Rosslyn's divisions bound for Antwerp to seek shelter in the East Scheldt anchorage of the Roompot, a measure which probably prevented the loss of numerous ships and lives.[58] Also, the opportunities of landing upon Cadsand were reduced by the inclement weather. These unexpected events necessitated new strategy by the expedition's joint commanders and made their already difficult task even more so. A new route to Antwerp was needed, but first the British position in Zealand would have to be secured.

5

Landing in Zealand

On July 26 General Monnet, French commandant of Flushing, alerted the war minister in Paris to a large contingent of English ships cruising off Walcheren. Although it was not uncommon to sight a squadron of British ships near the coast, these had anchored in the Stone Deep and their number had increased daily between July 23 and 26. Monnet's dispatch informed General Clarke, Napoleon's war minister, that rumors were flying in the islands and that Gen. Stewart Bruce, the Dutch commander of Zealand, had been receiving false reports of a British landing on Walcheren.[1] In view of the mounting English activity offshore, Monnet began to prepare his defenses and requested the mayor of Flushing, A. F. Lammens, to inspect the batteries and munitions "in case of the event."[2]

On the evening of July 28 the first wave of the British expedition, some sixty-four ships, was sighted north of Walcheren, and the following morning, after telegraphing this news to Paris, Monnet began organizing the defenses of Flushing and Walcheren.[3] The troops under Monnet's command consisted of a Colonial battalion, a battalion of returned French deserters, an Irish battalion, three Prussian battalions, and some detachments of veterans and gunners, totaling some 4,496 men.[4] These troops were augmented by the Dutch forces on the island under Gen. Stewart Bruce, stationed at Zoutland, Middelburg, Ter Veere, and Fort Ter Haak.[5] Monnet immediately dispatched his second-in-command, Gen. Pierre-Jacques Osten, to West Capelle with a detachment to observe the English movements and prevent, if possible, a disembarkation.

Upon his arrival at West Capelle, Osten learned that the English force was being increased by hourly arrivals of troops transports. The position of the English ships convinced Osten that the British intended to enter the Roompot and attempt a landing along the northern coast of Walcheren. He consequently sounded the general alarm and ordered the Irish and Colonial battalions to be brought up to oppose this expected invasion. With these troops General Osten followed the movements of the English ships conveying Sir John Hope's division into the Roompot on the afternoon of the twenty-ninth. Foregoing an attempt to land upon Walcheren at this time, the British ships moved farther up the anchorage. This puzzled Osten until he was apprised of a second wave of ships approaching the Stone Deep, apparently destined for Walcheren. The Irish and Colonials were deployed along the northern shore of Walcheren, and Osten remained for the night at West Capelle to observe the enemy buildup in the Stone Deep.[6]

On the morning of the thirtieth, Osten learned that the first wave of the English (Hope's division) had continued up the East Scheldt to an anchorage between North Beveland and Schouwen. He also was advised that the second wave was entering the anchorage of the Roompot. Therefore Osten dispatched an aide-de-camp to the village of Seroskirke to bring up the Second Prussian Battalion which had arrived the night before. Since the most logical point for a British landing appeared to be the Bree Sand, a beach between Fort Ter Haak and East Capelle, Osten also ordered the Irish and Colonial troops to join him there.

The immensity of the English expedition astonished Osten, for upon his arrival on the dyke near the Bree Sand, he was confronted with about three hundred ships "of all sizes" anchored between Fort Ter Haak and East Capelle. Aware that General Bruce was at Fort Ter Haak, Osten sent an aide-de-camp to inform him of the French dispositions and to seek the cooperation of the Dutch forces. Osten later recounted that "the general responded that I could take whatever measures I wanted to; but that I ought not to count on him; that the English were too strong to oppose their landing; that in consequence, if he were attacked he would destroy the batteries of the fort and retire to Ter Veere."[7]

Osten reported these circumstances to General Monnet and then took a position behind the dyke parallel to the Bree Sand, which would shelter his three battalions of Irish, Colonials, and Prussians, some twelve hundred men, from the fire of the English gunboats. Although Osten knew that his troops could not prevent an English landing, it was his goal to harass the English advance as he retreated across the island to Flushing. He deployed the Irish and Prussians along the dyke to the right near Fort Ter Haak with two pieces of artillery and stationed the Colonials, also armed with two field pieces, on the left.

Sir Eyre Coote's Left Wing had anchored off the Bree Sand before noon on the 30th. Immediate preparations were commenced for landing the army on Walcheren. Troops and equipment were lowered into the flatboats and ship's boats. By 4:00 P.M., the tide was ebbing and the gunboats were in a position to provide protection for the landing troops.[8] The First Division, under Lt. Gen. Fraser, disembarked first.[9] An eyewitness gave the following description of the landing:

The Gunboats had taken up their positions along the shore, the flats full of soldiers and towed by the ship's boats, formed in the rear of the Gunboats. On a signal the flats advanced. All now was solemn silence, saving the Gunboats, who were thundering showers of iron on the enemy. Their well directed fire soon drove them to shelter, behind the sandbank. The flats had now gained the Gunboats, shot through the intervals and gained the shallow water, when the troops leaped out and waded ashore, drove the enemy from behind the hills where they had taken shelter from the destructive fire of the Gunboats.[10]

The light infantry troops of the Irish and Colonial battalions, which had been driven from the beach by the English gunboats, were the front line of Osten's defense. These troops were to be supported by the grenadiers and light infantry from the Prussian battalion; however, the Prussians refused to advance to the Bree Sand and remained with their battalion behind the dyke. Upon discovering that they had no support from the Prussians, the Irish and Colonials withdrew from the beach under gunboat fire and were then routed by the landing British soldiers. As Osten later described it, "the troops which I had with me resisted the fire of the English; but assailed by the great number and the extraordinary fire of the gunboats, they began to disband in spite of all my efforts to hold them together."[11] Two pieces of field artillery which were being transported by horses owned by local peasants were abandoned when the peasants cut the harnesses and fled with the horses. Under such circumstances, Osten had no choice but to retreat to the little village of Seroskirke and attempt to regroup his forces.

As soon as Fraser's division had landed, Col. Dennis Pack marched a detachment of his Seventy-first Light Infantry to the left toward Fort Ter Haak, where the Irish and Prussian battalions had been posted with two six-pounders. Their position was soon abandoned, however, because of fire from the cutter *Idas* and the numerical superiority of the English.[12] The Seventy-first continued toward Fort Ter Haak where Gen. Stewart Bruce fired a few shots at the gunboats and landing British troops from the fort's batteries, but the targets were beyond range. Upon the approach of Colonel Pack's detachment, Bruce evacuated Fort Ter Haak in favor of the much larger and better-fortified town of Ter Veere.[13]

The remainder of the British army assigned to Walcheren was landed during the evening of July 30. Gen. Thomas Graham's division was landed about 7:00 P.M., followed shortly thereafter by Gen. Thomas Picton's brigade and some accompanying detachments from Gen. William Houston's brigade.[14] Headquarters was established at Ter Haak for the evening, and defensive positions were taken along the Bree Sand.

Colonel Pack, upon occupying Ter Haak, continued his march along the Veere Gat toward Ter Veere. Some resistance was encountered while approaching the town, but the skirmish was brief since the garrison retired into the town as darkness descended.[15] During the evening Colonel Pack learned from deserters that the garrison of Ter Veere had been weakened by the withdrawal of a number of troops to Flushing and South Beveland. Relying upon this information, Pack dispatched a party of night skirmishers.

With this view he again detached Captain Ness with a sergeant and a few men to reconnoitre the approaches. This officer and his party passed a French picquet unobserved, and had nearly reached the drawbridge, when a dog, which had followed them began to bark, and alarmed the sentries on the ramparts, who challenged. A brisk fire was quickly opened on the reconnoitring party and the support, which was then moving up to them and had already surprised and taken prisoners a picquet of the enemy's. As the alarm now became general in the place, the fire increased, and the British detachments retired along the dyke, suffering severely.[16]

The following morning General Fraser ordered his division, armed with five nine-pounders and a heavy howitzer, to invest the town. By 8:00 A.M. the troops had encircled the town and the British gunboats commenced firing from the Veere Gat. The barrage continued until early afternoon when the increasingly strong winds and adverse tide forced the gunboats to retire from action. Three gunboats were numbered among the casualties of the day.[17] That evening, Capt. Charles Richardson, a naval officer from the *Caesar*, fired some incendiary rockets into Ter Veere from his position atop a dyke. The damage from the rockets, combined with the earlier fire of the gunboats, achieved the surrender of Ter Veere. Early on August 1, the 519-man garrison surrendered as prisoners of war.[18]

Following the rout of his forces along the Bree Sand, General Osten had attempted to regroup at the village of Seroskirke. Many of the troops had fled to Middelburg, however, and on the thirty-first only a small force could be rallied at Seroskirke. Fearing that the British would cut off his retreat to Flushing, Osten fell back to Middelburg, but upon arriving, he was informed that the city officials had left to meet Sir Eyre Coote to negotiate surrender terms. The city was without fortifications and the Dutch garrison had been ordered into South Beveland by General Bruce. Under these

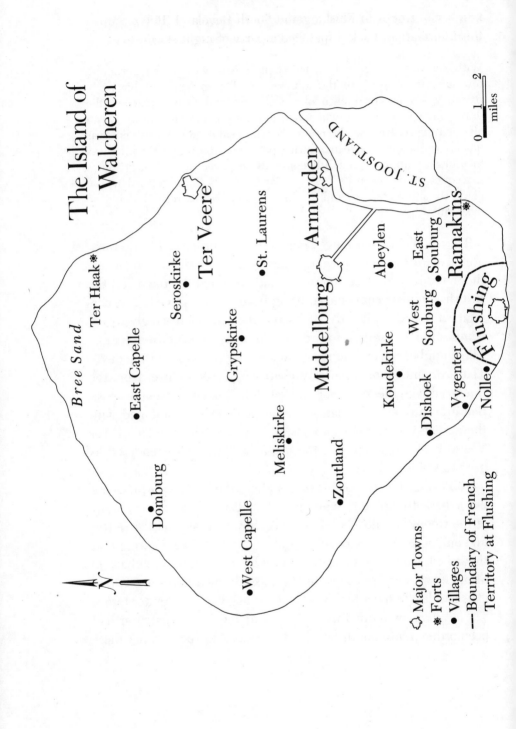

The Island of
Walcheren

Bree Sand

Ter Haak

Domburg

East Capelle

Seroskirke

Ter Veere

St. Laurens

Grypskirke

Meliskirke

West Capelle

Zoutland

Middelburg

Armuyden

ST. JOOSTLAND

Abeylen

West
Souburg

East
Souburg

Koudekirke

Dishoek

Vygenter

Nolle

Flushing

Ramakins

Major Towns
Forts
Villages
Boundary of French
Territory at Flushing

0 1 2
miles

conditions, the mayor of Middelburg had appointed representatives to arrange for the city's capitulation.[19] Osten, therefore, retired toward Flushing.

Several small villages between Flushing and Middelburg were suitable for the stationing of French outposts. Two such villages were East and West Souburg, where Osten positioned the Colonial battalion and the Irish battalion, respectively. The Second Prussian Battalion was posted along the dyke which paralleled the Middelburg-Flushing road, while a detachment of forty grenadiers from the Colonial battalion was dispatched to the village of Koudekirke. Several small patrols were directed to the left and right of Flushing to forestall any surprise attack by the English.[20]

Earlier the same morning, July 31, Sir Eyre Coote reorganized the British army on Walcheren into four divisions. The new Right Wing, commanded by General Graham, included 3,062 men and 6 artillery pieces. The Centre, under Lord Paget, numbered 4,055 soldiers. General Fraser's division, composed of 4,090 men, constituted the Left Wing and was supported by 6 artillery pieces, as was the Centre. General Houston was assigned the 2,676-man Reserve, accompanied by the reserve artillery. This reorganization was completed by 1:00 P.M., and the army moved forward from the Bree Sand in two columns. The first column, composed of the Right Wing and the Centre, marched through East Capelle to Grypskirke, where the Centre halted while the troops under General Graham continued to the village of Meliskirke. The second column, consisting of the Reserve, entered Seroskirke, which had been evacuated earlier by Osten, and continued to St. Laurens. The situation of the British on Walcheren on the evening of July 31 was described as follows:

Major General Graham was ordered to observe Zoutland on his right, and to communicate with Lieutenant General Lord Paget, at Grypskerke on his left. Lieutenant General Lord Paget was ordered to communicate on his right with Major General Graham at Meliskerke, and on his left with Brigadier General Houston at St. Laurens. Brigadier General Houston was ordered to communicate with Lieutenant Gen-

eral Fraser (before Ter Veere) on his left, and with Lieutenant General Lord Paget on his right at Grypskerke.[21]

After Ter Veere's surrender early on August 1, the British army
continued its move toward Flushing, reducing all defensive fortifications along the way. General Graham's Right Wing followed
the western coast of Walcheren and destroyed the abandoned
coastal batteries near Zoutland. At Dishoek and Vygenter, two
batteries west of Flushing, Graham's division encountered solid
opposition for the first time during the march. A detachment from
the Third Prussian Battalion attempted to defend the batteries but
was forced to withdraw to Flushing when its line of retreat was
threatened.[22] The Nolle battery, positioned on top of the dyke
west of Flushing, was captured also, and the Prussian detachment
then retreated into Old Flushing, a suburb outside the city's walls.
The Ninety-fifth Riflemen, serving with Graham's infantry, distinguished themselves in capturing the batteries.[23] Graham's division, now within full range of Flushing's guns, took shelter in
ditches and behind dykes.

Gen. William Henry Paget's column had been moving parallel
with Graham's. Initial resistance came at the village of Koudekirke, where Osten had stationed sixty men of the Third Prussian
Battalion and forty Colonial grenadiers.[24] The defensive troops
were pushed back toward Flushing following a brief skirmish, and
Paget continued to West Souburg, where more resistance was
encountered.

The enemy having brought forward a field piece which bore upon a
material picquet, Lt. Colonel Johnson with parts of the 68th and 85th
Regiments was detached by Brigadier General Rottenburgh to attack
him, and he succeeded in driving him into the town of Flushing.[25]

Paget promptly established his headquarters at West Souburg.

The left column, consisting of the Reserve under General Houston, had been ordered to march through Middelburg and take a
position at East Souburg, all the while watching the fort of Ramakins on the left and communicating with Lord Paget's position at

West Souburg. After passing through Middelburg, Houston found the road to Flushing blocked at the village of Abeylen, where Osten had established a breastwork and had cut a ditch across the roadway. Osten was apprised of Houston's advance upon the outpost at Abeylen and sent the light infantry of the Colonials to reinforce the position. Before this could be accomplished, however, the British charged the position, and Osten's original detachment of Colonials abandoned three six-pounders and fled along the road to East Souburg.[26] General Osten, supported by the arrival of General Monnet from Flushing, succeeded in halting the retreat and reorganizing the troops for battle. The Colonials were ordered to hold East Souburg as long as possible so that Osten could form a defensive line between that village and Flushing.[27]

As Houston's column approached East Souburg he came under fire from the Colonials. The English general ordered a frontal assault and at the same time made dispositions to turn the village, which resulted in the immediate evacuation and retreat of the Colonials.[28] The Prussian grenadiers posted along a nearby dyke joined the retreat and in so doing abandoned two six-pounders to the invaders. Houston exploited the confusion and pursued the fleeing troops along the road toward Flushing. Osten described his position as follows: "The enemy profited from the disorder of the 1st Colonial Battalion, and moved on me in force; my troops disbanded and I was obliged to lay my hands on the panic stricken; but in spite of all the efforts of my two aide-de-camps, the Battalion Commander, Maj. Serier, and myself, we could not rally them, it was impossible to accomplish it."[29]

The retreat continued to the walls of Flushing. The confusion was compounded by the large numbers of islanders retreating with the troops. These peasants came from East and West Souburg and from farther west, where Paget and Graham also were moving on Flushing. Into the midst Osten "arrived upon the glacis of Flushing with but seven men prepared to fight."[30] The fire of Osten's single piece of field artillery halted the nearest English column. The guns of Flushing, which could not fire previously because of Osten's retreating troops, now opened and forced Paget's Sixty-eighth and Eighty-fifth to retreat to West Souburg, with moderate casualties.[31] Once the English advance was stopped, Osten established several advance posts about seven hundred yards from the walls of Flushing and retired into the city with the remainder of his troops. Sir Eyre Coote, accompanying the Reserve, established general headquarters at West Souburg.

While the other three columns of the British army were engaged near Flushing, General Fraser marched his division from Ter Veere through Middelburg and moved toward Ramakins. This small fortress east of Flushing on the Slough Passage was of particular importance to the English since its guns controlled the navigation of the Slough at its junction with the West Scheldt. It would be virtually impossible to pass any large ships from the Slough into the West Scheldt without first securing Ramakins.[32] Fraser's division met no opposition during the march to Ramakins; and on the evening of August 1 his troops took up positions along a dyke less than a mile from the fortress. The following morning Col. William Fyers, the commanding engineer, reconnoitered Ramakins and recommended a heavy bombardment for a rapid surrender since Ramakins had no shelter from such an attack. Consequently, the engineers took advantage of some entrenching tools which were landed at Ter Veere the same morning and began construction of a battery of three twenty-four-pounders and two ten-inch mortars seven hundred yards from the fort.[33]

On the following day, August 3, the guns of Ramakins began firing on the work party at the battery. The Ninety-fifth Riflemen responded by using trees and hedges to cover their advance to within a few hundred yards of the fort, from where they fired upon the gunners of the garrison who were unprotected on low parapets and succeeded in driving them from their guns. By evening the battery was completed, but before it could commence firing, Ramakins surrendered. The 127-man garrison, commanded by Captain Wounier, marched out of the fort and yielded as prisoners of war.[34] By the evening of August 3 only Flushing remained to be captured for complete British control of Walcheren.

While entrenching equipment and artillery were being landed at Ter Veere for the siege of Flushing, news reached Walcheren of events in South Beveland. Sir John Hope's division had been conducted up the East Scheldt on July 30 and had anchored off the island of Schouwen near Zieriksee. Arrangements were made to land the troops on South Beveland on the thirty-first, but bad weather delayed disembarkation. On August 1, ships of shallow draft and small boats transported without incident six thousand of Hope's troops from their anchorage to a landing site near the village of Wemeldinge. The remainder was landed the following day.[35]

The grenadiers of the Guards Regiment and a detachment of the Ninety-fifth Regiment were disembarked first and moved inland, with patrols being dispersed to Capelle and Goes. The main body of Hope's division then marched toward Goes, the principal town on the island, detaching three companies of the Twentieth Regiment at the village of Kattendyke. As the advance guard of Hope's army approached Goes, they were greeted by the town's magistrates who yielded the city without opposition.[36] Hope stationed the Ninety-second Regiment at Goes and pushed his column eastward. During the course of the evening he learned that Dutch troops from Walcheren and from other areas of South Beveland had been converging near the fort of Batz. Foregoing any action that evening, Hope established his headquarters at Goes, stationed General Disney's brigade three miles east at Capelle, and ordered Erskine to encamp his brigade between the two.

At daybreak on August 2 operations in South Beveland continued. General Disney was ordered to advance toward Waarde, the anchorage of the French fleet when at neither Flushing nor Antwerp. Disney had expected the Dutch to defend Waarde's twelve-gun battery commanding the anchorage, but upon arrival he found it abandoned and the guns spiked. Later in the afternoon one of Disney's patrols ventured along the dyke toward Fort Batz and discovered that it too had been deserted.[37]

Gen. Stewart Bruce, the Dutch commander in Zealand, was responsible for the evacuation of Batz. He had been on Walcheren until the night of July 31, when he and his Dutch troops slipped out of Ter Veere and crossed over into South Beveland. He was soon joined by the remaining Dutch troops from Walcheren, including the garrison of Middelburg. With these forces, now totaling some nine hundred men, Bruce retreated along the West Scheldt as the French fleet ascended the river.[38] Once the fleet had sailed above Waarde, the Dutch general spiked the guns of the battery there and retired to Batz, where he arrived with a much depleted force.[39] There, on August 2, he received a dispatch from King Louis ordering him to defend Batz in order to retard the British advance. Although the fort was enclosed and protected by a moat, Bruce did not consider his position strong enough to pose a serious obstacle to the invaders. He therefore spiked the guns, dismounted their carriages, and crossed the Bergen-op-Zoom channel to the mainland via a little-known ford.[40]

General Bruce's evacuation of Batz without firing a shot not only jeopardized the defense of the Scheldt and endangered the French fleet, it was also a humiliation for King Louis. Napoleon saw this episode as just another example of Dutch perfidy and ordered that an example be made of Bruce. Louis consequently stripped the general of his command and had him court-martialed. When his first trial ended in acquittal, an outraged French emperor ordered Bruce tried again. The second trial, on 8 July 1810, resulted in Bruce's dismissal from the army and a short imprisonment.[41]

The value of Batz to the British was immediately evident. By the evening of August 2, all South Beveland was in British hands. The possession of Batz gave the British control of both the East and the West Scheldt, with the exception of Flushing, to within fifteen miles of Antwerp. Although the French fleet was now

above Batz, the expeditious occupation of this strategically located fort provided the British an excellent base from which to
expand operations against the Continent. It was apparent that the
Dutch and French were aware of their vulnerability when they
initiated defensive measures upon the first sighting of the British
in the Scheldt on July 29.

6

Cadsand or Antwerp

On the Continent, reaction to the expedition was immediate. The sighting of British ships was telegraphed to Paris from Boulogne, Dunkirk, Cadsand, and Flushing, and the news reached General Clarke, French minister of war, on July 30.[1] In response Clarke ordered Gen. Antoine-Guillaume Rampon not only to take command of the forces dispatched to the left bank of the Scheldt but also to direct the 6,000 National Guard from the camp at St. Omer to Cadsand.[2] Gen. Antoine-Alexandre Rousseau, the commander on Cadsand, received eight companies of reserve from Ecloo on July 30, and the following day Gen. Chambarlhac de Laubespin, the fifty-five-year-old commandant of the Twenty-fourth Military Division at Brussels, arrived to command the defenses of the island.[3] With Chambarlhac's arrival, followed later in the day by a detachment of cannoneers and military workers from Antwerp, the number of troops on Cadsand on July 31 rose to 5,744, including 309 cavalry.[4]

The circumstances surrounding Huntley's failure to land on Cadsand have already been discussed. Chambarlhac, however, had every reason to expect that the British assault on Cadsand was imminent. "I am about to be attacked," he wrote. "Send reinforcements immediately."[5] In addition to the 5,744 already on the island by July 31, additional French troops began converging upon Cadsand when, on August 1 and 2, Gen. Jean-André Valletaux's 1,500-man brigade arrived from Louvain and, on August 3, both General Rampon and Gen. Jean-Baptiste Olivier reached Cadsand. Rampon's 6,000 National Guardsmen had marched from St. Omer to Ghent and were immediately directed to Cadsand. General Olivier, commandant of the Sixteenth Military Division at Lille, took command of the 5,500 National Guardsmen from the

Department of the North and joined General Rampon on Cadsand on the third.[6]

Since Owen's squadron off Cadsand also posed a threat to the French ports between Cadsand and Boulogne, the National Guard was alerted at Ostend, Dunkirk, and Calais. Defensive measures were taken as far south as Le Havre, where Gen. François-Louis Lamorlière, commandant of the Fifteenth Military Division, reported that he had "taken measures to repulse . . . any attacks on the coast of the 15th Military Division." If the English did have objectives other than the Scheldt, the port of Boulogne appeared to be a likely goal. Weakened by the withdrawal of the 6,000 National Guard from St. Omer, General Sainte-Suzanne's camp at Boulogne was augmented by the Third and Fourth Demibrigades from Paris. By the time the Third Demibrigade arrived at Boulogne on August 5, Sainte-Suzanne was convinced by the movements of the British ships near Cadsand that the British had no intention of attacking Boulogne. Consequently, both demibrigades were ordered to the Scheldt.[7]

During the first few days of August, numerous small detachments, in addition to the large units already mentioned, were placed under orders for the defense of the Scheldt. On August 1 a 700-man detachment from the Legion of the Vistula, accompanied by ninety Polish Lancers, was directed to Lille to be deployed as required along the Scheldt or the coast between Cadsand and Boulogne.[8] On August 2, two Colonial battalions totaling 1,000 men were ordered to Boulogne; the following day, between 700 and 800 gendarmes were dispatched to Antwerp from Brussels; and on August 3, the detachments of the 113th Infantry Regiment and the Seventy-first Light from Paris were also ordered to Boulogne.[9] The gendarmes of the Sixteenth and Twenty-fourth Military Divisions were armed for action at Lille and Ghent, respectively. Responding to the crisis, the prefect of the Department of the North, François-René-Jean Pommereul, ordered all mayors and subprefects in his department to raise men to garrison the communes and reinforce the National Guard.[10]

Pictorial Plan of the West Scheldt

During these first days of August, the French were primarily concerned with fortifying the left bank of the Scheldt, especially Cadsand, and the coast of Flanders south of the island. The defense of Cadsand was important for three reasons. First, reinforcements to Flushing could be supplied most easily from the village of Breskens, opposite Flushing. Second, the batteries of Cadsand were essential in preventing the British from using the Wielingen channel to enter the West Scheldt. Also, these batteries could harass English ships attempting to bombard Flushing via the Deurloo channel. Third, the French considered it possible that the British might attempt to land on Cadsand and move south to attack other French ports with a combined land and naval operation.[11] For these reasons, the forces available for the defense of the Scheldt were initially directed to Cadsand.

Although most of General Clarke's attention was directed to Cadsand and the coast, he did not overlook the fact that Antwerp, with its weak defenses, was vulnerable. On August 1 Clarke had ordered Gen. Louis-Joseph Saint-Laurent, who was on leave in Paris, to assume command of the artillery at Antwerp and along the Scheldt. In addition, the minister of war's deployments were further strengthened by the dispatch of seven to eight hundred gendarmes from Brussels to Antwerp.[12]

Since the arrival of the British in the Scheldt, Antwerp had been foremost in the mind of King Louis of Holland. On August 1 at Aix-la-Chapelle, Louis had received the first reports of the British expedition, and he immediately returned to Amsterdam. Here he entrusted the defense of his capital and northern Holland to Marshal Jean-Baptiste Dumonceau and reinforced Gen. Jean-Joseph Tarayre with four thousand men at Bergen-op-Zoom. Louis also learned to his dismay that General Chambarlhac was massing troops on Cadsand and that Antwerp had not been reinforced. In his letter to Chambarlhac on August 1, Louis indicated the hazard involved in occupying Cadsand at the expense of Antwerp. On August 2 Louis again criticized the concentration of troops in

Cadsand, this time in a letter to Napoleon. "General Chambarlhac is concentrating his troops in the island of Cadsand; but since it seems certain to me that it is their intention to attack Antwerp and attempt to destroy the docks there, it appears that that measure is not at all sufficient and leaves Antwerp completely open to attack from the other side." Louis attempted to impress his brother with the seriousness of the situation and urged Napoleon to appoint "one of the marshals in order to take general command of all the forces of the land and sea, in order that there be a liaison between their efforts."[13]

Concern for Antwerp became more general on August 3, when news of General Bruce's evacuation of Batz and its subsequent occupation by the English became known on the Continent.[14] Admiral Missiessy's fleet had sailed above Batz on July 31, and on August 1 his ships of the line were behind the boom spanning the river between Forts Lillo and Liefkenshoek.[15] Although General Tarayre, commanding the Dutch forces, had over four thousand troops at Bergen-op-Zoom, Gen. Jean-Louis-François Fauconnet, the French commandant of Antwerp, had fewer than one thousand men to defend Antwerp. These were the only men immediately available to defend the right bank of the Scheldt between Bergen-op-Zoom and Antwerp. Neither Lillo on the right bank nor Liefkenshoek on the left were sufficiently garrisoned to sustain serious attack, and the British were less than fifteen miles away at Batz.[16]

Meanwhile, the situation on the left bank was somewhat relieved on August 3, when Generals Rampon and Olivier arrived on Cadsand with their respective National Guard units. Rampon assumed command of the forces on the left bank of the Scheldt and, learning of the evacuation of Batz, dispatched General Chambarlhac to Antwerp. The latter informed Paris: "Batz has been evacuated. General Rampon and 6,000 men have arrived in Cadsand. I am going to Antwerp with 2 battalions of infantry and any cavalry I can collect. In its present state nothing prevents them [the English] from becoming masters of the two branches of the Scheldt and turning the fleet and port of Antwerp."[17]

At Antwerp General Fauconnet reported to Clarke that he was cooperating with King Louis of Holland in defending the right bank of the Scheldt and that it appeared that his city was the English objective. "I have ordered the director of engineers to place the city and citadel in a state of defense." He could also report that work was being commenced between Antwerp and Bergen-op-Zoom, particularly at Lillo and Liefkenshoek. After dispatching General Chambarlhac to Antwerp, Rampon requested Clarke to order additional reinforcements there also, emphasizing that his own troops were needed to defend Cadsand and the left bank. However, Clarke's orders were already en route to Rampon, directing him to "take measures to prevent the English from attacking Antwerp by the right bank."

Send to Fauconnet all the battalions of military workers of the navy, with the gunners, and reinforce Antwerp with everything available in order to repulse an English attack there. General Charbonnier has arrived at Antwerp from Maestricht with 600 men and 200 cavalry. One detachment of Colonials, 700 or 800, are in route and will arrive on the 7th, [and] 100 Lancers on the 11th. I will also send part of the artillery company from Metz to Gand, arriving on the 18th. Three hundred men of the artillery train will arrive at Gand on the 10th.[18]

In response to the gravity of the situation in the Scheldt, the National Guard of six departments—Lys, Pas de Calais, Nord, Aube, Escaut, and Deux Nethes—were formed into companies for the defense of the Scheldt. On August 5 the situation on Cadsand was ameliorated by the withdrawal of Huntley's division from Owen's squadron. With the threat against Cadsand diminished to some degree, more troops could now be directed from the coastal areas to Antwerp and the right bank of the Scheldt. The Third Demibrigade was ordered to "march day and night" from Boulogne to Antwerp; General Sainte-Suzanne was ordered to organize the National Guard from the departments of Somme and

Aisne at Boulogne and, when 6,000 men were assembled, to dispatch them to Antwerp; and a detachment of 230 artillerymen from the Eighth Regiment of Artillery at Verdun also was placed under orders for Antwerp, scheduled to arrive on the eleventh or twelfth.[19]

General Saint-Laurent had arrived at Antwerp on August 3 and had immediately commenced work repairing the defenses of the city and citadel. In a meeting with Chambarlhac, Fauconnet, and the sixty-nine-year-old maritime prefect, Pierre-Victor Malouet, Saint-Laurent was successful in achieving agreement on a coordinated effort. The defenses of the city were in semiruin. Many of the guns on the ramparts were unserviceable and their carriages in need of repairs. Gunpowder was found stored on the ramparts and needed to be removed to shelter. Even had the guns been serviceable, the cannoneers had not yet returned from Cadsand, and the navy gunners from the fleet had not been organized for work on the ramparts. Saint-Laurent found the eighteen guns at Lillo and the eleven at Liefkenshoek in operating condition, but both forts needed palisades.[20]

Whereas General Fauconnet had only 900 men at Antwerp on August 2, when Batz was evacuated, by August 6 that number had been raised to almost 6,000. General Valletaux's 1,500 troops, comprising the Fourth Battalion of the Forty-eighth Infantry Regiment and the Fourth Battalion of the Thirteenth Light Infantry Regiment, had accompanied General Chambarlhac from Cadsand to Antwerp on August 3, covering the forty-odd miles in one day.[21] Furthermore, the minister of war could announce the following on August 7:

I have given orders that about 36,000 men, including the garrison of Flushing, be assembled under orders by the 12th, independent of the 2,500 men which will arrive on the Scheldt from the 12th to the 20th; which force will hold the enemy in check and cause them to fear for their line of communication in Walcheren and South Beveland. Because most of the enemy's force is in the Scheldt, I have directed most of the troops there from the camp at Boulogne. I have ordered the 6th and 7th Demi-brigades to proceed immediately to Antwerp, replacing them at Boulogne with the National Guard from the departments of the Seine and Somme.[22]

Upon his arrival on Cadsand, General Rampon proceeded to organize and deploy the troops which were collecting in the Scheldt. On August 5 King Louis wrote Rampon from Breda offering him the Dutch troops for the defense of Antwerp. "I place at your disposition my troops which are under the orders of General Tarayre. My troops are between Bergen-op-Zoom and Antwerp."[23] With the pressure on Cadsand relieved, Rampon reorganized his forces by returning the immediate command of Cadsand to Rousseau and giving General Olivier the overall responsibility for the troops on the left bank of the Scheldt between Antwerp and Cadsand. Rampon then proceeded to Antwerp and later consulted with Louis near Bergen-op-Zoom. On August 7 Rampon reported his deployments completed. On the right bank he had placed a division composed of two brigades and commanded by General Chambarlhac. The First Brigade, under General Valletaux, was composed of the 180th Regiment, 781 men; the Thirteenth Light Infantry Regiment, 724 men; and a detachment of 105 mounted troops of the Fourth Hussars. These 1,610 French troops were placed on both flanks of the 4,500 Dutch troops commanded by General Tarayre, which extended in a line from Bergen-op-Zoom to the village of Putten, with Huibergen in the center. The Second Brigade of French troops was commanded by Gen. Claude Rostollant and included a detachment of the Twenty-second Light Infantry Regiment, 208 men, and a detachment of the 108th Infantry Regiment with a strength of 300 men. To these regulars were added 1,100 military workers and seamen and 1,150 customs agents and troops from the Fourth Demibrigade. Detachments from the Tenth and Twenty-second Regiments of Light Cavalry, totaling 180 men, completed the Second Brigade, which took up a position near Fort Lillo. The Reserve was quartered at Capelle, about a mile from Putten, where Chambarlhac established his headquarters. The Reserve consisted of 179 dragoons and 130 gendarmes. Rampon also had garrisoned 366 men at Lillo and 240 men at Liefkenshoek.[24]

On August 7 the garrison inside the walls of Antwerp consisted of 907 men, most of whom were dragoons without mounts and customs agents and workers. The citadel's garrison numbered 225, and across the river at the fort of Tête de Flandre, 74 men were in garrison. As more troops arrived daily, they were added to the garrison at Antwerp, which was augmented by sailors from the fleet.[25]

General Olivier had overall responsibility for the left bank of the Scheldt, especially Cadsand, which was under the immediate command of General Rousseau. Olivier had organized the National Guardsmen into eight legions of 500 men each. In addition to these troops, 2,400 men of General Rampon's command still remained on Cadsand; an indeterminate number of National Guards were quartered at Ecloo, Ghent, and Olivier's headquarters at Bruges; and others were arriving so rapidly that "about 20,000 men, with about 16,000 or 17,000 National Guards" would fortify the left bank by August 12. Flushing already had received over 3,000 reinforcements from Cadsand by August 6, and more would be sent if communications remained uninterrupted.[26]

With such a large military force being collected on either bank of the Scheldt between Cadsand and Bergen-op-Zoom, there was a growing need for a commanding general, not only to coordinate the movements of the French army and navy but also to secure cooperation of the Dutch. When the English had first appeared off Walcheren, General Clarke had given temporary command of the French forces to General Rampon and had immediately written Napoleon in Vienna for instructions. Napoleon received the first reports of the expedition while at Schoenbrunn on August 6; consequently, his orders to Clarke did not reach Paris until August 12.[27] In the interval, Clarke was harassed by his own indecision and by urgings from King Louis of Holland that a French marshal be sent to direct the military affairs in the Scheldt. Louis had first made this suggestion in his letter to Napoleon on August 2 and had followed it on the same date with a letter to Jean Jacques Cambacérès, archchancellor of the empire. "It is urgent that there be at Antwerp, a Marshal who can unify the command of the land and sea, and give to the affairs the energy and unity of which there is a great need." Louis was apprehensive not only for the fleet and shipyards at Antwerp; he also feared a possible Dutch insurrection spurred on by the British presence. Additional troops were needed not only to protect the frontiers of Holland and France but also to "prevent an explosion in this country, and principally in the area of Antwerp, where the inhabitants are not content."[28] Louis considered the defense of Antwerp the primary goal of the troops in the Scheldt, but it was not until August 3 that an appreciable number of soldiers was placed under orders for Antwerp.

Although General Rampon was in command of the French forces in the Scheldt, Louis controlled his Dutch troops, thus posing the problem of a divided command above Antwerp. Furthermore, Admiral Missiessy, in charge of the French fleet, was under direct orders from Adm. Denis Decrès, minister of the navy; and General Fauconnet, commandant of Antwerp, had no definite orders concerning his relationship to Rampon. No chain of command had been established. Such was the situation in the Scheldt on August 7 when General Rampon announced his dispositions. On the same day, Louis again wrote Clarke urging the appointment of a marshal or someone with authority to command the army and navy. "It is necessary that there be here a marshal or grand officer of the empire, in order that he also give orders to the navy."[29] Louis later described the subsequent events of August 7 in the following manner:

I have not ceased to correspond with the general at Antwerp, the admiral and the maritime prefect, but I was upset to see the disunion or rather the confusion from several authorities and especially the lack of vigor and resignation to the events. I asked then for a conference with generals Rampon and Chambarlhac, and while I was meeting with them, I received the response from the Archchancellor and the comte d'Hunebourg, both asking me to take the position of commander in chief.[30]

Louis remonstrated that to be effective he would need to have Admiral Missiessy under his orders, but that he preferred to have Decrès, minister of the Navy, come to Antwerp to direct the activities of the fleet.[31] Later in the day, Louis issued a general announcement from his headquarters at Rosendaal that he had taken command of the Army of the Brabant, so named by Louis, and including all the French and Dutch troops along the Scheldt.[32] General Rampon was given the command of one of the two corps organized on the right bank in addition to the general command of Olivier's division on the left bank, although Olivier remained in immediate command. The second corps on the right was composed of Tarayre's Dutch troops, increased to six thousand men, now under the general command of Marshal Dumonceau. Generals Chambarlhac, Louis Charbonnier, and Claude Dallemagne, the latter commandant of the Twenty-fifth Military Division at Wesel, were given commands of divisions under General Rampon.[33]

In his report to Napoleon on August 9, Louis outlined the dispositions he had made and indicated that his position was still very weak. A large force had indeed been assembled, but its effectiveness in the field was questionable. Fort Lillo had only one officer to direct the work of the four-hundred-man garrison, and the boom, "the principal defense of the squadron," broke with each tide because of the strong current. Louis was preparing to inundate both sides of the Scheldt between Bergen-op-Zoom and Antwerp and had already ordered additional fortifications erected along that route.

I have ordered General Fauconnet, the Admiral, and Malouet to immediately find locations to erect three good forts, to prepare some merchant ships to sink in the passes if we are reduced to the last extremity, to prepare a great number of fireships, to work day and night . . . to put Lillo and the other forts in a formidable state, to raise four other batteries of twenty pieces of 36 each at the four bends in the river, with the artillery and equipment from the navy.[34]

Concluding his report to Napoleon, Louis advised that although the remainder of his kingdom was defenseless, he was doing everything possible to protect the fleet and Antwerp. Louis added that though king of Holland, "I will always be French at heart and always your brother."

General Rampon's reaction to Louis's temporary appointment as commander was one of resentment, although he indicated his willingness to obey the king of Holland until Napoleon's wishes were known.[35] Moreover, Rampon corroborated Louis's distressing report of the weakness of the French-Dutch troops in the Scheldt. Most of the troops were very young, many having never been under fire before. Consequently the initiative would be left to the English, since with troops of such caliber "it is necessary to assure them of success and not attempt anything which could affect their morale." On August 9 Louis complained to Clarke that the forces under his command constituted only a "moral force" and that "the English are much stronger than we are, in spite of the arrival already of reinforcements." Louis urged that additional troops be recruited to enable him to take the offensive and drive the English from the Scheldt. "If we do not get troops enough to take the offensive soon, we will be lost; they may be successful just as in Spain."[36]

As each day passed with the English remaining in Walcheren and South Beveland, the defensive position along the Scheldt improved. General Saint-Laurent, after organizing the work to repair the fortifications at Antwerp, began his inspection of the other significant forts along the Scheldt. He found the guns at Lillo and Liefkenshoek in good order. Crossing to the left bank, Saint-Laurent inspected the works at the Tête de Flandre, and at Terneuse he relocated the batteries in order to take advantage of protection afforded by the large dyke.[37]

Arriving on Cadsand, Saint-Laurent received a report on the defenses of the island. The coast was protected by six permanent and four mobile batteries. Of the permanent batteries, numbers one, two, and three constituted the Imperial Battery which defended the pass between Flushing and Breskens and totaled one twelve-pounder, ten twenty-four-pounders, eighteen thirty-six-pounders, and twenty-three mortars, fourteen of which were twelve-inch. The three remaining permanent batteries consisted of a total of ten guns and were designed primarily to protect the coastal waters. The port of Breskens was defended by a temporary battery of only two pieces of twelve, but thirteen mobile pieces were available if needed. Communications and reinforcements for Flushing were provided by means of small ships harbored in the Breskens port.[38] Upon completing his inspection tour of the defenses in the Scheldt, Saint-Laurent related to Clarke that although the Imperial Batteries were formidable, British ships of the line could probably pass up the West Scheldt between Flushing and Breskens in spite of fire from both shores.[39]

By August 11 daily arrivals of additional troops on both banks of the Scheldt had significantly raised the strength of Louis's Army of the Brabant (or the Corps of Observation of the Scheldt, as the French minister of war continued to designate it).[40] In addition to Dumonceau's 6,000-man Dutch corps, Rampon's French corps on the right bank now numbered 7,994 infantry, 1,070 cavalry and gendarmes, and 335 artillerymen. An additional 3,158 French troops and 150 Dutch were expected to arrive at any moment. On the left bank, from Antwerp to Cadsand, General Olivier's command had been increased to 20,101, including some 16,000 National Guards. Olivier also had 200 gendarmes, 582 artillerymen, and 26 field pieces. His entire force now totaled 20,883, and additional reserves were being directed to Ghent. The camp at Boulogne under General Saint-Suzanne included 8,000 troops by August 11, and sufficient troops were under orders to join the camp by the 20th to raise that total to 13,000. Consequently, the French forces in the Scheldt on August 11 totaled 15,399 troops on the right bank and 20,883 on the left bank with additional troops under orders for the Scheldt and the camp at Boulogne to serve as reserves.[41]

The following day the sluices were opened on both banks of

the Scheldt between Antwerp and Bergen-op-Zoom, flooding principally the areas around the Tête de Flandre, Antwerp, Lillo, and Liefkenshoek. On the same day, General Chambarlhac was directed to establish his division headquarters at Sandvliet, barely four miles from the English position at Batz.[42] Furthermore, Louis, in his zeal to protect Antwerp, proposed that stone-filled ships be sunk in the Scheldt below Antwerp to block the passage.[43] In his letter to Clarke on the twelfth, Louis again emphasized the vulnerability of Antwerp, the right bank, and indeed all of Holland to an English attack.

The reinforcements which you have ordered for General Rampon have arrived, nevertheless they will form only nine thousand infantry, among which 3,000 have never carried a rifle. They cannot adequately defend Antwerp. . . . The 6,000 men which General Rampon can rely upon, have almost no officers or sub-officers. . . . My ships, my docks are perhaps being burnt. East Friesland is perhaps at this moment occupied by the Duke of Brunswick.[44]

While Louis was writing this disheartening letter on the twelfth, General Clarke was receiving in Paris the first instructions from Napoleon concerning the Scheldt. In immediate response to Napoleon's orders, Clarke appointed Marshal Jean-Baptiste Bernadotte, Prince of Ponte-Corvo, commander of all French forces in the Scheldt, excepting the coast from Boulogne to Cadsand (including the camp at Boulogne), which remained under control of General Sainte-Suzanne.[45] Gen. Jean-François Dejean, French inspector general of engineers, was ordered to Antwerp to direct the construction and repair of fortifications along the Scheldt.[46] Napoleon also advised that he had appointed Gen. Claude-Sylvestre Colaud as governor of Antwerp. Moreover, he made it very clear to Clarke that he would not permit the British expedition to have much effect upon his operations in Germany. "At the most I will come myself, but I will not send a single man. . . . In general, all that I have asked for is useful to me, but not indispensable; it is for you to distinguish what you should send me and what you should retain."[47]

Napoleon also had ordered Marshal François-Etienne Kellermann, duke of Valmy, commander of the reserve army on the
Rhine at Strasbourg, to retain all reinforcements passing through
his depot en route to the Grand Army. Kellermann was directed
to form a corps at Wesel to protect northern Germany and to
serve as a reserve for the troops on the Scheldt.[48]

Two weeks had now passed since the British had landed in the
Scheldt, and during that period the French and Dutch had
strengthened their defenses and collected an army. On August 3
the total French and Dutch force from Cadsand to Bergen-op-
Zoom, a distance of approximately forty-five miles, numbered
fewer than 20,000 men, of whom only 900 were stationed at Antwerp. More than half of these 20,000 were National Guardsmen
who had never been under fire and were poorly armed and trained
and unfit to meet an army in the field. However, by August 13,
the combined French-Dutch force on both banks of the Scheldt
had risen to almost 46,000 men, more than half located between
Antwerp and Bergen-op-Zoom, and new confidence had been
instilled in the officers and troops by the appointment of Marshal
Bernadotte as the commanding general.[49] Such was the situation
on the Continent when the first sounds were heard of the British
bombardment of Flushing.

7

The Siege of Flushing

The occupation of Fort Batz on August 2 placed the British in a position to achieve all the objectives of the expedition. Flushing was the only obstacle which prevented their controlling the Scheldt to within fifteen miles of Antwerp, and although the weather had forced the expedition into the East Scheldt, neither Lord Chatham nor Sir Richard Strachan seemed perplexed with the turn of events.[1]

On August 1, while the British troops were occupying Ter Veere and moving across Walcheren to surround Flushing, Chatham and Strachan met at Middelburg to plan future operations. Since the division originally scheduled to sail to Sandvliet via the West Scheldt was now anchored in the East Scheldt, a new route to Sandvliet was necessary. The shallow East Scheldt was quickly eliminated from consideration and two other routes were studied. Strachan favored landing the troops, ordnance, and cavalry on the north side of South Beveland, marching the thirty-odd miles to Batz, then crossing the Scheldt to Sandvliet. Such a plan would not clutter the narrow Slough passage with so many transport vessels and would enable the warships to reach Batz more rapidly to support the army on its march toward Antwerp.[2] Chatham, however, considered this plan impracticable; he believed that landing the army, crossing the island via its narrow muddy roads, and reembarking to Sandvliet would result in considerable delay. Consequently, Chatham adopted the plan of transporting the troops, cavalry, ordnance, and other supplies by ship through the Veere Gat and Slough into the West Scheldt and then sailing directly to Sandvliet.[3]

On August 3 Ramakins surrendered while the British were commencing the bombardment, thus opening the Slough passage to the British from the East Scheldt to the West Scheldt.[4] Immediately thereafter, orders were issued to the ships of the squadron conveying Rosslyn's troops and equipment, as well as all the cavalry and ordnance, to pass through the Veere Gat and the Slough into the West Scheldt in order to proceed to Batz. Once all the armament and warships were collected at Batz, the advance to Antwerp could be attempted.[5] Several gunboats had succeeded in passing Ramakins prior to its surrender and were attempting to unite with Owen's ships at the mouth of the West Scheldt to complete the encirclement of Walcheren and to cut off communications between Flushing and Cadsand.[6]

Commodore Owen had remained off Cadsand with Lord Huntley's division until August 3, when orders were received to send Huntley's troops to the Roompot. Prior to that time, most of Owen's ships and smaller vessels were engaged in maneuvering to land on Cadsand, thus preventing him from devoting full attention and effort to blockading Flushing. By Thursday, August 3, only a few gunboats had reached the West Scheldt above Flushing through the Slough passage and with Gardner's squadron downwind and Owen otherwise occupied, General Chambarlhac seized the opportunity to reinforce Flushing. Six hundred and sixty men of the Sixty-fifth Infantry crossed into Flushing on August 1, and there followed the next day an additional 1,003 soldiers from the Fourth Battalion of the Eighth Demibrigade, and the Seventy-second and 180th Infantry Regiments.[7] The following day, the boats which had carried these reinforcements into Flushing attempted to return to Breskens. Owen, anchored off the Elboog in the estuary of the West Scheldt, ordered some of his boats to attack. Capt J. M. Hanchett, who was described by Strachan as a real "fire-eater," also joined in the chase in the sloop *Raven* to give some protection to the smaller British vessels. A sudden change in the wind blew the smaller English boats toward the sea batteries of Flushing, and the *Raven* followed to attract the fire of the town. Benefiting from Hanchett's diversion, the boats returned safely to the squadron, but the *Raven* was heavily damaged.[8]

The *Raven* incident seemed to confirm the opinions of the most experienced pilots in Lord Gardner's squadron, for just hours before, they had responded to an order from Strachan to state their opinion concerning the practicability of attempting to force the West Scheldt between Flushing and Cadsand. Gardner reported that "it is in their opinion impossible to pass the ships into the Scheldt, either by the Deurloo or Weiling [Wielingen], without probable destruction, as long as the enemy possess Flushing and the Cadsand shore."[9] While Strachan studied the situation, Gardner and Owen executed plans to sever communications between Flushing and Cadsand. By anchoring ships above and below Flushing out of range of the land batteries, rowboats could be stationed in the river between the two squadrons to prevent effectively any reinforcements from being passed from Cadsand to Flushing. As this plan was being put into operation on August 4, a severe gale forced the English flotilla, commanded by Capt. Philip Carteret, to take shelter in the Slough above Flushing. However, this same south-southwesterly wind enabled the French to reinforce Flushing from Cadsand with some 320 men from the Forty-eighth Infantry, having crossed the river in only seventeen minutes. Two days later, a similar situation occurred and 1,160 more troops were passed into Flushing. By the seventh, however, the British naval blockade was effected, and other attempts by the French to reinforce the besieged town were unsuccessful.[10]

After its surrender on August 1, Ter Veere had become the principal port of disembarkation for stores and equipment for Sir Eyre Coote's army on Walcheren. Entrenching tools and ordnance were the most essential equipment required on Walcheren after Coote's forces had invested Flushing. A small number of tools had been landed on August 2, but these had been only barely adequate for constructing the batteries against Ramakins, and it was not until after surrender of that fort that the first work party be-

gan breaking ground before Flushing on the evening of August 3.
Stores and equipment were slow in transit. This delay can be
partially explained by examining the scene of disembarkation.
"The beach at Ter Veere was of small dimensions, and by the
second day, it was literally covered mast high with guns, carriages, artillery and engineer stores of every description, in one vast
heterogeneous mountain; the lighter articles, required in the first
instance for batteries, lay at bottom, the heavier at top."[11]

Once these items were separated, there remained the problem
of transporting them to the scene of action, some eight miles
across the island. The narrow roads, bound on each side by deep
ditches and made almost impassable by incessant rains, made it
difficult to use artillery horses to pull the guns and carriages. A
brigade of seamen under Capt. Charles Richardson was finally
employed to assist in bringing the heavy ordnance forward.[12] With
some difficulty, enough wagons were soon procured from the
island to transport stores and equipment to the engineers' park at
West Souburg.

The engineer initially in charge of establishing the batteries
against Flushing was not the commanding engineer, Col. William
Fyers, but rather Lieutenant Colonel D'Arcy. It was originally
planned that only a small force would be placed against Flushing
while the primary force of the army marched on Antwerp; therefore Colonel Fyers accompanied the Right Wing of the army
destined to land at Sandvliet. Consequently, although he landed
on Walcheren on July 31, Fyers did not take direct command of
the batteries until August 8, when, due to numerous enemy reinforcements, Lord Chatham made the decision that Flushing would
have to be reduced before the expedition could advance.[13]

Placing the batteries against Flushing posed a difficult engineer-
ing problem.

The fortress of Flushing was enclosed by a line of nine bastions; seven
of these were unrevetted, being protected by a broad ditch too deep to
be forded. The demi-bastions at the extremities were on the sea dyke,

and having no ditches, their escarps were revetted. There were only two ravelins in the whole line, but the dyke bastions were covered by advanced flèches, closed at the gorge with heavy iron chevaux de frise. The whole of the ground outside the line, except certain detached points, was below the sea level at high water, and could be inundated by sluices constructed in the counterscarp. It was therefore impracticable to form the ordinary approaches or to attack *en regle* [in the standard manner].[14]

Consequently, the highest ground within reasonable distance of Flushing was selected for each of the British batteries. During the evening of August 3, work was commenced on the first battery, F, which included six ten-inch mortars fourteen hundred yards from Flushing.[15] Work was expanded as more equipment arrived at West Souburg. On August 5 a second battery, E, was laid out for ten twenty-four-pounders; and on the following day Battery G was marked off on the east dyke to contain three pieces of twenty-four. Construction also continued on the communication trench from Batteries E and F to broaden and deepen it to form a shielded road by which men and equipment could move sheltered from the fire of Flushing. The protective trench was then continued toward the right, eventually forming a parallel from the west dyke to Battery F in front of West Souburg.[16]

The British army retained the positions it had occupied on August 1, with General Fraser's division extending from Ramakins to East Souburg. Because the naval blockade of Flushing had not been achieved, thereby allowing French reinforcements to enter the town, Lord Chatham considered it necessary to strengthen his army on Walcheren. Such a measure would also expedite the siege of Flushing. Consequently, on August 2 General Grosvenor's division had begun landing on Walcheren and on the third had taken a position between Graham and Paget near West Souburg. Grosvenor was ordered to keep his troops ready to reembark "the moment circumstances admitted of the armament proceeding to its ulterior destination."[17] On August 5 the Light Brigade of the

King's German Legion was also landed to serve in the advance posts of the besieging army, bringing the total number of British troops to over twenty thousand.[18]

Meanwhile on August 1, General Monnet's French troops had retired into Flushing after first establishing advance posts along a perimeter several hundred yards from the town's wall and extending from the east to the west dyke, including Old Flushing. The garrison had been increased by approximately sixteen hundred reinforcements from Cadsand on August 1 and 2 and the total Monnet entrusted to the personal leadership of General Osten. On August 3 Osten ordered the newly arrived detachments from the Sixty-fifth and Seventy-second infantries to the Ramakins gate. The former detachment was to man the ramparts while the latter occupied the demilune (a small fortified position defending the gate) outside the wall. If the British attempted a general assault, the Seventy-second was to evacuate its position and reenter the town, burning the suburbs behind it. Osten also strengthened his advance posts: the Third Battalion of Prussians was ordered to bivouac outside the walls east of the city; a detachment of one hundred men of the Third Battalion was dispatched to reinforce the outpost on the West Souburg road, where a traverse had been constructed; and the battalion of French ex-deserters was sent to occupy Old Flushing and provide support for the advance post on the west dyke and the small force protecting the traverse on the road leading to Old Flushing.[19]

On August 4 General Monnet ordered a reorganization of the Flushing garrison into two demibrigades. The right consisted of the troops of the Sixty-fifth Infantry and the Prussian battalions under the command of Major Gauthier, who had the responsibility for the advance works on the east dyke and outposts on the east side of the town. The left was placed under Major Serier and included the Irish battalion, the Colonials, the battalion of returned French deserters, the fourth battalion of the Eighth Provisional Demibrigade, and detachments of the Seventy-second Infantry. Serier's forces were more numerous than those under Gauthier

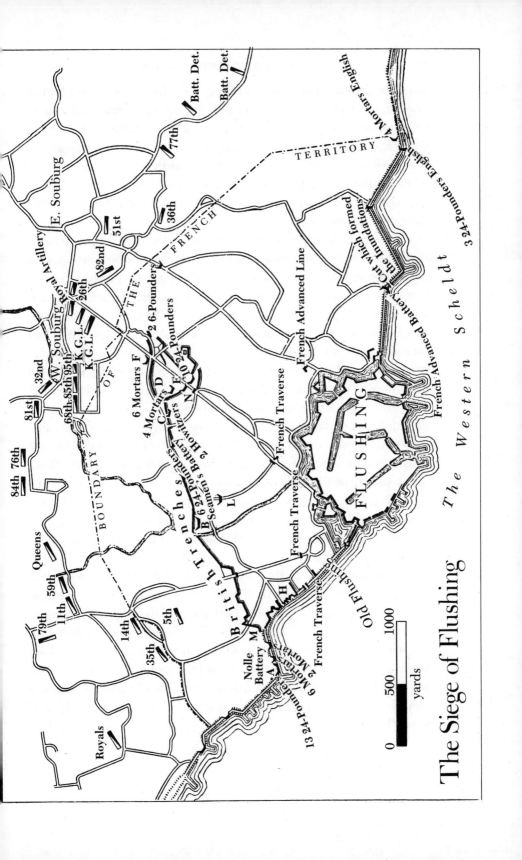

The Siege of Flushing

since the British were concentrating their batteries on the higher ground west of Flushing. The left demibrigade was ordered to deploy along the west dyke and defend the two traverses outside Old Flushing and on the West Souburg road. The few remaining troops of the garrison, augmented by additional reinforcements received between August 4 and 6, were held in reserve.[20] Flushing's National Guard patrolled the streets in both day and night shifts to maintain order.[21]

The French attempted no sorties before August 7, but prior to that date there were numerous minor skirmishes between opposing advance posts, and occasionally the guns of Flushing would fire in an attempt to disrupt the work on the British batteries. During the night of August 1, General Graham's advance troops had begun a breastwork across the road near the west dyke, but rifle fire from the French traverse caused work to be temporarily suspended. On the fifth, pickets from the twenty-sixth Regiment in front of Battery F exchanged fire with the French advance post near the traverse on the West Souburg road, with the English suffering five casualties.[22] The same day, Sir Eyre Coote dispatched Captain Wounier, the captured commander of Ramakins, toward Flushing with a flag of truce. The French pickets fired upon Wounier's party, but it returned to the British lines unharmed. The following day, the Ninety-fifth Riflemen, occupying an advance post in front of West Souburg, had a brief skirmish with about thirty of Major Serier's troops, during which two Frenchmen were killed.[23]

Meanwhile, in South Beveland Gen. Sir John Hope had secured his positions in the island. By the time the troops of General Disney's brigade had occupied Fort Batz on the night of August 2, all the batteries and villages in the island were in English hands. Hope's headquarters on South Beveland was established at Goes, while Disney occupied the southern portion of the island, including Waarde and Batz. Lord Dalhousie's brigade was bivouacked near Schore, and General Erskine remained with his brigade near Goes.[24]

Sir Richard Keats had landed on South Beveland on August 3, and after surveying the situation, he reported to Sir Richard Strachan. The French flotilla had assumed a position near Fort Lillo and appeared to be ready to "move as circumstances may determine them." Keats stated that the Bergen-op-Zoom channel "will not admit of our smallest Brigs going that way; it is a Gulley difficult by all accounts, as the Enemy had removed the Marks for even Pilots to keep in it."[25] Although the larger men of war could not reach Batz via the shallow East Scheldt Keats reported that two gunboats using that route had arrived. Several more gunboats as well as some thirty flatboats armed with carronades were under orders to proceed to Batz via the same route. This was the only British naval force immediately available to move upon Batz. The frigates and ships of the line, stationed below Flushing without sufficient pilots, were intimidated by the batteries on both sides of the entrance to the West Scheldt. The smaller British vessels were employed either in blockading Flushing and preparing to support the land batteries against the town or were in the Veere Gat and Slough attempting to expedite the numerous transports into the West Scheldt. As soon as additional vessels became available, they were directed up the West Scheldt to Batz, buoying the channel as they went.[26]

Since no English naval force was available to defend Fort Batz, it was essential that the fort's guns be made serviceable as quickly as possible. A detachment from the Royal Artillery under Captain Wilmot was immediately set to the task, and by August 4 they had unspiked ten pieces of twenty-four and three howitzers and replaced them on their carriages ready for action. The twelve twenty-four-pounders at Waarde also were unspiked.[27] These measures were completed just in time, for late on the afternoon of August 5, twenty-five French brigs descended from their anchorage point near Forts Lillo and Liefkenshoek and attacked Batz. General Disney's troops and the Royal Artillery manned the guns of the fort and returned fire. After nearly two hours of action, the French brigs retired, neither side receiving any serious damage.[28]

On Walcheren, Chatham and Strachan met again at Middelburg on August 6 to discuss the measures each was taking to hasten the expedition toward its primary objectives. While officially both seemed optimistic about the future of the campaign, their correspondence suggests that each had developed serious doubts about their ultimate success. Rumors circulated that the duke of Danzig [Marshal Lefebvre] had arrived at Antwerp at the head of 30,000 reinforcements, and while the news was quickly discounted, it caused both British commanders concern.[29] As early as August 5, Strachan wrote that "the intelligence of the French resources puts us to a stand and I fear it will not be practicable to get to Antwerp."

If the French have put reinforcements into Antwerp, more will come, and when it is ascertained that they have received reinforcements and that a French General of Rank is there, I shall advise our turning our thoughts to some other point than embarrassing ourselves by entangling the army and navy in an extensive and intricate navigation. I wish this trying business were well over.[30]

Meanwhile, Sir Home Popham, who enjoyed the confidence of both Chatham and Strachan, was also getting discouraged. On August 5 he presented to Chatham a memorandum which appears to have had a significant influence on the commander in chief's subsequent actions.

The various reports of the immence force collecting under the orders of the Duke of Dantzick [Danzig] at Antwerp, makes it necessary to take such precautions, and make such arrangements, as will prevent the possibility of disaster, and at the same time offer some prospect of accomplishing further objects of national importance, with a well ground hope of success.
The object of the present expedition, was, to capture Flushing, and destroy the Naval Depots and capabilities in the Scheld. If Flushing is captured, whether the fleet is captured or not, it cannot get out of the Scheld; in short, Flushing is the key to the Scheld, and with that in our possession, the Enemy is always liable to be destroyed by our Fire Ships, . . . they will rot at Antwerp.[31]

Popham's role in the expedition has never been fully explored, but evidence suggests that it was crucial. Not only does it appear that he was one of the masterminds behind it,[32] but he undoubtedly influenced Strachan's decision to concentrate the expedition in the East Scheldt,[33] and on August 5 he suggested to Chatham that the mere capture of Flushing would make the expedition a success.

The war office, however, did not seem to share the growing pessimism of the expedition's leaders. In a letter to Chatham on August 8, Castlereagh indicated no regret in not having captured Cadsand and expressed his great pleasure in the progress of the campaign. "You have not, however, suffered any obstacles to impede the progress of your operations which have been commenced with less delay, prosecuted with more rapidity, and pushed further towards the main object, than I could have hoped for in the time."[34] Castlereagh's optimism suggests, perhaps, that he did not fully understand the problems confronting the expedition.[35]

At the August 6 meeting, Chatham and Strachan exhibited differences of opinion and, to a lesser degree, dissension. Their correspondence reveals at least two incidents which created tension between the two men. The first occurred during the attack on Ter Veere when Chatham ordered some of the naval force to go into action without previously consulting Strachan.[36] The second occurred a few days later: Amelius, Lord Beauclerk landed provisions at Ter Veere late on August 1 but could get no receipt from the commissary officer, who said "he should not work until nine tomorrow, and not then if it did not suit his convenience." Strachan remonstrated that "the seamen work from dawn of day till dark night, and the captains and officers attend them."[37] Chatham evidently did little to correct this situation.

The meeting lasted through dinner and late into the evening. Chatham queried the admiral concerning the naval blockade of Flushing and how soon the various elements of the military could be transported through the Slough passage and into the West Scheldt. Strachan had written Chatham the previous day advising him of the difficulties the navy was experiencing, especially those due to the squally weather, but he stated that he was ordering some frigates to force the passage between Flushing and Cadsand. At the meeting on the 6th Strachan emphasized further the navy's problems: "I stated fully the difficulties I had to encounter from the untoward state of the weather, and from the intricacy of the channel in passing the vessels through the Slough, as also from the difficulties made by the pilots, who refused to take charge of these vessels, or even to carry the line of battle ships into the West Scheldt."[38]

Strachan concluded that in view of these difficulties, he now considered his suggestion of August 1, which concerned landing troops, ordnance, and cavalry on South Beveland, as the only practical plan which could be adopted. Under this plan, fewer ships would have to navigate the complicated passages of the West Scheldt, and a limited number of ships transporting essential provisions to the army could first be hurried up to Batz. Strachan warned that if the entire expedition continued to Batz through the Slough, an indefinite delay could result.

Chatham was aware of the difficulties the navy was experiencing, or so he stated, but he was not convinced that it was practical to land on South Beveland and transport all the cavalry and ordnance to Batz only to reembark. The roads on South Beveland were no better than those on Walcheren, and the entire operation would require a great deal of advance preparation. Consequently, Chatham rejected Strachan's suggestion. Furthermore, Chatham was probably influenced in his decision by several other factors. Flushing had received numerous reinforcements by the sixth, and a much larger besieging force was now necessary to contain the garrison. Also Chatham could hardly consider leaving Flushing to his rear and advancing upon Antwerp while there was a possibility that more reinforcements could be thrown into Walcheren from Cadsand if unfavorable weather conditions made the complete blockade of Flushing impossible. Until Flushing capitulated and a significant naval force assembled near Batz, an advance to Sand-vliet and operations against Antwerp seemed to Chatham impracticable. Finally, the general must have been influenced by intelligence reports received from the Continent and more especially by Popham's memorandum of August 5. Adjourning the conference, Strachan left with some vague idea that the commander in chief had acquiesced to his proposals concerning disembarking the remainder of the expedition on South Beveland, or at least he later so stated. Consequently, the men's differences of opinion extended then even to what was determined at this important conference.[39]

Although Chatham did not adopt Strachan's proposal, he did compromise somewhat the following day by ordering Huntley's division and the infantry of Rosslyn's division to disembark on South Beveland while their materiel and cavalry were forwarded through the Slough. This order was canceled on the seventh but reversed again on the eighth, and the following day both Huntley's and Rosslyn's divisions were finally landed; Rosslyn immediately assumed command of all British forces on South Beveland. Chatham also canceled his plan of establishing his headquarters at Goes, on South Beveland, and determined that until the naval blockade of Flushing was effective and ships of the line were able to proceed up the West Scheldt past Flushing, he would continue on Walcheren.[40]

By August 7 General Monnet's garrison had been cut off from the remainder of Walcheren for almost a week, although reinforcements continued to arrive from Cadsand. This too was severed on the seventh, and Flushing was completely invested by land and sea. He was, however, still able to communicate with Breskens via his telegraph set high atop the Hotel de Ville, but this was also knocked out early on the afternoon of August 13 when the bombardment of Flushing began.[41] Consequently, Monnet's knowledge of British troop strength and positions was weak, and on the afternoon of August 7 he ordered a large party to reconnoiter the British positions west of Flushing. Major Serier's demibrigade was given the assignment and was instructed to probe the enemy positions behind the parallel but to avoid an engagement with a superior force. Serier's forces were formed into three numerically equal columns for the sortie. The left column under Major Bockmann was composed of three hundred returned French deserters who were to attack the breastwork on the sand hills near the west dyke in front of the Nolle Battery. The center column, composed of the grenadiers and light infantry of the Colonial battalion and ninety men of the Forty-eighth Regiment under Major Bouis, was to seize the redoubt in the meadow adjoining the sandhills near the Nolle, coordinating its movements with those of the left column. Finally, Major Serier and three hundred men from the Forty-eighth Infantry made up the right column, which was to move along the road from Old Flushing paralleling the movements of the other two units. A four-hundred-man detachment of Prussians under Major Direek was left in reserve in Old Flushing.

The columns moved out at 5 P.M. on August 7 and were soon under fire from the Royals and the Fifth Regiment. The left column stopped almost immediately and refused to advance and engage the Royals posted on the west dyke; they remained a short distance from Old Flushing and directed their fire in the general direction of the Royals. Osten later recorded that this fire "not only was useless, but equally dangerous for our troops which were in front." [42]

Under such circumstances, Major Bouis and his troops soon found their position desperate. While moving on British Redoubt M, they received fire from Royals posted on the dyke and were charged by their light company.[43] At the same time, Capt. Weber Smith of the Royal Artillery opened with a piece of six from behind the breastwork. This fire, combined with the arrival of Lieutenant Colonel Pratt's two companies of the King's German Legion, made Bouis's position untenable.[44] By the time his column could extricate itself and retreat into Old Flushing, 133 men were either killed or wounded and several more captured, including Major Bouis himself.[45]

The third column, meanwhile, had been advancing a few hundred yards to the right on the Koudekirke road and, supported briefly by the guns of Flushing, was engaged by elements of the Fifth Regiment under Major Emes. The Fifth Regiment was quickly reinforced by troops from the King's German Legion, including a 5½-inch howitzer, which was brought to bear upon a house used by Serier's advance pickets. Finding the English well entrenched and in superior numbers and learning of the retreat of Bouis's column, Serier was forced to withdraw immediately to escape encirclement by the Royals and the light infantry of the King's German Legion. As darkness approached, Serier's column, supported by the Prussian reserve, fought its way back to the shelter of Old Flushing. The reconnaissance effort cost Serier 251 men killed, wounded, or missing, while the Prussians, in covering the Forty-eighth's retreat, lost 36 men. The returned French deserters, although not closely engaged, nevertheless suffered 53 casualties and some deserters to the English.[46] The British losses were somewhat lighter: only 14 were reported killed and 141 wounded during the entire action. This action on the seventh was the only significant sortie attempted by Monnet during the siege.

On August 8 the French flotilla again bombarded Batz, but the fort, with all its guns and fortifications in order, drove the vessels back up the river with damage to several gunboats.[47] Meanwhile, Sir Home Popham, commanding a flotilla of brigs and sloops, advanced up the West Scheldt, buoying the channel along the way. Popham approached Batz on August 11, as Sir Richard Keats was arriving via the East Scheldt with thirty flatboats armed with carronades. The arrival of these two English naval forces coincided with a third attack upon Batz by the French flotilla, and six of its gunboats attempted to pass the fort and sail into the Bergen-op-Zoom channel. Fort Batz opened fire, and in the ensuing action all six gunboats grounded and were set afire. With the approach of the two English naval contingents, the remaining vessels of the flotilla retired up the river near Lillo. Both Keats and Popham took up anchorages at the fort.[48]

It should be noted here that Sir Richard Strachan had originally scheduled the ships of the line and frigates to pass into the West Scheldt on August 2, at which time he planned to be able to attack the French fleet and flotilla once its retreat further up the river had been cut off by Sir John Hope's capture of Fort Batz. When this proved premature, Strachan decided to hold these ships at the estuary until the various elements of the expedition had proceeded up the West Scheldt toward Sandvliet, assuming that these ships might be needed against Flushing.[49] Although on August 3 he had received opinions of the pilots which described the difficulty of attempting to force the entrance of the West Scheldt while both banks were occupied by the French, Strachan issued orders to prepare the frigates and ships of the line to force the passage but not to act until he so ordered.[50]

As the siege of Flushing developed into a protracted operation, Strachan finally decided to force the entrance to the West Scheldt on August 6 with his frigates, but contrary winds prevented this until August 11.[51] On August 8 Lord Gardner, replying to Strachan's orders, reported that the frigates would advance as soon as the winds became more favorable but that more pilots should be available before the ships of the line attempted to advance. On the same day, Strachan wrote Chatham offering the use of the ships of the line against Flushing if the land batteries proved insufficient in forcing the besieged town's rapid surrender. This offer, Strachan declared, would have been made before, but since Flushing was not the sole objective of the expedition, he wished to keep the ships of the line effective.[52] But now, since the success of the expedition depended so much upon the rapid reduction of Flushing, Strachan was willing to use the ships against the town and cooperate with the army in any manner desired.

In a letter also dated August 8, Strachan indicated to Lord Gardner that he did not think Flushing would surrender under a land bombardment alone and that ships of the line might be needed to accomplish that end.

I very much apprehend that the Enemy will hold out till he is attacked by sea, it will therefore be proper to have six sail of the line ready to go against his sea defenses. . . . I do not propose to expose the Ships of the line to this risk of being fired, if the town can be reduced by other means, and therefore, the effect of the bombardment will be waited for, which I hope will take place today or tomorrow; our Flotilla at the same time will open from their present position.[53]

While the ships of the line were awaiting additional pilots to direct them into the West Scheldt once the land batteries had commenced the bombardment of Flushing, unfavorable winds had prevented the frigates from effecting the same objective. On August 11, however, the winds became more favorable, and Sir William Stuart, Captain of the *Lavinia*, led his ten frigates into the West Scheldt and passed the guns of Flushing and Breskens.[54] General Osten turned all the sea guns of Flushing upon the squadron in a fruitless attempt to prevent their passage, while General Picton ordered Battery G to open fire upon the town in a diversionary effort.[55] Stuart's ships were exposed to the fire from both banks for more than two hours, but the only significant damage was to the *L'Aigle*, which was hit by an exploding shell which killed one seaman and wounded four others. The total casualties for the ten frigates were two killed and nine wounded.[56] Strachan had intended to accompany the frigates up the West Scheldt once they had cleared Flushing, but since the land batteries were almost ready to commence the bombardment, he instead joined the ships of the line to direct their operations against Flushing.[57]

Inside Flushing, General Monnet had decided to execute a measure which he had hoped to avoid. The situation in Flushing was now gravely serious, and Monnet realized that the town could be saved only by cutting the dykes and inundating the island. So

long as the communications with Cadsand had been open and
reinforcements and supplies continued to arrive in the town, Monnet thought he could eventually accumulate a sufficient force to
drive the British from the island.[58] But with the isolation of Flushing, the dykes seemed to be the only remaining weapon. Napoleon had made it a standing order that the dykes were to be cut if
the town were ever besieged. He had communicated this order to
Monnet and had repeated it to General Clarke, minister of war,
on several occasions.[59]

On August 1 General Monnet had called a council meeting to
discuss the possibility of cutting the dykes but indicated that he
was hesitant to do so since he had lost Napoleon's order.[60] The
council unanimously agreed, however, that the dykes should be
cut if Flushing were in danger of a forced surrender. Monnet ultimately consented, but he delayed execution of the order until
Flushing was completely cut off. On August 6 he finally ordered
the east dyke cut directly in front of the French advance battery
and the sluices opened in the counterscarp of the moat surrounding Flushing. These limited measures were taken in an effort to inundate only the areas occupied by the besiegers.[61] The initial cut
in the dyke was only deep enough to allow water to flow into the
island at high tide, but it was gradually deepened as the situation
in Flushing became more critical.

On the following day Chatham was informed that the water
was rising in the drainage ditches and canals of Walcheren. Cognizant of Monnet's strategy, Chatham consulted some of the local
inhabitants and learned that since Flushing was some three feet
higher in elevation than Middelburg, opening the flood gates in
the latter and also at Ter Veere would drain off much of the water
via the island's drainage network.[62] These measures were immediately executed and this relieved somewhat the effects of the inundation attempt.

The British army continued the work of completing the parallel
and preparing the batteries for bombardment of Flushing under

the direction of Col. William Fyers, who had replaced Colonel
D'Arcy as commander of the engineers on August 8.[63] Construction continued on Batteries E and F, and new batteries, A and G,
were begun on the west dyke and the east dyke respectively. Mor-
tar Battery D was laid out on August 10, and during the day it
was noticed that the water in the ditches was rising and that it
flowed with a perceptible current. Work on the batteries was in-
terrupted by occasional fire from the guns of Flushing, which
General Osten ordered fired every half hour for several hours
daily in an effort to hinder completion of the batteries.[64]

Even though the British had learned how to drain off much of
the water pouring through the cut dyke, the break was now being
deepened and the canals and drainage ditches were not sufficient
to handle the water. The water was almost overflowing the drainage passages by the tenth, and the area immediately around
Flushing was slowly being flooded by the sluices in the counterscarp of Flushing's moat. The Colonials, whom General Osten had
posted at the traverse outside Old Flushing, were forced to evacuate their position temporarily because of the rising water.[65]

In spite of the rising water and inclement weather, work on the
British batteries continued and neared completion. The work was
temporarily suspended during the night of August 10 because of a
violent thunderstorm. "The ground very soon became impassable
for the guns and heavy Carriages, and the trenches were so filled
with water that the men could not work." [66] On the eleventh work
resumed, and a new battery, B, manned by seamen under Capt.
Charles Richardson, was laid out and work begun. During the
same day most of the low-lying areas near Flushing were flooded
and various elements of the British army were forced to move to
higher ground.[67]

By August 12 all the batteries were completed with the exception of Battery B, the seamen's battery, where a large work party
was employed in bringing up the guns and finishing preparations
for putting the pieces in place.[68] As the water in some of the drain-

age ditches began to overflow the banks, the local inhabitants made further suggestions to the British to prevent flooding of areas occupied by the troops.

The country people represented the necessity of stopping up the ditches, running in the Meadows in front of the lines of the 11th and 59th regiments, from the great ditch which runs from Flushing towards Middleburgh. They also recommended, that the bank of the great ditch should be heightened, in order to confine the water entirely to that channel, so that it may be carried off by the sluices opening to the Middleburgh channel.[69]

The drainage ditches near the position occupied by the Fifth Regiment overflowed on the twelfth, putting some of the trenches and the nearby road under water. Several of the communication trenches near Battery E were also flooded with water three and four feet deep in places, and on the left, in front of Fraser's division, the flooding reached such proportions that poles were placed to mark the roads. Work parties were constantly employed in attempting to keep the water out of the trenches. On the twelfth, as the flooding became a serious threat to the army and its fresh water supply, Lord Chatham announced that the guns would open against Flushing the following day.

At 1 P.M. on August 13, fifty guns from the British batteries commenced the bombardment of Flushing. At the same time, a flotilla of gunboats and brigs under Captain Cockburn attacked from above Flushing and another flotilla directed by Commodore Owen moved against the town from its anchorage in the Deurloo Channel.[70] Some frames for Congreve rockets which had been erected near Battery G on the east dyke fired a few missiles into Flushing during the early hours of the bombardment, causing several fires and tremendous panic in the town. By sunset on the thirteenth, many of Flushing's guns had been dismounted by the barrage, and several others had remained unserviceable since August 11 when the frigates had fired on the town while forcing the entrance to the West Scheldt.[71] The bombardment on the thirteenth continued into the night but slackened somewhat after dark, when the British flotillas withdrew from action after expending their ammunition.[72] Meanwhile, the water continued to rise and overflow more land near the British positions. On the west side of Flushing, the road from West Souburg to the right of British lines was now almost impassable, and the batteries and trenches were threatened in spite of all the British efforts. Batteries D, E, and F were particularly menaced, and sandbags were brought up to protect the guns and ammunition.

During the night of August 13, General Graham ordered an attack upon the French post atop the west dyke. Under cover of fire from Battery A, commanded by Lieutenant Wood, the Third Battalion of Royals and the Fourteenth Regiment, Second Battalion, with a detachment of light infantry from the King's German Legion, advanced toward the French position. Colonel Hay, commanding the Royals, moved along the dyke and attacked the French traverse held by Major Bockmann and a detachment of returned French deserters who fired a few shots and retired into Old Flushing, abandoning the post to the Royals.[73] Meanwhile, Colonel Nicholls with the Fourteenth Infantry and the German troops attacked the French traverse on the road outside Old Flushing and forced the Colonials and Irish to evacuate their position and withdraw into that suburb also.[74] Major Serier, seeing all his advance posts now abandoned, retreated into Flushing, setting Old Flushing ablaze. This action during the night of August 13 cost the French about one hundred casualties, while the British losses numbered one killed and six wounded.[75] The newly gained position on the west dyke was immediately reinforced, and a work party under Captain Birch of the Royal Engineers began digging a 600-yard communication trench back to the redoubt located at the southern extremity of the British parallel.

At daybreak the bombardment recommenced with added fury as the seamen's battery with six twenty-four-pounders finally opened. The battery, which had been under constant fire on the thirteenth, was completed then only because "the smoke from Old Flushing, which the enemy set on fire, being driven by the wind along the front of the town, prevented the enemy from seeing our work."[76] The seamen's battery then opened a devastating enfilading fire which soon silenced the guns of the demilune on the west dyke and the bastion adjoining it. Although none of the British batteries was yet flooded, the water had risen five inches during the preceding twenty-four hours, and if that rate continued new arrangements would be necessary if the town continued to resist.

The British flotillas had returned to the attack early on August 14, and by ten o'clock in the morning, the wind was strong enough for the ships of the line to move into the river. Sir Richard Strachan described the action:

The squadron was led in by the *St. Domingo*, bearing my flag, and I was followed by the *Blake*, with the flag of Rear-Admiral Lord Gardner; the other ships advanced in succession. Soon after we had opened our fire, the wind came more southerly, and the *St. Domingo* grounded inside of the dog-sand. Lord Gardner, not knowing our situation, passed inside of us, by which the *Blake* also grounded. The other ships were immediately directed to haul off, and anchor as previously intended.[77]

Strachan's ships of the line were fortunate in that the sea batteries of Flushing near the west dyke which might have been opened on the grounded ships had been silenced by the enfilading fire of the seamen's battery. With the aid of Commodore Owen of the *Clyde*, both the *St. Domingo* and the *Blake* were soon afloat.

The superior fire power of the British land batteries and the ships of the line and flotillas was taking a toll in Flushing. General Osten recorded the following:

All these forces fired a most terrible fire without example. More than 1100 cannon rained death and desolation on the town. In the beginning our batteries responded rather vigorously, although we did not have nearly enough gunners to service all the pieces, since we had only a company of the First French Regiment and a company of Dutch and we had already lost many artillerymen when the frigates forced the passage.

In a very short time many of our pieces were dismounted; a number of the gun carriages were very old and shattered after one report from their pieces and several mortars from the Dutch foundries were *hors de service* because of a malfunction of their vents. In less than an hour we lost half of our artillerymen. I visited the batteries often, where I found several absolutely without gunners; many of them were not accustomed to war and had abandoned their pieces and were hiding in order to escape a service which terrified them so. The braver ones died uselessly at their posts since they were not supported. Finally our batteries were reduced almost to silence by the extra-ordinary fire of the enemy.[78]

In the process of silencing Flushing's guns, the town itself was being reduced to ruins. The incendiary rockets caused extensive fires which became increasingly difficult to extinguish as the water pumps were rendered inoperative. The Hotel de Ville was set afire during the afternoon of August 14 and General Monnet and his staff were forced to flee. Fires were now raging out of control throughout the town and nearly caused the explosion of the principal powder magazine.[79]

The British guns continued to fire upon the town, and an additional battery was established on some high ground 250 yards in front of the seamen's position, at the edge of the flooded area around Flushing. The rising water was now reaching critical proportions all along the British lines.

Great exertions were required during these 24 hours to preserve the communications from being inundated by the sudden rise of the water. Parties were everywhere at work to let off the water from the trenches, and to prevent its further entry. The inundation had by this time spread all over the space between the parallel and Flushing, and in some places had risen to the height of the parapet of the parallel.[80]

At 4 P.M. on the fourteenth, Chatham, seeing that the guns of Flushing were almost hushed, ordered a cease-fire and directed Sir Eyre Coote to summon the town. Coote dispatched Lieutenant Colonel Walsh, his assistant adjutant general, with a flag of truce and a letter demanding the surrender of the town and its garrison. Two hours later Coote received Monnet's reply, which stated that as soon as the French commandant had consulted his council, he would answer the summons. At 8:45 P.M. no answer had been received from Monnet; therefore Coote dispatched another message into Flushing warning the commandant that unless the town surrendered immediately, hostilities would be resumed. Still no answer was forthcoming, so Coote ordered the British batteries to open fire once again. General Monnet quickly dispatched a letter to Coote demanding a forty-eight-hour cease-fire, to which the British general replied that the only terms he would discuss further would be those calling for the immediate surrender of Flushing.[81] Consequently, the bombardment continued.

During the evening the British erected a small battery for one gun and a howitzer on the east dyke about seven hundred yards from the point where the French had initially cut the dyke. Primarily constructed to cover an attack upon the French advance post which protected the cut dyke, the battery was completed about 11 P.M. Colonel Pack, with some detachments from the Thirty-sixth and Seventy-first as well as the King's German Legion's light infantry, then attacked the position manned by detachments of the Sixty-fifth and the Prussian battalions.[82] After a brief encounter, Major Gauthier's detachment retreated into Flushing. Pack's forces experienced some difficulty in crossing through the deep water at the cut in the dyke; consequently, before a position could be secured at the evacuated French battery, a reinforced company of Gauthier's demibrigade returned to recapture the position. Pack's troops were forced to retreat but were successful in spiking the guns.[83]

The bombardment continued into the early morning of August 15, when, at 2:30 A.M., General Coote received Monnet's offer to surrender. General Monnet's sole request was that his multinational garrison be treated as French troops. Coote agreed and insisted that the French close their sluices and stop all efforts toward inundation.[84] The naval attack, however, continued until after 3 A.M., when Sir Richard Strachan received Coote's letter to cease fire.

General Monnet had been induced to surrender Flushing because of several factors. His guns were either unserviceable or dismounted, his troops demoralized, and the town's inhabitants suffering greatly. As early as the afternoon of the thirteenth, Monnet had been approached by Flushing's mayor, Adriaan François Lammens, acting as an intermediary for the citizens of the town, urging that since there was no hope of receiving reinforcements, the town be surrendered. Monnet's reply to this was that "a besieged city never surrenders on the first day of bombardment."[85] On the fourteenth, as fires raged throughout the town, the inhabitants increased their pleas to Monnet to stop the destruction of life and property. Realizing that a council of war would probably suggest continuing the struggle, Monnet surrendered Flushing without consulting the other military officers.[86]

Colonel Long, Lord Chatham's adjutant general, and Captain Cockburn of the navy entered Flushing early on the afternoon of August 15; by evening they had signed the terms of surrender. Following the ratification of the surrender terms, a detachment of Royals on the west side of the city and troops from the Seventy-first Regiment on the east took possession of the gates of Flushing.[87] On the following day, arrangements were made to embark the captured garrison on transports to England and to march the troops out of Flushing on the morning of August 17; but when a complication arose, the actual surrendering of the town was postponed until the following day.[88] Consequently, it was not until the morning of August 18 that the garrison of Flushing filed out of town, stacked their arms, and marched under escort to Fort Ter Haak to be embarked to England. Generals Monnet and Osten were allowed to remain in Middelburg and Flushing for two additional days to settle their personal business.

Flushing presented a dismal sight to the British troops when they entered the city on the eighteenth. The Hotel de Ville, the commissary warehouse, two churches, and 247 houses were completely destroyed, and many other buildings were damaged to a significant extent.[89] Gen. William Dyott, commander of a brigade in Lord Huntley's division, had come over from South Beveland on August 13 to review the batteries as they opened on Flush-

ing; he recorded this scene on entering Flushing following its
surrender:

The next day, I went into Flushing and so sad a spectacle I never saw.
There was not a house that had not been shot through and through,
many battered to dust, and many others burnt to ashes. . . . It is utterly
impossible to describe the horror and dismay exhibited in the coun-
tenances of the poor, miserable, wretched beings observable in the
street, who remain to lament the loss of their family and friends.[90]

Since Flushing was taken by long-range bombardment without
a breach in the fortifications, the English losses appear slight in
comparison to those of the French. The official English returns
from the army and navy show only 50 killed and 208 wounded
during the period from August 8 until the surrender of Flushing
on the fifteenth, including the losses sustained by the frigates on
August 11 and the flotilla and ships of the line during the siege.[91]
It is more difficult to determine the French losses on Walcheren
during the period from July 30 to August 15, since the French and
British returns indicate the strength of the garrison in Flushing
only at the moment of surrender, and an indeterminate number of
sick and wounded men were evacuated to Cadsand prior to the
naval blockade.[92] The number of troops in Flushing, including reinforcements up to the time the British completed the naval blockade, numbered 7,639.[93] The British captured 1,816 men, including
deserters, of which 519 were taken at Ter Veere and 127 at Ramakins.[94] These troops, however, were mostly Dutch and had never
been counted among Flushing's garrison. Most of the remaining
1,170 prisoners came from Flushing, since these were the only
troops left in the island after August 2. The difference between
the total number of troops composing Flushing's garrison after
the last reinforcements arrived (7,639) and the strength of the
garrison on August 16 (5,539) indicates that more than 2,100
troops were lost—either killed, wounded, captured, or deserted.[95]
These 2,100 casualties, exclusive of the 618 sick and wounded in
the hospitals of Flushing, compare favorably with the figure given
by General Osten and are a relatively accurate estimate of the

losses sustained by the garrison of Flushing during the action on Walcheren.

General Monnet's surrender of Flushing after thirty-eight hours of bombardment astonished Napoleon, who believed the town should have held out indefinitely. "Flushing is impregnable. . . . It is impregnable because to reach it one must cross a moat filled with water; whilst as a last resort the dykes can be cut."[96] The bombardment alone could not cause the town to surrender, Napoleon insisted. "They will demolish a few houses, but that has never caused a town to surrender."[97] Upon learning of General Monnet's action, Napoleon attributed the surrender to cowardice or treason and ordered the French general's conduct investigated. On November 25 the court of inquiry ruled:

That General Monnet, contrary to his duty, did not fulfill the order of his Imperial Majesty, in case of his being hard pressed by the enemy, to cut the dykes rather than surrender;

That he surrendered the fortress at a time when it had only sustained a bombardment of thirty-six hours; when the garrison was still composed of more than four thousand men; when no breach had yet been made in the rampart, and the enemy were yet more than eight hundred metres distant from the fortress, when our troops were yet in possession of the outworks; and when consequently, the place was not really besieged;

That the general is therefore guilty of gross misconduct, which cannot be attributed to any motive other than cowardice and treason.[98]

Contrary to what later appeared in the British press, Monnet was neither court-martialed nor sentenced to death. He was, however, not anxious to return to Napoleonic France. Unlike General Osten, who violated his parole and escaped to France in February 1810, Monnet remained a prisoner in England until the fall of the empire. On his return in May 1814, he resumed active duty and was created a baron by King Louis XVIII.

No matter how poor Monnet's conduct may have been judged by his superiors, it was his defense of Flushing which stalled the British expedition for more than two weeks. Taking into consideration the quality of the garrison at Flushing, Monnet and his second-in-command, General Osten, appear to have conducted themselves about as well as possible under the circumstances.[99] Lord Chatham considered any advance by the army impossible so long as Flushing held out, for almost one half of his army was encamped on Walcheren engaged in the siege, and he did not consider the remaining forces sufficient to pursue the other objectives of the expedition.[100]

With Flushing reduced, Chatham now turned his attention toward the prospects of attacking Antwerp. As the British commander in chief prepared to transfer his headquarters to South Beveland, Marshal Jean-Baptiste Bernadotte, the prince of Ponte-Corvo, was in Antwerp inspecting his defenses and anxiously watching the British movements.

8

Bernadotte at Antwerp

The condition of the 46,000 French-Dutch troops which had been aggregated in the Scheldt between August 3 and 13 caused King Louis to note that "an army has been collected, but it needs to be organized."[1] The organization of this army was the primary problem confronting Bernadotte when he arrived at Antwerp on August 15 to take command of the Army of the North.[2] Both Louis and General Rampon had welcomed Bernadotte's appointment and met with the French marshal to brief him on the situation of the Scheldt army.[3]

Bernadotte's arrival at Antwerp coincided with the *fête de Napoléon* (celebration of Napoleon's birthday), and during the day Bernadotte and Louis reviewed the troops, affording the new commander a look at the soldiers placed under his command to defend Antwerp and the frontiers of France. A contemporary recorded the following: "The Dutch Guard was conspicuous in their bright uniforms. The French troops presented, on the contrary, the appearance of a weak mass, incoherent and poorly disciplined. One saw sailors, dragoons, lancers, light cavalry, hussars, even cuirassiers, equipped to be mounted, follow slowly on foot the infantry drummer."[4]

The following day, King Louis left for Amsterdam to organize his National Guard and take charge of defending the other coastal areas of Holland which might be a target for British attack.[5] Half of the 4,000 Dutch guards accompanied him, while the remainder formed the nucleus of troops at Bergen-op-Zoom under Marshal Dumonceau and were expected to cooperate with Bernadotte in defending the right bank.[6]

On August 14 the minister of war had ordered Marshal Bon-

Adrien-Jannot de Moncey, duke of Conegliano, to Lille to organize and command a corps of gendarmes and establish a reserve for the Army of the North.[7] Clarke also called up 4,400 additional reinforcements who were scheduled to arrive in Antwerp by August 25.[8] Other military detachments were being directed to the Scheldt from the depots of Metz, Strasbourg, Paris, Verdun, and more distant points. In addition, 60,000 National Guard had been placed under orders for service in the Scheldt by August 15, 30,000 as a result of Napoleon's August 6 decree.[9] These National Guard units were drawn from twenty-one departments and were commanded by generals, most of whom had been in Paris serving in the senate.[10] The initial mobilization of guardsmen was in dispositions as follows: 6,000 at the camp at Boulogne under General Sainte-Suzanne; 8,000 commanded by General Rampon in Cadsand; 8,000 at Ghent under Gen. Jerome Soulès; and an additional 8,000 men quartered at Ghent to form a reserve under the command of Gen. Pierre Garnier.

The National Guard mobilized on August 15 as a result of Napoleon's decree were formed into five divisions of 6,000 men each and constituted a second line of defense for the troops already in positions on both banks of the Scheldt. The First Division was stationed at Antwerp under Gen. Claude-Sylvestre Colaud; the Second at Brussels under the seventy-nine-year-old Gen. François d'Aboville; the Third Division at Lille commanded by Gen. Marie-Charles, comte de Latour-Maubourg; the Fourth Division at Ostend under Gen. Charles-Henri Vaubois; and the Fifth Division commanded by Gen. Louis-Jean-Baptiste Gouvion (brother of the marshal) at St. Omer.[11]

Bernadotte's front line of defense from Cadsand to Bergen-op-Zoom included some 19,000 infantry troops as well as the 16,000 National Guards commanded by Generals Rampon and Soulès.[12] The infantry detachments were from various light and regular regiments of the French army and included 900 artillerymen. The mounted troops numbered 2,300, including light and heavy cavalry and gendarmes from nearby departments. On August 15 the

Army of the North, excluding its reserves and the Dutch troops at Bergen-op-Zoom, totaled 39,800.[13]

The command of the Sixteenth Military Division, which included all military forces north of the Somme River but excluded the camp of Boulogne and Bernadotte's forces on both banks of the Scheldt, was given to Marshal Moncey on August 16.[14] The cities of Antwerp, Ghent, Ostend, Lille, and the fortresses of Sas de Gand and Ecloo were placed in a state of siege and emergency provisions were ordered for each.[15] Although work was progressing rapidly and reinforcements were arriving daily, the condition of the troops troubled Bernadotte.

Since arriving here, we have been most active, . . . but nevertheless, one can only do what is humanly possible; we do not sleep, and the work continues night and day. . . . Of the troops, some of the corps of National Guard are nonexistent; more than one half have already deserted; those that remain are poorly armed, without cartridge pouches; without uniforms for the most part, and consequently return to their departments.[16]

Bernadotte further reported that most of the artillery arrived at Antwerp in poor repair; of eleven field pieces arriving on August 18, for example, nine were found unserviceable. Moreover, the British appeared ready to attack from Batz. Although the Army of the North was in poor condition, Bernadotte assured General Clarke that every effort would be made to repulse the British forces.

Immediately after the fall of Flushing, the British forces on Walcheren (with the exception of General Fraser's 6,000-man garrison, which remained to maintain the island) began moving into South Beveland.[17] General Grosvenor's division and part of General Graham's division were embarked on transports from Ramakins on August 19 and 20, respectively. The remainder of the British troops crossed into South Beveland via the ferry near Armuyden and marched to encampments near Batz. The cavalry and ordnance transports and numerous stores ships were still having difficulty navigating the Slough passage, resorting "to warping because of the adverse winds."[18] These ships finally entered the West Scheldt and reached Batz on August 24 and 25.

Lord Chatham had begun moving his headquarters to South Beveland on August 19, but financial problems delayed his departure from Middelburg. Chatham's commissary general had strict orders from William Huskisson at the treasury to pay nothing more than the current market price (at the time the expedition sailed) for all supplies purchased in the islands of Zealand and then only in bills on London. This proved impracticable, however, partially because the exchange rate was against England by eighteen to twenty percent. The inhabitants insisted that payment be made in specie, since this had been agreed upon in the terms under which the islands had surrendered. Chatham therefore considered himself obligated to pay in specie for items purchased, and realizing too the necessity of maintaining goodwill in the occupied islands, he requested more dollars for the expedition's use. Although London was hard pressed for foreign specie, £40 thousand in Dutch dollars was sent out the first week in September.[19]

Money matters settled, Chatham moved his headquarters to Goes on South Beveland on the twenty-first, advanced to Crabbendyke on August 23, and finally arrived at Batz on the twenty-fourth. This leisurely pace would suggest that the commander in chief had no intention of pursuing further operations, although Chatham later argued that his presence was not needed at Batz until all the naval forces had arrived. Still, his actions drew criticism from among other officers. Frederick William Trench (later general), serving with the Quartermaster General Corps under Sir John Hope, recorded his impressions:

After three days lost in Walcheren with the ceremony of laying down arms he . . . arrived at Ter Goes the day before yesterday. He came as far as Schore to consult with Sir John Hope—they had a long conference and then L. C. resolved to take up his quarters at Crabbindyke— but instead of going on to Bathz to see the Admiral, he returned to Ter Goes to dinner! Nor could he be persuaded to make a little circuit for the sake of seeing a little more of the country, but went back the way he came; that being the shortest. Yesterday, about 12 o'clock he got under way being preceded by a column of waggons in the first of which was a live turtle; he had a fresh horse at Schore, but did not attempt to go further than Crabbindyke tho' Bathz was but 7 miles off. . . . This apathy is so extraordinary that I can account for it only on a supposition that he waits the return of orders from England.[20]

Upon his arrival at Batz, Chatham found that the last transports conveying General Graham's troops and the remaining cavalry had arrived, thus placing the total forces of the expedition in a position to advance toward Antwerp and the French fleet.

The British movements up the West Scheldt to Batz were closely observed by the French from their positions in Cadsand, Terneuse, and along the left bank of the West Scheldt. Terneuse was situated at a bend in the West Scheldt where the river's deep channel passed near the southern bank, close enough for the fort's guns to annoy the larger British ships. On August 17, as the British frigates moved up the West Scheldt they exchanged fire with Terneuse, garrisoned by fifty French cannoneers and three companies of Swiss troops.[21] Little damage resulted to either the ships or the fortress until a British shell hit the fort's powder magazine, causing an explosion and one hundred casualties.[22]

The British movements toward Batz following the capitulation of Flushing indicated to Bernadotte that Antwerp's docks and the fleet were additional objectives of the English expedition. After studying the British positions, Bernadotte arranged his defenses upon the assumption that Chatham would attempt to approach Antwerp via the Scheldt and its right bank. Consequently, he prepared to meet the attack with the following measures: first, he extended the areas to be inundated below Antwerp; second, he ordered his engineer, Louis Victor, vicomte de Caux de Blacquetot, to rebuild the old abandoned forts of la Croix, St. Marie, St. Philippe, Frederick Henry, Perle, and Isabelle, all of which were situated at strategic locations along the river between Sandvliet and Antwerp; third, the more formidable forts of Lillo and Liefkenshoek, opposite each other on the Scheldt, were strengthened.

Lillo was manned by 400 men and 50 guns, while Liefkenshoek was garrisoned with some 250 men and 50 guns.[23] Across the river between the forts a boom which completely blocked navigation of the Scheldt had been constructed of heavy logs and cables. Ships attempting to break the boom would come under fire from the two forts. Above the boom, the French flotilla was stationed in strategic positions to be supported by the guns of forts la Croix, St. Marie, Perle, and St. Philippe. The navigation was obstructed again further up the river by several ships bound together by chains and cables. Finally, three ships of the line were stationed at the approach to Antwerp, supported by newly installed riverfront batteries on the right bank and the forts of Isabelle and Tête de Flandre directly opposite the city. Fire ships and the remainder of Admiral Missiessy's squadron also were in Antwerp's port as a last resort to protect the docks and arsenals.[24]

Napoleon had made it very clear, in his letter to the minister of the navy on August 18, that he wanted Admiral Missiessy's squadron to play an active role in the defense of Antwerp. During the first two weeks of August, Missiessy had vacillated between moving his ships to safety above Antwerp and keeping them along the riverfront where they would receive protection from the guns of Antwerp and the forts of Isabelle and Tête de Flandre. The former measure was finally adopted, thereby making available some six thousand sailors for garrison duty and to serve as cannoneers in the recently armed forts along the Scheldt.[25]

While these defensive preparations were being implemented, on August 20 General Clarke announced a reorganization of the Scheldt forces. Bernadotte continued to command the Army of the North, but the size of his command on the left bank was reduced to the inundated area between Hulst and Tête de Flandre. Marshal Moncey was given the command of the forces on the left bank from Ostend to Hulst, now designated as the Corps of Observation on Cadsand.[26] Moncey's 16,000-man corps was to include 4,000 troops of the line and 12,000 national guards, 8,000 of whom were to be withdrawn from Bernadotte's Army of the

North. The withdrawal of these troops solicited a protest from the marshal, who stated that this measure would reduce his force to only 8,000 men to "defend Antwerp, support the navy, occupy the forts, and carry out campaigns on the two river banks." [30] He refused to transfer them to Moncey.

As Bernadotte complained of his troop shortages, the minister of war was issuing new orders which placed an additional 9,265 troops under Bernadotte and Moncey. Detachments of infantry, cavalry, and artillerymen were ordered to the Scheldt from the military depots at Metz, Ghent, Nancy, Strasbourg, and Rochefort. Clarke calculated that these reinforcements, all of whom were scheduled to arrive on the Scheldt by the first week in September, would bring the total strength of the Army of the North and the Corps of Observation on Cadsand to 56,120, excluding the 30,000 National Guardsmen held in reserve and the Dutch troops under Dumonceau stationed on the right bank.[28] Of the total 56,120 men, 20,000 were to serve under Marshal Moncey.

Although the above figures issued by the minister of war would indicate that a formidable force was bivouacked in the Scheldt, there was a vast difference in the army on paper and that actually commanded by the two French marshals. On paper, Bernadotte had 27,380 men at or near Antwerp, of which 14,800 were troops of the line. However, on August 22 Bernadotte indicated he had only 12,000 combat-ready troops to face an English force of 35,000 or 40,000.[29] Moncey reported on the following day that his forces on the left bank were so thinly spread between Cadsand and Hulst that he was unable to establish the armed camp at St. Nicholas of 5,000 or 6,000 troops as requested by Bernadotte.[30] From a more positive viewpoint, however, Jean Dejean, inspector general of engineers now serving under Bernadotte, considered the real danger passed by August 23. Dejean reasoned that although the British had collected a substantial force at Batz by August 19, five days later they were in their same positions. Had the English been more daring and attacked via the river and the right bank of the Scheldt, he wrote, "they could have forced the imperfect and incomplete defenses we had here . . . and could have burned the city and docks of Antwerp." After the nineteenth, additional reinforcements and improved and expanded defensive works had given new confidence to the French troops and "lessened the chance of success of the enemy."[31]

Bernadotte and Moncey, however, shared a different picture of the situation. Even as reinforcements arrived and the defensive positions along the Scheldt improved, Bernadotte reiterated that his and Moncey's forces were too sparse along the banks of the Scheldt. "If it is wished to guard everything, it will be weak everywhere. The forces spread around over 30 leagues would be necessary here in order to save Antwerp, the fleet, the docks, and the glory of the army of the Emperor."[32]

The British concentration at Batz on the twenty-fourth prompted Bernadotte to appeal for all forces in the Scheldt area to be concentrated in the vicinity of Antwerp. "It is Antwerp, the fleet, the docks, these only that the enemy want; and it is here that all the troops should be."[33] The Army of the North had little field artillery, and there was no officer "worth his merit" to supervise the artillery train. In an attempt to bolster the defenses near Antwerp, Bernadotte asked Moncey to send a corps of 8,000 to 10,000 men to Hulst to cover the left flank of the Army of the North. Moncey replied that he was strengthening the garrison at Terneuse and could not send additional troops to Hulst without weakening the defenses of Cadsand.[34] Because Bernadotte had not dispatched Rampon's 6,000 National Guards and the 2,000 troops of the line from the Army of the North to Moncey, the Corps of Observation on Cadsand, in addition to being poorly equipped, had remained below strength. "My army is composed of detachments from numerous depots, without overcoats, and various accouterments, with the least instructions; diminished each day by desertion; and destined to guard a line twenty leagues long. . . ."[35] In spite of these conditions, Moncey had provisioned and strengthened the several depots between Cadsand and Antwerp, specifically Hulst,

Sas de Gand, St. Philippe, Axel, and Yzendyke, where the munitions depot for Cadsand was located.

By August 26, the French had over 100,000 men under orders for service in the Scheldt. The Army of the North, including its reserve national guard units at Brussels, numbered 32,957. The Corps of Observation on Cadsand totaled 41,448, including the reserve at Ostend and Ghent.[36] Marshal Jean-Baptiste Bessières, duke of Istria, was en route from Vienna to take command of the Army of the Reserve, which was headquartered at Lille and consisted of 12,000 National Guardsmen, half of which were quartered at St. Omer.[37] General Sainte-Suzanne commanded 11,136 men at the camp at Boulogne; and another 3,219 men from various military depots were encamped at Chartres and Etampes awaiting orders. Therefore Clarke reasoned that the total number of troops available for service in the Scheldt if the threat of English invasion continued was 100,600.[38] And in addition to these troops, Marshal Dumonceau commanded some 6,000 Dutch troops at Bergen-op-Zoom and the island of Toleland, should the British attempt to disembark in that area. All these forces were at the complete disposal of Bernadotte if a direct confrontation with the British army occurred.[39]

Meanwhile, the British flotilla under Sir Home Popham ventured up the Scheldt near the forts Frederick Henry and Doel on August 24 and 25 and attempted to impede the construction of their batteries and fortifications. Gen. Louis Charbonnier, in charge of the advance French fortifications, returned the fire, and during the evening of the twenty-fifth the work on the batteries continued.[40] Bernadotte's intelligence reported on August 27 that all British transports had arrived at Batz and the British attack on the mainland was imminent. Bernadotte still considered his situation critical though decidedly improved since his arrival at Antwerp on August 15. During the course of the twenty-seventh, General Colaud arrived in Antwerp to assume the post of governor of Antwerp and commander of the city's forces. This new

appointment resulted in some initial confusion between Bernadotte and Colaud concerning each other's authority and their relationship, but these problems were quickly resolved by clarifying
instructions from Paris.[41]

On August 28 while awaiting the next British move, Bernadotte
received additional instructions from Napoleon concerning the
defense of Antwerp. Napoleon was aware of the low caliber of
troops composing the Army of the North and ordered Bernadotte
not to venture a battle "except to save Antwerp; or unless you
outnumber the English four to one and have a good position, covered by redoubts and batteries." Napoleon also stressed that Antwerp and Cadsand were to be the primary focal points for the
defensive measures in the area. The former was vital for obvious
reasons, and the latter because it "endangers cities in France and
its loss would cause disorder on the west bank."[42]

Supported by Moncey on the left, Bernadotte was ordered to
remain at Antwerp and prevent the British from effecting a landing on the right bank between Bergen-op-Zoom and Antwerp.
Antwerp was to be considered an entrenched camp, and the Army
of Antwerp, as Bernadotte's forces were renamed (Moncey's army
was renamed the Army of Tête de Flandre), was to be used only
defensively and as a corps of observation until the British withdrew their expedition, which Napoleon was certain would occur
in a short time. "Independently of the fever which ought to have
taken already an enormous toll in the island of Walcheren, the necessity of reinforcements for the army of Portugal will force the
ministers to promptly recall the expedition."[43] However, if the
English did attempt to attack Antwerp, Moncey would move his
headquarters to Tête de Flandre to reinforce Antwerp from the
left, while Marshal Kellermann's ten-thousand-man reserve army
from Wesel attacked the English from the rear. The Army of the
Reserve, commanded by Marshal Bessières at Lille, also would be
available if needed. Napoleon's words seemed prophetic, for on
the same day his letters were being relayed to the Scheldt, the

British ships at Batz began a retreat down the river, announcing the end to further British operations.

On August 25 Sir Home Popham and General Brownrigg had reconnoitered the right bank of the Scheldt above Batz near Sand-vliet and selected a favorable landing site for the British army. On the following day Lord Chatham, Sir Richard Strachan, Sir Richard Keats, and the lieutenant generals of the army met to discuss further operations of the expedition. "So many difficulties appeared to present themselves to our further progress, that the commander of the forces determined to convene a meeting of the Lieutenant Generals of the Army the following day, to obtain their opinion previous to his Lordship's sending his dispatches to England."[44]

At the meeting of the lieutenant generals on August 27, General Brownrigg presented a memorandum outlining what he considered to be the most practicable plans for carrying out operations against Antwerp and the many difficulties involved.[45] The latest intelligence received in South Beveland concerning French and Dutch forces indicated that there were about 8,500 Dutch and French troops in Bergen-op-Zoom and vicinity, including 2,000 men at Breda and 500 in Tolen. Fifteen thousand men reportedly were between Bergen-op-Zoom and Antwerp, with an additional 11,000 troops stationed in Antwerp itself. The British sources further revealed that there were 3,500 men on the left bank of the Scheldt, placing the entire French-Dutch force at 35,500 and increasing daily.[46]

In contrast, the British strength was diminishing daily. As early as August 20, large numbers of British soldiers were becoming seriously ill with a fever, and by August 27 the number of sick totaled 3,467 and was increasing hourly.[47] If the sickness continued to spread at the current rate, further operations would necessarily be prohibited; but even assuming that the fever grew no worse, the British forces available for extended operations were still insufficient to combat the opposing forces already in defensive positions along the Scheldt. Brownrigg reasoned that of the 30,000 British effectives,[48] including infantry, cavalry, and artillery, 6,000 were needed to garrison Walcheren and 2,000 for South Beveland. This left 22,000 men to commence operations on the Continent, and regardless of the plan adopted for the attack on Antwerp, at least 8,000 men would be required to observe Bergen-op-Zoom and protect communications.

Two basic plans seemed feasible to Brownrigg for the advance upon Antwerp. The first was a cooperative effort of the army and navy: the army would land on both banks of the Scheldt to protect the navigation of the navy. This plan had the advantages of combining the total military and naval power of the expedition and utilizing it against the powerful French defensive positions on both banks of the Scheldt. By landing 4,000 men on the left bank, supported by the flotilla and squadron, it was conceivable that the boom could be broken, Lillo and Liefkenshoek reduced, and the remaining obstacles removed in order to reach Antwerp.[49] However, it was apparent that by dividing the army in such manner, the remaining 10,000 troops advancing along the right bank to besiege Antwerp would be insufficient to cope with the French forces entrenched along the route and in the city itself.[50] An alternate plan called for landing the entire army on the right bank and advancing all 14,000 troops directly to Antwerp. While this plan did not divide the forces and consequently provided a larger force for the siege of the city, it had several significant disadvantages. If the left bank were not occupied, support of the naval force would necessarily be forfeited above the initial landing site near Sandvliet. Additional troops also would be needed to mask Fort Lillo, since this fort was thought to be almost impregnable to an attack from the land side alone, and naval assistance would be impossible without occupying the opposite shore. Furthermore, the second plan would not achieve complete investment of Antwerp since Tête de Flandre would be unmolested on the left bank and could serve as a source of reinforcements and supplies.[51] "Thus the safest and best way of attacking Antwerp far exceeds our means; while the alternative is liable to all disadvantages of a want of naval co-operation, and an incomplete investment of the place." [52]

The seven lieutenant generals, after reviewing the circumstances of the army and the intelligence reports, rendered an opinion to Lord Chatham following the council of war on August 27. They concluded that "under all the circumstances that have been laid before us, the undertaking of the siege of Antwerp is impracticable." [53] Admiral Strachan followed the report with a suggestion that if no action could be taken in advancing on Antwerp, the army might cooperate with the navy in an attack on the forts of Lillo and Liefkenshoek. Strachan hoped to break the boom and attack the flotilla anchored behind it. [54] After considering the proposal, the council of war decided that little would be gained by such an operation. "We are of the opinion, that as the siege of Antwerp cannot be undertaken, the success of which could alone accomplish the ultimate object of the Expedition, no possible advantage can result from attempting to reduce the forts of Lillo and Liefkenshoek; or from undertaking any minor operations." [55] After deciding to abandon any further operations, Chatham notified Castlereagh of the decision and stated that he planned a gradual withdrawal from South Beveland to Walcheren. [56]

Meanwhile, Chatham and Strachan were no longer on friendly terms. Disagreements between them had been numerous from the beginning of the campaign, and now that further operations had been suspended and failure was a reality, their relations became even more strained. Strachan evidently had believed that with the fall of Flushing immediate operations farther up the Scheldt would follow. With this in mind, he invested Sir Richard Keats, on August 16, with full power to act in conjunction with Lord Rosslyn's forces on South Beveland against enemy positions upriver. [57] Rosslyn, however, had no such instructions, assuming rather that Chatham was coming to South Beveland to direct operations himself. Four days later Chatham arrived on South Beveland, but did not establish his headquarters at Batz until August 24. Meanwhile,

Strachan was growing impatient with inaction and Chatham's seeming indecision, and on the twenty-sixth he penned the following letter to the commander in chief:

I consider it impossible for the navy to move higher up the Scheldt than its present situation, while the enemy is in possession of Lillo and Liefkenshoek. An attack upon these fortresses is, I think, more a military than a naval question; though in consideration of the means for such a measure, I beg of you to be assured, that every co-operation which can be devised shall be most cheerfully given on the part of the navy. The command of these fortresses may open some field of enterprise to us, and present an opportunity of obtaining more local information than we have at present; but I do not imagine that all the objects of the Expedition can be fully accomplished without the possession of Antwerp.

Your Lordship is, no doubt, aware of the propriety of coming to an immediate decision as to the line of our future operations, in consequence of the advanced state of the season, and the shortness of our provisions and water.[58]

Later in the day Strachan, Keats, Chatham, and the lieutenant generals met, and the following day the decision was made to suspend operations.

Strachan evidently did not understand fully the military problems presented in Brownrigg's and Hope's reports which convinced Chatham to bring an end to the expedition, or perhaps he wanted it to appear that the navy was willing to continue operations, but that the army had refused. His letter to the secretary of the admiralty on the twenty-seventh suggests this, and on the same day he wrote Commodore Owen "the Army is so sickly and the Enemy gaining strength that Lord Chatham has given up the object of the expedition notwithstanding the difference of opinion in regard to that measure with the Navy."[59]

With the decision to abandon further operations having been made, Strachan immediately offered the full cooperation of the navy in reembarking the troops in South Beveland, but he asked that a force large enough to secure the island be retained on the island until the navy had an opportunity to sink ships in the narrow passages of the Scheldt near Batz. Strachan estimated that this operation would require from ten days to two weeks.[60] Chatham refused this request, emphasizing the seriousness of the epidemic on the island and questioned the necessity of retaining South Beveland for the navy's protection.

I cannot help observing, that as there is no armed force of the Enemy in South Beveland, and as all the guns are removed from the batteries, I should have hoped that the extensive naval force under your command, if not able to prevent the landing of troops, would at least render it impossible for the Enemy to disembark heavy guns and stores, and reestablish his batteries, which would alone impede your progress down the river.[61]

Strachan retorted that his ships could be effective in protecting the island only if they were not involved in evacuating soldiers.[62] This dissension was soon common knowledge among the expedition's forces and in fact was even reported to Bernadotte at Antwerp on August 30. "Some of my men have been obliged to serve as pilots for their British ships, and they assure me that there exists a great disagreement between the two commanders of the military and the navy, and they no longer hide their blame for each other's operations."[63] Sir Home Popham intervened on September 1. In a letter to Chatham, he attempted to apologize for the admiral, assuring the general that nothing improper was meant in Strachan's letters concerning further operations or embarking the troops, but that Strachan merely wanted to follow his instructions from London. "If you have been offended, I am sure he will apologize. I work to keep even the smallest disagreements from arising between the two of you."[64] The rift, however, was already too wide for Popham to accomplish a reconciliation.

On August 31 Strachan agreed to abandon his attempt to block the navigation of the Scheldt and to devote his full attention to the evacuation of the army on South Beveland.

9

Fever and Retreat

Lord Chatham's decision to terminate operations in the Scheldt was prompted not only by the formidable opposition now encamped near Antwerp but also by the ill health of the British army. He concluded his letter to Castlereagh on August 29 declaring, "I am concerned to say, that the effect of the climate at this unhealthy period of the year is felt most seriously, and that the number of sick already is little short of 3,000."[1] Chatham, in fact, understated the seriousness of the situation, since the number of sick on the twenty-ninth had reached almost four thousand men.[2] With the sickness spreading so rapidly among the troops, Chatham determined to evacuate the marshy lowlands of South Beveland as quickly as possible. Nevertheless, he hoped a reply from London concerning further operations would arrive before the tedious operation was completed.

Preparations for evacuating South Beveland were commenced on August 28. Since it was no longer necessary to detain the cavalry transports, most of which had never been unloaded, they were ordered to sail for England immediately. On August 29 the artillerymen began dismantling the guns of the island with the exception of those at Fort Batz, which remained armed as a security measure until the troops had been evacuated. As these batteries were being removed, additional guns were erected on Walcheren along the Slough and Veere Gat to command these channels. Guns were also placed on St. Joostland Island near the ferryhouse, where numerous boats were being accumulated to transport the troops from South Beveland to Walcheren. A floating bridge across the canal separating Armuyden and St. Joostland was constructed by the Royal Staff Corps to facilitate the evacuation.[3]

Meanwhile, the fever was increasing with astonishing rapidity among the troops. Having first appeared in South Beveland in early August, it spread to Walcheren just prior to the fall of Flushing; and by September 1, the sick numbered almost five thousand men.[4] John Harris of the Rifle Brigade described the situation on South Beveland soon after the fever appeared among the troops.

The first I observed of it was one day as I sat in my billet, when I beheld whole parties of our Riflemen in the street shaking with a sort of ague, to such a degree that they could hardly walk; strong and fine young men who had been but a short time in the service seemed suddenly reduced in strength to infants, unable to stand upright, so great a shaking had seized their whole bodies from head to heel. The company I belonged to was quartered in a barn, and I quickly perceived that hardly a man there had stomach for the bread that was served out to him. . . . In fact, I should say that, about three weeks from the day we landed, I and two others were the only individuals who could stand upon our legs. They lay groaning in rows in the barn, amongst the heaps of lumpy black bread they were unable to eat.[5]

The fever continued unabated as the evacuation of troops on South Beveland began on August 30. The soldiers bivouacked on the northern side of the island were embarked on transports and men of war at Kattendyke and Wemeldinge in the East Scheldt. On the following day, Major General Dyott's brigade marched to the Slough to be ferried across to Walcheren. Six hundred men of Dyott's brigade were sick and were transported to the Slough by wagons, only to be delayed several hours upon reaching the Walcheren side because vehicles were not available there to transport them to hospitals.[6]

There also were many difficulties in embarking the sick troops on board the transports. The vessels converted into hospital ships were allotted on the basis of number of sick indicated in the returns. As a result of this confusion, "the sick were embarked with the well, from the want of sufficient means."

The embarrassment had now unfortunately far exceeded what could have been speculated on even by those who best knew the effects of this unhealthy climate, and it was consequently beyond the means of our hospital establishment, either to furnish attendants or comforts to the extent required. The officers of the medical staff suffered very much from the disease, and deserved the greatest credit for their unremitting attention to their painful duties.[7]

On September 1 Lord Chatham dispatched General Brownrigg to discuss with Sir Richard Strachan the final arrangements for the evacuation of the remaining troops on South Beveland. Monday, September 4, was the day designated to complete the evacuation and withdraw all British forces from the upper regions of the Scheldt. More sick were evacuated during September 1, and some small detachments of healthy troops were embarked at Batz in canal boats for Ramakins. Additional soldiers were marched to the Slough to be ferried across to Walcheren, while Sir Richard Keats supervised the embarkation of other regiments on transports and men of war in the East Scheldt.

All the artillery attached to the army was embarked during September 2, except three guns which were posted at Goes for security. The remaining troops quartered in the northern areas of South Beveland were embarked during the day in small vessels at Wemeldinge, along with their baggage and stores. Sir Richard Keats had been hesitant to send the large transports and men of war into the East Scheldt beyond the anchorage at Zieriksee to embark the sick troops because the ships might be exposed to fire from the Dutch batteries on Toleland and detained by adverse winds. Keats, therefore, collected small boats at Wemeldinge to transport the men to the larger ships down river. Other troops were embarked from the dyke on North Beveland. The spreading fever continued to hinder the evacuation, and by September 3 the sick numbered 8,194 and were increasing hourly.[8] John Webbe, inspector of hospitals, had written Sir Eyre Coote as early as August 31 that the medical supplies and staff would likely be insufficient to cope with the fever if it continued to spread as rapidly as it had the last few days of August. Coote, who had been appointed commander of Walcheren on August 28, immediately dispatched an

urgent letter to Castlereagh requesting additional medical supplies and personnel.[9] Increased medical assistance, however, was
needed by the troops long before Castlereagh had an opportunity
to respond to Coote's request.

The evacuation of South Beveland continued. At Borselen,
Major General Montresor's brigade was being prepared to embark
on transports as well as ships of war. However, Sir Richard Strachan deemed it wise to maintain some of the ships of war in a
battle-ready condition to protect the retreat and had issued such
an order.[10] Consequently, when Montresor's brigade appeared for
embarkation with some six hundred sick troops, they were refused
accommodation on the men of war, even though not enough
transports were immediately available to receive them. Rear Admiral Otway, learning of the situation, ordered every available
transport to Borselen to accommodate the sick, but the scene remained a distressing one. "The Army want Men of War for their
sick, as they say when they are divided into Transports they have
not sufficient medical men to attend them. We have some sick
here without advice or assistance of any kind whatever. The
scene is just now a most melancholy one. God send us better prospects."[11] Early the following morning, three transports arrived at
Borselen to embark Montresor's sick troops, and on September 4
the last British soldiers were evacuated from South Beveland. Sir
John Hope, directing the final withdrawal, then embarked the
remaining guns, stores, carriages, and platforms and destroyed the
magazines left on the island. About 3:00 P.M., the evacuation was
completed, and the rear guard of the British expedition descended
the Scheldt.[12]

By September 6 all British troops were either garrisoned in
Walcheren, aboard ships anchored at Flushing, or in the Roompot. Lord Chatham, prompted by "the crowded state of the men
on board, and the increasing sickness among officers and men,"
asked Sir Richard Strachan to direct the troop ships to proceed
immediately to England, anticipating Castlereagh's orders.[13] On
September 8 the sick of Chatham's army, including the troops

which sailed for England the preceding day, numbered 10,948.[14] Chatham meanwhile remained on Walcheren, anxiously awaiting a reply from Castlereagh concerning future measures to be taken. On September 10 Chatham received Castlereagh's orders to return to England with the army after first leaving a sufficient force on Walcheren to garrison the island. Sir Eyre Coote, therefore, was stationed on Walcheren with 16,766 men, while Chatham and the remainder of the army returned to England.[15] However, adverse winds detained Chatham's departure until September 14. Moreover, by the sixteenth Coote's army on Walcheren had already been reduced by almost half, with sick troops numbering 7,853 and 309 deaths reported the preceding week.[16]

Meanwhile, the movements of the British ships retiring down the river completely bewildered the French command. Bernadotte refused to believe these operations were anything but new strategy attempted by the British. "It appears that the enemy has renounced for the moment his project of attacking us . . . and prefers to keep us uneasy by threatening us on several points."[17] Bernadotte alerted Moncey, headquartered at Ghent, of the British movements downriver. Furthermore, Bernadotte reasoned that Antwerp would now be the pivotal point of the French defense. If the British attacked on the right or left bank, his forces at Antwerp were well positioned to bolster the defenses in either area.

Cadsand appeared to be the most likely objective of the British forces, if they intended to continue operations near the mouth of the Scheldt where their ships were assuming new stations. On paper, Moncey's Army of Tête de Flandre consisted of 38,187 men. However, Moncey revealed that he had only 10,000 troops prepared for combat on August 29. The remainder of his forces were "either too old, too young, or invalids—useless for service."[18] Considering the area from Cadsand to Antwerp vulnerable, Moncey called up his reserve at Ghent. His army also was augmented by some 3,600 men from the camp at Boulogne, including 1,000 naval cannoneers with thirty guns, 6,000 National Guards from Brussels, and a similar force from Ostend. In his dispositions made on the thirty-first, Moncey placed General Olivier in command of the area from Terneuse to Hulst; General Rampon, headquartered at Hulst, commanded in turn the area from Hulst to Tête de Flandre; General d'Aboville and his 6,000 National Guards were ordered to establish a camp at St. Nicholas; and General Soulès was given command of the forces on Cadsand. Moncey moved his own position to Cadsand to observe the movements of the British force in the Scheldt.[19]

Meanwhile, Marshal Jean-Baptiste Bessières arrived at Lille on August 30 to assume command of the Army of the Reserve. In addition to the National Guards under Bessières, the camp of Boulogne and the National Guards along the Atlantic coast from Cadsand to Dunkirk were alerted to the British descent to the mouth of the Scheldt. While these defensive measures were being executed, the French observed with amazement the evacuation of South Beveland. By August 30 only sixty British ships remained anchored near Batz, and on September 4 the last of the British ships descended the Scheldt. Immediately following their departure, the French flotilla ventured down the river to the anchorage above Batz, and later that evening a detachment of Dutch troops, commanded by Gen. Ghisbert-Martin Heyligers, forded the Bergen-op-Zoom channel north of Batz and occupied Batz itself.[20] The following day, the fifth, Marshal Dumonceau's Dutch troops accordingly occupied all of South Beveland.

Thus far Napoleon's strategy had been successful. By concentrating superior numbers of troops (though inferior in quality) and avoiding confrontation with the English long enough for the unhealthful climate of the islands of Zealand to take its toll among the British troops, the invasion was repulsed without a major encounter. Upon learning of the British evacuation of South Beveland, Napoleon determined to continue his defensive policy and thereby allow the British to retain possession of Walcheren. On September 11 Napoleon announced the reorganization of the army in the Scheldt with the appointment of a new commander; the latter measure was prompted by the French emperor's dissat-

isfaction with Bernadotte's latest actions at Antwerp. Becoming
confident that the crisis at Antwerp had passed, Bernadotte had
issued "an order of the day" on September 1, congratulating his
soldiers on their courage and stating that with only 15,000 men in
his Army of Antwerp, an English force of 40,000 had been re-
pelled.[21] Napoleon was incensed at this display, primarily because
he had publicly announced, for Austria's benefit, that the French
army in the Scheldt exceeded 60,000 men. Napoleon therefore recalled Bernadotte to Paris and appointed Marshal Bessières as the
new commander of the Army of the North, as the combined
armies of Antwerp and Tête de Flandre were now designated.[22]
Marshal Moncey assumed command of the Army of the Reserve
at Lille, filling Bessières's vacated post. Napoleon also was fearful
that the French troops bivouacked along the Scheldt might con-
tract the Walcheren fever. He consequently ordered the Army of
the North to bivouac several miles from the marshy areas along
the banks of the river.[23]

Although the British cabinet had agreed that no further operations could be conducted in the Scheldt, a decision had not been
reached concerning whether or not to retain Walcheren. It was
decided to await news of Austria's peace negotiations with France,
since Walcheren might still offer an avenue for later operations on
the Continent.[24] Therefore Chatham, prior to his departure from
Walcheren, had been ordered to ascertain the number of troops
necessary to defend the island and the expense involved.

On September 9 Sir Eyre Coote issued his report to Lord Chatham concerning the defense of Walcheren. He stated a force of
20,000 men would be necessary to defend the island against an
attack by combined French-Dutch forces estimated at that time
to be between 35,000 and 40,000 men. Chatham, however, had already decided to garrison the island with fewer than 17,000 soldiers in an effort to expose as few men as possible to the fever.
Furthermore, the immense British naval force positioned in the
waters surrounding Walcheren offered additional protection and
thereby permitted a reduction in the garrison. Coote's report had

also indicated that extensive repairs to the key forts of the island would be necessary in order to adequately defend Walcheren. Ter Veere and Flushing were considered the most important and formidable positions on the island; yet repairing and strengthening only these two fortresses would require a great deal of time and money. Coote also observed that the approaching winter would force the ships of war from their protective positions in both Scheldts, the Veere Gat, and the Slough because of the ice. "After such an exposition [Coote concluded], his Majesty's ministers will be the best judges of the propriety or possibility of keeping the island. The advantages must indeed be great that can compensate the loss of lives and treasure which the retention must necessarily occasion." [25]

While peace negotiations continued between Austria and France, the British cabinet agreed to retain Walcheren. Though garrisoned by an insufficient number of troops, which was reduced further by the daily additions to the sick list, Walcheren was relatively safe from attack so long as the navy continued to control the waterways of the Scheldt. Sir Eyre Coote, in command of Walcheren, still was apprehensive of his army's position on the island. By September 17, 8,200 men were on the sick list. [26] One week later the number had increased to 9,836 men, and the epidemic gave no indication of abating. These circumstances prompted Coote to exclaim in his letter to Castlereagh on September 23 that "the alarming progress hourly made by this fatal disease, is such that if it should continue in the same proportion for three weeks longer . . . our possession of this island will become very precarious." [27]

The spreading sickness among the troops on Walcheren strained the understaffed medical corps to the limit. When the expedition sailed from England in July, it carried the standard number of doctors and medical assistants allotted for an army of its size. The medical board, however, had not been informed of the secret destination of the expedition, and consequently no special precautions or additional medical supplies were taken. [28] As a result, the doctors were overworked. To further complicate matters, many of the doctors themselves became victims of the fever. In an effort to alleviate some of the pressure on the medical staff and also to provide better care for his men, Coote appealed to Castlereagh on September 23 for additional medical assistance.[29] Actually, it was not doctors but semiskilled hospital mates who were so badly needed on Walcheren. However, once it was known in England that the fever was taking such a heavy toll in the island, few men could be found for work among the troops on Walcheren. Castlereagh attempted to explain the shortage of medical men available for such service. "When you consider the number of medical assistants already sent to Walcheren, and reflect upon the previous necessity of succouring the demands for aid to the wounded in Spain, you must feel how extensively difficult, if not impossible, it must be to provide an adequate and immediate supply for a calamity so sudden and so extensive."[30] During the following weeks, a few doctors and hospital assistants volunteered for service on Walcheren. In addition to these, Coote received permission to employ the residents of the island as mates at the hospitals, which reduced to some degree the burden on the medical staff.[31]

Another problem occasioned by the spreading fever was the insufficient number of buildings suitable for use as hospitals on Walcheren. Major General Dyott accompanied Sir Eyre Coote on an inspection of the hospitals of Walcheren and recorded the following: "I don't suppose it ever fell to the lot of a British officer to visit in the course of three days the sick chambers of nearly 8,000 men in fever; and the miserable, dirty, stinking holes some of the troops were from necessity crammed into, was more shocking than it is possible to express."[32] After the bombardment of Flushing, scarcely a structure was left completely whole. Consequently, the few hospitals established in undamaged buildings were overcrowded, and in many instances, damaged and unheated buildings were forced into use.[33] Of the other towns on the island, only Middelburg had buildings suitable for use as hospitals, and several hospitals were established there. It was preferable, however, to have the sick near the coast to facilitate evacuation. As a result of crowded hospital conditions, many troops were released prematurely, unfit for duty, and often suffered relapses. The sick men also needed bedding as much as proper hospital accommodations. As originally planned, the expedition was intended as a brief campaign, and therefore only blankets and large coats were furnished for the army. It was not until the beginning of October that sufficient beds and sheets arrived from England to accommodate the sick.[34]

Although no one could have foreseen the epidemic which spread among the British troops in Zealand, the general unhealthfulness of the islands of the Scheldt was not unknown to the British government. British armies had frequently been in Holland during the eighteenth century; in fact, as late as 1794 British troops were at Antwerp. Sir John Pringle, in his *Observations on the Diseases of the Army*, had described the fever which attacked the British forces bivouacked in Zealand during the campaign of 1747, concluding that "the British soldiers have always been subject to these fevers in the Netherlands."

It ought also to be remarked, that the sickness never begins till the heats have continued long enough to give time for the putrefaction and evaporation of the water. The epidemics of this country may therefore be generally dated from the end of July or the beginning of August, under the canicular heats; their sensible decline, about the first falling of the leaf; and their end, when the frost begins; the rest of the year is much less disposed to produce any distemper.[35]

The British cabinet, therefore, was well aware of the risk involved, but since this was designed as a brief campaign directed primarily against the more healthful environs of Antwerp, the danger to the troops was considered slight.[36]

Soon after the fever began to attack the troops, John Webbe, inspector of hospitals, was asked to investigate the causes of the disease and to determine its effect. Webbe submitted his report on September 11, two days before he himself fell ill with the fever. His report stated:

Independent of the existing records of the unhealthfulness of Zealand, every object around us depicts it in the most forcible manner; the bottom of every canal that has communication with the sea is thickly covered with an ooze, which, when the tide is out emits a most offensive and noisome effluvia; every ditch is filled with water which is loaded with animal and vegetable substances in a state of putrefaction; and the whole island is so flat, and so near the level of the sea that a large proportion of it is little better than a swamp, and there is scarcely a place where water of a tolerably good quality can be produced.[37]

Webbe observed that although most of the men attacked by the fever would recover, the fever probably would be recurring and would have long-range effects. Of the troops who survived the Walcheren fever in 1809, many later demonstrated the truth of Webbe's observations, especially those who served with Wellington in the Peninsula.[38]

Another analysis of the causes of the disease was offered by Dr. Robert Renny, assistant surgeon to the forces. Renny contended that the soldiers' diet and poor lodgings were sufficient in themselves to have caused the epidemic.

The food issued to the troops, those in hospitals excepted, consisted of salt beef, or pork, and ship's biscuit. The animal food was extremely salty, and the biscuit was far from being easy on digestion. Thirst was a necessary consequence. The men now had recourse to their spirituous liquor (rum, gin, or brandy), which they too often drank with more haste than prudence dictated. A partial intoxication and extreme thirst succeeded. Tankwater was now had recourse to, and drunk without limit. Pain in the head, back, and limbs, anorexia, heat of skin, quickness of pulse, and the other symptoms of fever succeeded; and they soon, in great numbers, required hospital treatment and comfort.[39]

While diet and improper lodgings undoubtedly exacerbated the soldiers' condition, the real cause of the Walcheren fever lies elsewhere.

Numerous other medical studies quickly followed the reports of Webbe and Renny and these indicate that not one, but several diseases were responsible for the epidemic which attacked the British forces in the Scheldt islands.[40] First, it appears that malaria formed a significant substrate of the disease. It is interesting to note that George Hargrove, in his account of the expedition, makes the observation that "we were much annoyed by a description of Moschetos, who attacked us in immense swarms; the sting of this fly does not produce pain at the moment, but is uniformly succeeded by an unpleasant degree of inflammation and tremefaction."[41] Second, lack of sanitation, compounded by overcrowded conditions in barracks, hospitals, and transport ships; improper diet; and finally, shortage of medical personnel, supplies, and facilities all contributed to serious outbreaks of dysentery, typhus, and typhoid. Each of these diseases appears to have been present to some degree and combined to produce the epidemic of the Walcheren fever.[42]

Throughout October the number of new cases of fever continued to increase. Meanwhile, there had been no military action since the fall of Flushing on August 15, and following the evacuation of South Beveland on September 4 the troops on Walcheren had been employed in erecting batteries and preparing the defenses of the island. The navy continued to retain command of the Veere Gat and Slough passage as well as the two branches of the Scheldt as far inland as South Beveland. The largest concentration was in the Veere Gat and Slough, protecting Walcheren from invasion by the Dutch troops occupying South Beveland. The navy also was employed in transporting the numerous sick from Walcheren to the various hospitals established along the east coast of England.[43] Of the approximately 17,000 men left to garrison Walcheren, 9,300 were sick by October 1, and the total deaths from the fever had reached 1,728.[44] By the first week of October, although the fever continued to spread, conditions for the sick improved somewhat when adequate bedding arrived and when repairs were completed on the buildings serving as hospitals.

The British cabinet continued to vacillate between retaining Walcheren, which would entail construction of permanent fortifications, and ordering its evacuation. The decision hinged primarily upon events in Vienna. Until a definite peace between Austria and France was concluded, the retention of Walcheren increased the bargaining power of the English ally. If war were resumed between the two continental powers, the possession of the "key to the Scheldt" could provide a staging point for future action. On October 8 a dispatch was received in London from the Austrian government urging the British cabinet to retain Walcheren. "It would give us pain if after all that has been done on the banks of the Scheldt, the British Cabinet were to withdraw the troops from that point."[45] Prompted by these urgings, the English maintained control of the Scheldt estuary, although the cost in human lives continued to mount.

On October 24 Lt. Gen. George Don arrived on Walcheren to relieve Coote of the command of the British garrison. The English cabinet also underwent some changes during the last weeks of October, with both Castlereagh and George Canning, the foreign secretary, resigning their offices.[46] The earl of Liverpool assumed the office of secretary of war and the direction of activities on Walcheren. Liverpool had just taken office when rumors began filtering into London that a peace treaty was about to be signed between Austria and France in Vienna.[47] The British cabinet, assuming these rumors had some basis, urged preparations to evacuate Walcheren as soon as definite news of a treaty was received in London. Consequently, on October 24 Liverpool instructed General Don to determine the length of time required to destroy the fortifications of Walcheren and the basin of Flushing and to evacuate the army.[48] Three days later Liverpool addressed another dispatch to Don, emphasizing that no definite orders to evacuate Walcheren would be forthcoming until the "peace rumors" could be verified.[49]

Prior to relinquishing command of Walcheren, Sir Eyre Coote had conducted General Don on an inspection of the island. After seeing the numerous sick men in the hospitals throughout the island, Don dispatched a request to Liverpool for transports to convey 5,638 sick to England. The men, according to the medical

staff on the island, might never fully recover from the disease
unless they were quickly removed from Walcheren. Don also
reported his apprehension for the safety of the army on Walcher-
en; in its weakened condition, the French-Dutch forces needed
only to pierce the naval defenses between Walcheren and South
Beveland to gain control of Walcheren. If this were to occur, most
of the British sick would undoubtedly fall into enemy hands. "The
rank and file for duty this day amount to 4,534, and from this
number must be deducted the attendants on the sick . . . besides,
as I have already observed, one-third is incapable of considerable
exertions."[50]

The danger of attack from South Beveland was, in fact, a real
one. Throughout September Napoleon had been content to allow
the British to retain Walcheren, confident that the fever would
soon force them to evacuate the island. However, as the first week
of October passed and the British remained on Walcheren, Napoleon grew impatient. Consequently, on October 8 he ordered
Marshal Bessières to prepare a plan for an attack on Walcheren.[51]
Napoleon also requested his brother Louis to increase the number
of Dutch troops on South Beveland from the current 3,000 men to
16,000 in order to cooperate with the French in driving the British
from the Scheldt. Bessières reported to Napoleon on October 21
that a successful attack upon the British positions was almost impossible because of the large British naval force protecting Walcheren. Napoleon responded that as soon as the ice forced the
British ships from the Scheldt, Walcheren should be taken.[52]

On October 14 the Treaty of Schoenbrunn was signed, restoring
peace between Austria and France. By November 2 Napoleon had
returned to Fontainebleau, and he now considered the British
troops remaining in Walcheren as little more than an annoyance.
"The Walcheren expedition appears to be of so little importance
to me, that it is my intention not to go there myself; I give that
responsibility to the duke of Istria [Bessières]."[53] On November 11
Bessières was ordered to erect mortars and cannon in South
Beveland along the Veere Gat and the Slough in order to drive the

British naval vessels from their defensive positions. Once this was accomplished, Napoleon considered expulsion of the British forces from Walcheren practically accomplished. To Bessières, he wrote on November 20, "You hold command of all the Dutch fortresses and troops, of my fleet, my arsenals, and my troops. Act swiftly and vigorously . . . and let me soon hear that the Slough is rid of the enemy."[54]

Before Bessières could execute his orders, however, the British began evacuating Walcheren. General Don had responded to Liverpool's queries on October 29, reporting that it would require at least twenty days to remove the stores and sick troops from the island and to destroy its major fortifications and naval facilities at Flushing. In view of the increased enemy activity on South Beveland, General Don requested Liverpool to have the naval vessels between the two islands augmented; if these ships were driven from the Veere Gat and Slough, his forces on the island would be at the mercy of the invading army.[55] On November 4 Don was authorized to commence the destruction of the naval facilities of Flushing and the sea fortifications of Walcheren. To expedite the work of the Royal Engineers in destroying the various works on the island, one hundred civil artificers were sent from England to serve under Lt. Col. Robert Pilkington, who was directing the demolition.[56] Liverpool suggested, however, that these measures be delayed until the sick troops had been evacuated from the island, since he feared an attack as soon as the destruction of the defensive capabilities of Walcheren was begun. Liverpool also considered it possible that the inhabitants of Walcheren, fearing the island would be inundated as a result of the destruction of the locks and the basin of Flushing, might attempt to prevent the British from executing these measures. Therefore, the evacuation of the sick men was ordered to commence before the Royal Engineers, Royal Staff Corps, and navy technicians began work.[57]

The transports for the evacuation of sick troops, which Don had requested on October 27, were prepared to sail from Harwich

November 3, but adverse winds delayed their arrival at Walcher-
en. Additional ships soon were equipped at Harwich to accommodate the remaining sick troops on the island. By November 26
the troop transports had arrived at Flushing, and the last of the
sick soldiers embarked for England.[58] A frigate, the *Fidelle,* which
had been under construction in the basin of Flushing when the
city capitulated, and a brig were launched from the port. An un-
completed ship of the line, the *Royal Hollander,* was taken apart
and sent back to England along with a large quantity of naval
supplies. The ship reportedly was rebuilt in Britain and christened
the *Chatham.*[59] By December 11 Pilkington's engineers had completed the work assigned to them, including the destruction of
"the dockyards, arsenal, magazines and every building belonging
to the naval establishments" at Flushing. The Royal Navy had
blocked the entrance to Flushing's harbor by sinking vessels
"filled with heavy materials, so as to render the passage for ships
of war impracticable." Captain Rudyard of the Royal Engineers
and a detachment of the Royal Staff Corps had destroyed the sea
defenses of Flushing by dismantling the batteries and leveling the
parapets. Finally, mines were placed at the base of the flood gates
to destroy the foundations, thereby completing the destruction of
the naval facilities of Flushing. Colonel Pilkington had effectively
accomplished this destructive work without subjecting the island
to inundation.[60]

Meanwhile, General Don was supervising the evacuation of the
ordnance, stores, and, on December 9, the last of the garrison.
However, unfavorable winds and stormy weather prevented the
British ships from clearing their anchorages in the East and West
Scheldt. The situation might have become critical had it not been
for the British men of war, who, under Commodore Owen in the
Veere Gat and Captain Mason in the Slough, held their positions
and prevented Bessières from occupying Walcheren until December 23, when the entire British force sailed for England.[61] With
General Don's departure from the Scheldt, the disastrous expedition was brought to an end.

10

British Reaction:
The Parliamentary Inquiry

Until the commencement of the siege of Flushing in early August, the British press seemed optimistic concerning the Grand Expedition and its chances for complete success. However, after the initial victories of the English forces in Zealand deteriorated into a protracted siege of Flushing, the comments in the newspapers became more guarded.[1] By August 13, scarcely two weeks after the expedition had been launched, private reports began circulating that early failures had already precluded full success of the expedition.[2] The earl of Rosslyn wrote a friend on August 10 from his command in South Beveland that the expedition would probably do little more than capture Flushing; consequently, he expected to be back in England before the middle of September.[3] The dissension between Chatham and Strachan hit the press as early as August 14, when the *Morning Chronicle* published an account from a private correspondent, which included the following:

Indeed, I fear the enemy begins to draw some inferences favourable to themselves from our inaction and seeming indecision. Ask any of our naval men the cause, and they say it rests with our military commanders, who in their turn complain of the delay that has taken place in landing the heavy ordnance, and of course impeding the necessary operations for a bombardment.[4]

As the end of August drew near with little more than the capture of Flushing accomplished, the British newspapers became increasingly skeptical and critical of the Scheldt operation. The *Times* reported on August 29 that "most of the officers are sick enough of the climate, if not of the expedition"; and the following day it suggested that since "it took a month for Flushing, so it probably will for Fort Lillo also." On September 2, when it was learned in London that further operations were uncertain, the press became more outspoken. The *Times* editorialized:

Who is going to announce the decisions of the expedition? The same men, therefore, who told us yesterday that we were using their patrons with great injustice, by insinuating that their grand expedition would do no more than take Walcheren, can hardly have the face to tell us today that it has done as much as could be expected, though it has done nothing but capture this island. Yet we are afraid that the "murder will out," and somebody else must therefore be found to announce it. We shall endeavor to pave the way for them, by stating our strong suspicion, of what it would have been almost treason to say ten days ago; namely, that Antwerp, and the naval and military stores at Antwerp must all be left at Antwerp. Lord Chatham has, we fear, got to the end of his tether.[5]

A few days later, when news of the British withdrawal was announced, the *Times* carried comments requesting a trial or court-martial to determine the party or parties responsible for the failure. The criticism of the expedition became more specific when Lord Chatham came under direct attack. "Such is the conclusion of this unhappy business, upon which we shall say the less for the present, as there can be no question but that the conduct of the Commander-in-Chief will receive the investigation of a Court-Martial."[6] The *Times* continued its attack on September 5, calling the failure of the expedition a national disaster and criticizing Chatham not only for his conduct of the expedition but also for "the intrepid indifference with which the determination to retreat was announced." Chatham, the paper continued, gave "no soothing expression to mitigate the grief, or assuage the shame of an overwhelmed and downcast nation."

During the following weeks, criticism often took the form of squibs subjecting various aspects of the expedition to ridicule but generally singling out Lord Chatham as the object of their derision. One such lampoon referred to the commander in chief of the expedition as "turtle Chatham," the name probably being derived from a story then current in London concerning Chatham's possession of two tortoises during his stay in Walcheren and South Beveland.[7] Even on the Continent, caricatures appeared at Chatham's expense. At Ghent, the *Journal du commerce* ran one which depicted Chatham seated in a chariot pulled by two turtles and six snails, holding the reins and crying, "not so fast."[8] On September 11 a letter from a private correspondent on Walcheren appeared in one of the London papers. "I assure you, this great armament has failed through the mismanagement of both ——— and ———. Of these, ——— is said to have generally breakfasted at 2 p.m., dined at seven, and gone to bed about two in the morning. He amused himself a good deal with playing at chess with his aides-de-camp."[9]

Although Chatham suffered the brunt of the criticism from the English press, all connected with the enterprise came under attack. Charges were raised against the ministers for planning an expedition which had so little chance of success. Others, when learning that Walcheren was to be retained, considered it treason to hold English troops in such unhealthful conditions.[10] Furthermore, the medical board received criticism for not anticipating the epidemic and taking preventive measures.[11] As the comments against the expedition became less restrained, a new development occurred which was initially attributed to the failure of the expedition. In mid-September the cabinet dissolved, primarily because of secret maneuvering by the foreign secretary, George Canning, in an effort to oust Castlereagh. Four cabinet members resigned, including the prime minister.[12] Immediately following these resignations, Canning and Castlereagh fought a duel on September 21, which naturally led to a national scandal. These events pushed the expedition from the public eye momentarily, although some saw the unsuccessful expedition to the Scheldt as a source of the cabinet's problems.[13]

Although the clamor for an investigation into the failure of the expedition did abate somewhat during October and November, an occasional article from the French newspapers reprinted in the London press served to keep the expedition before the public.[14] Daily reports of the fever among the troops on Walcheren also aroused popular indignation, especially after October 31 when it was learned that even though peace had been signed between Austria and France, the troops still would not return immediately.[15]

By December a new cabinet had been formed and the demand for an investigation was renewed by the press. On December 1 it was reported that Lord Castlereagh had suggested that a parliamentary inquiry be conducted into the failure of the expedition. Following a stormy debate on December 7, the Court of Common Council of the City of London petitioned the king to call for a parliamentary inquiry. George III replied that "it will be for my parliament, in their wisdom to ask for such information, or to take such measures upon this subject as they shall judge conducive to the public good."[16] The *Times*, commenting on the City of London's petition, demanded a parliamentary inquiry and stated that "this is not a matter of litigation between this party and that . . . for the contending parties here are the nation and the nation's enemies."[17]

Parliament convened 26 January 1810. The opening speech by the lords commissioners to both houses set the stage for the inquiry.

His Majesty commands us to express to you his deep regret that the exertions of the Emperor of Austria against the ambitions and violence of France have proved unavailing, and that His Imperial Majesty has been compelled to abandon the contest, and to conclude a disadvantageous peace. Although the war was undertaken by that Monarch without encouragement on the part of His Majesty, every effort was made for the assistance of Austria which His Majesty deemed consistent with the due support of his allies, and with the welfare and interest of his own Dominions.

An attack upon the naval armaments and establishments in the

Scheldt, afforded at once the prospect of destroying a growing force, which was daily becoming more formidable to the security of this country, and of diverting the exertions of France from the important objects of reinforcing her armies on the Danube, and controlling the spirit of resistance in the north of Germany. These considerations determined His Majesty to employ his forces in an expedition to the Scheldt.

Although the principal ends of this expedition have not been attained, His Majesty confidently hopes that advantages, materially affecting the security of His Majesty's Dominions in the further prosecution of the war, will be found to result from the demolition of the docks and arsenals at Flushing. This important object His Majesty was enabled to accomplish in consequence of the reduction of the island of Walcheren, by the valour of his fleets and armies.

His Majesty has given directions that such documents and papers should be laid before you as he trusts will afford satisfactory information upon the subject of this expedition.[18]

In its first regular session, the House of Commons voted to investigate the expedition and selected a committee to hear testimony from the various individuals involved. The committee was to meet in closed hearings and at regular intervals report its progress to the Commons.[19] The investigation was to proceed chronologically, questioning those persons concerned with the planning, execution, occupation, and retreat, in that order. Papers and documents relative to all phases of the expedition also were to be examined by the committee. The evidence as it was presented fell into five general categories, each pertaining to specific aspects of the expedition. The first concerned the conception of the expedition, especially the financial arrangements and other factors which prevented the troops from being sent to Portugal or perhaps Germany or Italy. The committee then heard evidence relating to operational plans, medical preparations, the conduct of military and naval affairs, and finally, the retention of Walcheren.

William Huskisson, one of the secretaries in the treasury office during the planning of the expedition, testified that the foreign exchange on the Continent was against Great Britain at that time to the extent of about twenty percent. Furthermore, it was impossible to arrange the large amount of credit necessary to finance the operations of an extensive campaign. When asked if the British government could have sent an army to northern Germany, Huskisson replied that the difficulty in raising credit prohibited such an operation. "I have no hesitation in stating as my opinion, that no army to that amount could have been sent to the Elbe or Weser." Huskisson was then asked if any army could have been dispatched to Portugal to reinforce the British troops there. He responded that the expense would have been too great and that "the demands on the military chest in the Peninsula . . . were such as to create the greatest apprehension that the chest would be entirely exhausted if the expenditure should be considerably increased." Italy presented the same problem. Consequently, Holland was the only strategic area on the Continent where the English could afford to employ an army of any magnitude. Huskisson further testified that although the treasury did have more specie available for operations in Holland than any other country on the Continent, the amount was sufficient only for a brief campaign.[21]

Richard Warton, also of the treasury office, testified concerning the actual expenses of the expedition, which had been speculated as high as £5 million sterling. Warton stated that the cost of the expedition, above the normal expense of maintaining the army and navy, amounted to £834,375. Of this, about one-half was incurred in procuring transports and providing for the occupation of Walcheren.[22] Much criticism had been levied against the cabinet for not launching the expedition earlier in the year when the weather would have been more favorable and, more important, the diversion for Austria more efficacious. These critics were silenced to some extent by the testimony of Sir Rupert George, chairman of the transport board, who emphasized the difficulty in procuring such a large amount of shipping as that required by the expedition. Numerous measures to provide the necessary tonnage had been taken (even the idea of requisitioning neutral ships was up for consideration at one point) but in spite of their efforts, sufficient shipping could not be provided until July.[23]

In his testimony before the committee, Lord Castlereagh defended the expedition on grounds that it offered the advantage of a brief operation close to England, a diversion for Austria, a significant opportunity for protecting England's security, and relatively little risk. Castlereagh emphasized that the expedition was not intended to be a full-fledged campaign but rather a *coup de main* with limited objectives. In describing the type of operation planned against the Scheldt, Castlereagh recalled his instructions to Chatham and observed, "my notion of the operation was that it was not to be a protracted operation, that it was neither to lead to a campaign nor to a regular siege."[24] Although perhaps envisioned as a *coup de main* by Castlereagh, what actually sailed from England was a massive force of some 44,000 men, over 4,000 horses, 206 pieces of artillery, over 200 wagons, carriages, and carts, 10 million rounds of ammunition, and 110,000 artillery shells, all conveyed in a naval force in excess of 600 ships.[25] When asked who was responsible for such a large body of cavalry and vast train of heavy artillery which would necessarily "impede the mode of advance by the Scheldt," Castlereagh testified that all military provisions had been requested by Chatham.[26] In his testimony, Chatham defended his arrangements, arguing that the cavalry and heavy ordnance were necessary to accomplish his assigned task.

The government's military advisers were questioned on the plan of attack on Antwerp. The opinion held by most of the military is exemplified in the testimony of Gen. Robert Brownrigg, who testified that given favorable weather and possession of either Cadsand or Flushing, the armament destined for Antwerp could have sailed from the Downs and reached Sandvliet in four days.

I think, if the armament destined to act against Antwerp had been assembled at Sandvliet by the 3rd of August, which would have been seven days after the first division sailed from the Downs, the whole might have been before the place by the 8th. . . . I think the French force at Antwerp on the 8th is reported to have been about 5,000 troops in addition to the armed burghers and artificers.[27]

Brownrigg contended that if the armament had arrived at Sandvliet on August 3 with 23,000 men, 17,000 troops could have marched immediately upon Antwerp, leaving 6,000 troops to invest Lillo and Bergen-op-Zoom. This force might have taken Antwerp by assault; but even if it had not, batteries could have been erected near the walls of the city by using the houses of the suburbs for cover. In such manner, a breach in the wall could have been made quickly. The fleet, meanwhile, might have forced the boom across the river and attacked Antwerp from the Scheldt while the army bombarded it from land. The entire area was reported to be poorly defended during the first two weeks of August; and had the attack been made promptly, there seemed to be "a very fair prospect of success."

The members of the medical board were then examined.[28] Each testified that if he had been informed of the destination of the expedition he would have recommended sending more medical supplies, especially bark.[29] However, testimony established that there was actually no deficiency of medicine on the expedition.[30] The adequate supply of medicines, however, was solely attributed to the efforts of the medical staff on Walcheren. Numerous requests for bark were dispatched to the medical board from the island during the first weeks of September, but the arrival on Walcheren was delayed. On September 28 Francis Burrows, acting inspector of hospitals on Walcheren, reported that there were only 300 pounds of bark remaining in store; and this amount diminished to 50 pounds, scarcely enough for one day, before a new supply was obtained.[31] Sir James McGrigor, who arrived on Walcheren at the end of September to assume the position of inspector of hospitals, learned that an American vessel had arrived at Flushing and carried, in addition to champagne and claret, several chests of bark. By purchasing some 1,400 pounds of this bark and supplementing it with additional quantities found on unloaded transports in the harbors of Ter Veere and Flushing, enough medicine was available until the shipment from London arrived.[32]

Thomas Lidderdale, a member of the medical staff serving on Walcheren, testified that the bedding for the sick was ordered as soon as it was learned that the troops would remain on the island.[33] The shortage of beds and sheets continued, Lidderdale stated, until the first week of October. Sir Lucas Pepys, physician general to the forces, then appeared before the committee and acknowledged that the soldiers had suffered as a result of an insufficient number of hospital workers, but argued that such an epidemic could not have been anticipated. He further assured the parliamentary committee that every effort had been made to recruit additional hospital mates once the fever broke out on Walcheren.[34] Pepys and the other members of the medical board admitted that they were fully aware of the health problems associated with the islands of Zealand, but they contended that an epidemic of such proportions was totally unexpected. The medical men concluded their testimony by agreeing that the Walcheren epidemic was attributable to several factors, including diet, drinking water, dampness of lodgings, unusually low land level, and generally unhealthful climate.[35]

The various military and naval officers serving on the expedition presented evidence concerning their specific operations. Regarding the abortive landing on Cadsand, Owen reported that he could have disembarked about seven hundred men of Huntley's division on several occasions had the general so desired. Huntley agreed, but testified that he considered seven hundred men too few to be landed on the island in one operation since reinforcements would be at least two hours in arriving; had they landed, they probably would have been sacrificed. Lord Gardner's landing boats were the key to the operation against Cadsand. Nevertheless, Gardner testified he was never ordered to assist Commodore Owen in the landing.[36]

Two misunderstandings appear largely responsible for the con-

fusion surrounding the operation against Cadsand. The first concerned Huntley's instructions. General Brownrigg's orders to
Huntley did not specify any definite number of men to be landed
in the initial disembarkation but simply stated that two thousand
men should be sufficient for the operation. Huntley, in a later
conversation with General Brownrigg, was informed that Strachan
had made arrangements for the operation against Cadsand and
"that there would be ample means for landing a great part of my
[Huntley's] division." This "ample means" was never actually de-
fined, but Huntley interpreted it to mean about two thousand
men. Strachan later testified that he considered his arrangements
sufficient since Gardner's squadron could reinforce Owen.[37] The
second misunderstanding resulted when Lord Gardner failed to
receive Strachan's dispatch of July 24 ordering Gardner to assist
in the Cadsand operation by supplying Owen with launches and
sloops of war to cover the beach. Had this letter been received,
however, the execution of this order probably would have been
impossible since Gardner was to the leeward and had no pilots to
guide his ships into the Wielingen channel.[38]

The final general category of information presented to the committee dealt with the retention of Walcheren. Sir Eyre Coote and
Gen. George Don, the two former commanders of Walcheren,
testified that it would have been impossible to hold Walcheren
for a prolonged period. With winter approaching, the naval protection would end; the ice in the channels surrounding Walcheren
would force a withdrawal. Both testified that it would have been
an expensive project to repair the fortifications of Walcheren and
provide an adequate garrison to defend the island. With the river
frozen and Walcheren confronted on three sides by hostile forces,
Don and Coote agreed that it would have been impractical to attempt further defense of this small enclave on the Continent, particularly after the peace agreement between France and Austria.[39]

The most significant evidence presented to the investigating
committee was contained in the narratives and testimonies of
Lord Chatham and Sir Richard Strachan. Upon his return from

Walcheren in September 1809, Chatham had prepared an account of his proceedings which he withheld pending an investigation into the causes of the failure of the campaign. When it became evident that a parliamentary inquiry would in fact take place, Chatham presented his narrative directly to George III on January 15, bypassing the secretary of war.[40] Chatham requested the return of his paper a few days later in order to make several changes and then resubmitted it on February 14 through proper cabinet channels.[41] Chatham's paper was then placed in evidence before the investigating committee.

Sir Richard Strachan, meanwhile, had learned from the newspapers that Chatham had prepared a report; he, consequently, began preparing his own account of the expedition.[42] Before his narrative was completed, however, Strachan heard rumors that Chatham's account contained charges against himself and the navy; Strachan was eager to obtain a copy of Chatham's paper in order to answer any such accusations. When the inquiry opened, Strachan was given a copy of Chatham's paper, and he subsequently submitted his observations on Chatham's narrative. These were placed in evidence before the committee on 5 March 1810.[43] Both papers, in addition to Chatham's and Strachan's actual testimonies, revealed significant areas of disagreement over specific plans of the expedition and what actually transpired during the operations in the Scheldt.

Chatham's narrative was based on the assumption that only two basic questions concerning the expedition required answering. The first was why the expedition could not have continued operations against the Continent once it arrived at Batz on August 25. Chatham replied that the reason was obvious: the size of the army had been reduced daily by the spreading fever, while the French and Dutch had concentrated an overwhelming force to oppose any British advance.[44] The more troublesome second question was why the army took almost four weeks to arrive at Batz. This, Chatham suggested, was "purely a naval consideration . . . and the delay in no shape rests with me, or depends upon any arrangements in which the army was concerned." In support of his statement, Chatham recounted the events of the expedition, explaining:

I have confined myself to stating the facts; abstaining as it became me, from all comment, and leaving it to the Admiral, in such report as he may make of his proceedings, to bring under your Majesty's view the circumstances which may have occasioned them [disappointments], and, above all, to account for the difficulties which prevented the investment of Flushing . . . as well as to shew the obstacles which presented themselves to the early progress of the armament up the West Scheldt, which operation I had always looked upon as the primary object of his instructions, and on the accomplishment of which our best hopes of success in any of the ulterior objects of the Expediton principally, if not wholly, depended.[45]

A comparison of the testimony and statements of the two men reveals several areas of conflict. Chatham stated he was disappointed that the troops, when marching to invest Flushing, did not have naval support, since "it was distinctly agreed upon, that a vigorous attack by the navy upon the sea front should be made" at that time. If this had occurred, Chatham believed Flushing might have been forced to surrender immediately, thereby making a regular siege unnecessary. Strachan, however, denied that any such cooperation was ever "distinctly agreed upon."[46] Early plans for the attack upon Walcheren support Chatham's contention, but these appear to have been contingent upon landing the troops near Zoutland. Since the landing took place on Bree Sand, located on the opposite side of the island where the British flotilla was employed to cover the landing and bombard Ter Veere, no naval vessels were available to attack Flushing at the time the army was approaching the town. It was only after Ramakins fell, on August 3, that a significant number of ships were able to enter the West Scheldt and reach a position to attack Flushing; by that date, the army had already invested the town on the land side. Strachan commented that any hope the commander in chief had that such an operation would persuade Flushing to surrender immediately must "appear very chimerical."

Chatham agreed with Strachan that although the expedition was forced into the Roompot, such unfortunate necessity should not have delayed the expedition more than three or four days. Their reasons for such opinions, however, were quite different. Chatham declared that once South Beveland was occupied and Ter Veere and Ramakins were captured, the Veere Gat, Slough, and West Scheldt were open for the expedition's advance to Batz. Since these military impediments were removed by August 3, any delay in assembling the expedition at Batz necessarily rested with the navy.[48] Strachan agreed that there was no military justification for the armament's not reaching Batz a few days after these forts were reduced, especially since the French fleet and flotilla were above Batz and offered no resistance. He contended, however, that the narrowness and intricacies of the Slough coupled with the inclement weather and continual adverse winds caused the extended delay.[49]

Strachan further testified that he had anticipated the difficulties in moving several hundred vessels through the Slough under the prevailing adverse weather conditions; in fact, during his conference with Chatham at Middelburg on August 1, he attempted "to impress them on his lordship's mind." Strachan related that at the meeting he received the impression that the general intended to change his plans, and that instead of moving all the heavily loaded transports through the Slough and West Scheldt to Batz, Chatham would land most of the infantry and cavalry on South Beveland.[50] Under such an assumption, Strachan stated that he prepared the flotilla to move up the West Scheldt on the shortest notice in order to cooperate with the army in "prosecuting the ulterior objects of the Expedition." By the sixth, when Chatham had not ordered any additional forces landed on South Beveland, Strachan again recommended this procedure. In a meeting with Chatham on August 6, Strachan emphasized the difficulties experienced by the navy in moving the numerous ships through the narrow Slough passages; he "ventured to propose to his lordship to commence the disembarkation by landing the cavalry immediately on South Beveland and marching them to Batz, which might be followed by the infantry now occupied in the siege of Flushing." Thus a "limited number of transports as might contain articles essential to the first advance of the army" could be expedited through the Slough.[51] Chatham did consent to land Huntley's and Rosslyn's forces on South Beveland, but he had no intention of disembarking all the cavalry, heavy ordnance, artillery horses, and stores and moving them across the island to Batz, only to have them reembarked for the Continent.[52] Furthermore, he did not consider it possible for the army to commence operations on the mainland until the cavalry, ordnance, ammunition, provisions, stores, and troops were assembled near Batz. The poor roads on South Beveland, almost obliterated by continuous rains, made the movement of the heavy guns along the overland route almost impossible.[53] It is interesting to note that the testimonies of naval officers on the expedition gave full support to Strachan's recommendation and that the military officers testified to complete agreement with Chatham's position.[54]

Chatham and Strachan agreed that an additional delay was caused by the navy's inability to completely blockade Flushing, thereby permitting reinforcements to enter the besieged town. Chatham attributed the prolonged siege of Flushing to this factor, charging that reinforcements in Flushing not only forced the army to attack the town in a more formal manner but also necessitated the landing of General Grosvenor's division on Walcheren to support the siege. Grosvenor's troops had been prepared to cross into South Beveland as soon as the transports began moving up the West Scheldt, but their necessary diversion to Flushing delayed further action against the Continent until Flushing capitulated.[55] Strachan admitted that French reinforcements were able to enter Flushing from Cadsand until August 7, but he declared that the navy did everything possible to halt this. The same wind which slowed the ships' advance through the Slough enabled the French to reinforce Flushing, in spite of the British navy's efforts.[56]

Chatham and Strachan were in general agreement on the Cadsand operation. After the Right Wing, destined for Antwerp, was forced into the Roompot, Cadsand possessed little value for the English, and a landing there by Huntley would have only divided the troops of the expedition. Neither could foresee the continued inclement weather which prevented the naval blockade of Flushing and allowed the French to reinforce that besieged town. Chatham attributed the failure against Cadsand to bad weather and to insufficient boats for putting an adequate force ashore during the initial landing. Strachan contended that the French defenses on the island were too strong to effect a landing. There appears to have been some truth in both statements.

In concluding his explanation for why the expedition was not assembled sooner at Batz, Chatham emphasized the fact that the first frigates did not pass up the West Scheldt until August 11 and that the ships of the line did not enter the West Scheldt until August 14, insinuating that an advance would have been impossible until these large ships were in a position to protect the advancing forces.[57] Strachan countered by stating that these large ships could have entered the river earlier; but since the French fleet was above the boom, the large vessels were not needed until the transports were in the West Scheldt.[58]

Both Chatham and Strachan concluded their respective reports by disclaiming any responsibility for the failure of the expedition. Each insinuated that the other had caused the delays which spelled defeat for the operations in the Scheldt. Chatham stressed that until the entire expedition was assembled at Batz, no operations against the mainland could be attempted. The responsibility for transporting the army to that location rested with the navy.[59] Strachan, on the other hand, emphasized the adverse wind and inclement weather, charging these climatic conditions with the delay in transporting the expedition to Batz.[60] Strachan did state, however, that had Chatham proceeded by South Beveland instead of attempting to assemble the entire operation at Batz via the Slough and West Scheldt, the campaign might have succeeded.[61]

From the conflicting narratives and testimony of the two commanders, it can be concluded that neither fully understood nor appreciated the problems confronting the other. Chatham showed indifference to the difficulties encountered by the navy in completing the blockade of Flushing and in pushing the numerous vessels through the narrow Slough passage under adverse weather conditions. There was almost unanimous agreement among the naval and military officers that Strachan had no choice but to order the entire expedition into the Roompot on July 30 and 31 because of the bad weather, yet Chatham seemed almost oblivious to these same weather conditions.[62] The factors of wind, current, tides, obscure channels, and paucity of pilots appeared unimportant to the military commander. Strachan, for his part, exhibited little understanding of the difficulties confronting the army. After the ships had been forced into the Roompot, Ter Veere was necessarily selected as the primary port for disembarking all stores, guns, and equipment to be used against Flushing, although Zoutland, closer to Flushing by approximately four miles, had originally been intended for this service. Consequently, everything used against Flushing had to be brought from the opposite side of the island along muddy, narrow roads, which naturally caused delay. Strachan seemed unaware of the disadvantages and difficulties forced upon the army because of this change from the original plan. Furthermore, Strachan's insistence upon landing on South Beveland also belied his understanding of military problems involved in such an operation. Although this procedure would undoubtedly have saved the navy much labor in navigating the Slough, it was impractical from the military standpoint, as confirmed by testimony of the military officers on the expedition.[63] This lack of basic understanding of the other's problems led Strachan and Chatham to incriminate each other for the failure of the expedition.

On March 26, after having heard all the evidence collected by the investigating committee, Lord Porchester began the debate in the House of Commons. Porchester gave a lengthy summation of the expedition from its conception to its return to England, charging that although no fault could be found with the military and naval commanders, the ministers should be censured for having planned such a campaign. In concluding his speech, he moved two resolutions, one concerning the policy and conduct of the campaign and the other on the retention of Walcheren after the "ulterior objects of the expedition were found impracticable." Porchester's first resolution proclaimed that the expedition to the Scheldt was undertaken under circumstances offering no rational hope of success at a time of year when the islands of the Scheldt were known to be most unhealthful; consequently, "the advisers of this ill-judged enterprise are, in the opinion of the House, deeply responsible for the heavy calamities with which its failure has been attended." [64]

Porchester's second resolution concerned the decision to retain Walcheren. This charged that although the primary objectives of the expedition had been abandoned, a significant portion of the British forces had remained on the island of Walcheren, exposed to imminent hazard from fever and to attack by the enemy for three months "without any urgent or determined purpose in view, or any prospect of advantage to justify such hazard, or to compensate such a sacrifice." The conduct by the ministers, Porchester's resolution concluded, called for the severest censure by the House of Commons.

Lord Castlereagh then spoke in defense of the expedition, maintaining that if the weather had been more favorable the expedition could have succeeded; the Government, he argued, could not be held responsible for the weather or fever which crippled the campaign. [65] General Craufurd then spoke at length defending the authors of the expedition. He stated that a diversion had been made in favor of Austria by the attack in the Scheldt and that under the unfortunate circumstances, the expedition had accomplished everything that could have been expected. Craufurd then moved for an amendment to Lord Porchester's resolution, omitting everything except the word "that" and substituting the following:

That this House taking into consideration the extreme importance of destroying the extensive and increasing naval means and arsenals in the Scheldt, where a considerable navy has been already constructed, which was growing with great rapidity, and to a formidable extent, and also taking into consideration the expediency of making a diversion in favour of Austria in the critical state of the war on the Continent, at the period of the undertaking of the expedition; considering also the probability of success arising from the reduced state of the forces in the neighborhood of the Scheldt, is of opinion that his Majesty's Ministers were justified in applying the naval and military means in a manner which combined a great national object with the prospect of affording essential assistance to our allies in advising the undertaking of the expedition, notwithstanding the difficulties with which it seemed to be attended—difficulties which have appeared to a degree not to be provided against by a state of wind and weather altogether unusual at that season of the year which was more unfavorable to the projected operations.

That the House sees with the deepest regret the loss of valuable lives, which by the diseases of the climate had been occasioned in that unhealthy situation; yet taking into consideration the state of the negotiations between Austria and France, and the grounds possessed by Ministers of renewing hostilities, that the retention of the island of Walcheren was likely to effect both of these objects; and considering also the time which must necessarily elapse under any circumstances before the island could be evacuated, the House is of opinion, that no blame can be attributed to his Majesty's Ministers for not having at an earlier period ordered the evacuation of that place.[66]

The debate continued three days longer. Finally, on March 31, after more than two months of investigation and debate, the Commons was ready to vote on the various resolutions.[67] The first division was on Lord Porchester's original motion censuring the ministers for the policy and conduct of the expedition. By a vote of 275 to 227, the resolution was defeated. Next came General Craufurd's amendment stating that no blame could be placed on the ministers for the policy adopted concerning the expedition. The amendment was carried by a vote of 272 to 232. The third division was on censure of the ministers for retaining Walcheren, as put forth in Lord Porchester's second resolution. This measure was defeated by the Commons 275 to 224. Finally, a resolution was adopted by vote of 253 to 232 approving the ministers' policy of retaining Walcheren until peace had been declared between Austria and France.[68] With the voting upon this final resolution, the inquiry into the expedition to the Scheldt ended, having found neither the ministers, the navy, nor the military commanders responsible for the failure of the campaign.

This exoneration by the Commons was not well received in the British press. The *Times* expressed the feelings of many when it declared on 5 April 1810:

The nation has now waited nearly half a year, from the failure of the Walcheren expedition to the close of its investigation, in patient hope of redress. It has now seen, with inexpressible concern, that this expedition is to be numbered, if not among the happy, yet among the wise and vigorous measures upon which our means have been exhausted.

If the Walcheren expedition is to pass unmarked by the general censure, then can no calamity happen on which the British nation will deserve to be heard? They who can be silent under the miseries of this infliction, will merit as much in contempt as they have suffered in injury; and may be justly esteemed by those who have wronged them, to have relinquished altogether the right to be heard on public measures.[69]

These remarks in the *Times* ended the public debate on the expedition. Lord Darnley, in a speech in the House of Lords on April 5, attempted to revive interest in the expedition and proposed another investigation into its failure.[70] But his speech fell on deaf ears, and a second investigation was never undertaken.

11

An Evaluation

An evaluation of the British expedition to the Scheldt must be made by considering its original objectives and how many of these were attained or ever were attainable. The expedition had two basic goals: to destroy the French naval power concentrated in the Scheldt River and to form a diversion for Austria. Had these two objectives been wholly achieved, the expedition might have had considerable impact upon the European scene.[1]

The primary objective of the expedition was to capture or destroy the French fleet concentrated in the Scheldt River, destroy the docks and arsenals at Flushing, Terneuse, and Antwerp, and obstruct the Scheldt, making it no longer navigable for ships of war.[2] Of these objectives, only the destruction of the docks and arsenals of Flushing were accomplished. In the 31 January 1810 issue of *Le Moniteur universel*, Napoleon admitted publicly that the damages inflicted by the British in the Scheldt amounted to two million francs, but in a letter to his stepson, Eugène de Beauharnais, he put the figure at fifty million.[3]

Still, few would argue that these accomplishments were worthy of the effort of some seventy thousand soldiers and seamen, the cost of almost one million pounds sterling (about twenty-five million francs), and the loss to the British army of over four thousand dead and some twelve thousand men incapacitated for an indefinite period.

The second objective of the expedition was to form a diversion for Austria, which had joined Britain in the war against Napoleonic France in April 1809. However, by the time the expedition was prepared to sail, the news of Napoleon's victory over the Austrians at Wagram (July 5–6) and the signing of the armistice at

Znaim (July 12) had already reached London. In light of these events, was a significant diversion in support of the Austrian war effort still possible? Evidently both Britain and Austria believed so. First, the battle of Wagram had been a "near run thing." Casualties had been extremely high on both sides, and although the archduke Charles had retreated from the battlefield, his army was still intact. Wagram was, therefore, no Austerlitz or Jena. In fact, Napoleon apparently came away from Wagram with a new respect for the Austrian army. On more than one occasion he reprimanded those who belittled the Austrian effort, by stating, "It is obvious that you were not at Wagram."[4] Second, although an armistice had been signed following the battle, the campaign was not necessarily over. As late as July 29, two days after the expedition had sailed, Benjamin Bathurst, the British envoy to Vienna, wrote London, "I have the strongest reason to believe the war will be continued here with great activity."[5] Austrian forces were still equal in numbers to those of Napoleon, and the Tyrolese revolt led by Andreas Hofer might cause additional problems for the French emperor. Consequently, the Austrians did consider the expedition of some value and repeatedly asked the British to maintain their positions in the Scheldt as long as peace negotiations continued. The Austrians were hopeful that the expedition might be sufficiently successful to force Napoleon to divert some of his forces from Germany, thereby strengthening Austria's bargaining power. The British maintained hopes that success in the Scheldt might persuade Austria to resume the struggle against France.[6]

To some degree, the British expedition did form a diversion for Austria, but it was too little and too late. When the expedition first appeared in the Scheldt, Napoleon directed all reinforcements under orders for the armies in Germany to march toward the Scheldt, emphasizing, however, that he would not reduce his forces on the Danube nor allow the expedition to affect his plans in Germany. It was obvious to Napoleon that the Austrians were delaying negotiations until the results of the expedition were known.[7] It soon became apparent, too, that the expedition would accomplish very little; consequently, the only significant effect it had upon the events in Germany was to delay the actual peace negotiations.[8] Six weeks earlier, such might not have been the case.

Although the expedition sailed too late to affect appreciably the events in Germany, the question remains whether even its limited objectives in the Scheldt could have been accomplished given favorable weather conditions. Historians are divided on the issue, although some maintain that the basic plan was "strategically sound."[9] Even though the unseasonal stormy weather was only partially responsible for the failure of the operation, there appears little doubt that had the winds permitted the main division of the army to reach its original destination in the West Scheldt, the expedition would have been more successful.

According to the original plan, the main division, consisting of approximately twenty-three thousand men, sailed from the Downs on July 28. This division was instructed to sail up the West Scheldt as soon as either the Wielengen or Duerloo channel was opened by the capture of Cadsand or Flushing and to proceed immediately to Sandvliet on the Continent. Had this been achieved, it was believed that a landing could have been made at Sandvliet by August 3 and an attack commenced against Antwerp by August 8.[10] Since the defenses of Antwerp during this period were inadequate, success appears likely. General Fauconnet had fewer than six thousand men at Antwerp on August 6, and by August 8, when, theoretically, the British would have attacked, General Rampon had arrived at Antwerp and organized its defenses; but of the twelve thousand Dutch-French troops immediately available, most were inexperienced National Guardsmen, poorly led, trained, and equipped.[11] In addition to these weaknesses, there was friction between Rampon and King Louis of Holland, the latter assuming temporary command of the Scheldt forces a short time later. Additional troops were arriving daily and reinforcements were available from the left bank, but even these could not constitute an army ready to meet the British forces in the field. Equally important were the dilapidated defenses of Antwerp and the two major forts further down the Scheldt—Lillo and Liefkenshoek.[12]

When the confusion and lack of leadership among the defensive forces at Antwerp are considered, combined with the weakness of the forts on the Scheldt and their insufficient garrisons, it appears quite possible that the British naval forces could have forced the boom at Lillo-Liefkenshoek and approached Antwerp while the army marched along the right bank. Jean Dejean considered this possible as late as August 19.[13] The British were frustrated in their design, however, primarily because of the extraordinarily bad weather, conflicting opinions between the naval and military commanders, and the fever epidemic. Concerning the latter, it is interesting to note that while Napoleon seemed ever cognizant of the health problems inherent in an operation among the islands of the Scheldt, none of the British leaders expressed similar views even though English troops had suffered from fever epidemics there in previous campaigns.

Napoleon's correspondence reveals the concern with which he viewed the British invasion of the Scheldt.[14] It is evident that he knew only too well how poorly defended and vulnerable to attack the western coast of Europe was, although years later he insisted the expedition could not have succeeded because of his strong fortifications. In 1809, however, most of these existed only in his mind. Napoleon did make an acute observation which in part illustrates why the expedition failed. "You had too many and too few men; too many for a *coup de main;* and too few for a regular siege."[15] Had the expedition been on a smaller scale without heavy ordnance and large cavalry units, it not only might have been prepared to sail earlier, but the navy would have been relieved of much of the rigors of navigating the heavy and cumbersome ships through the intricate passages of the Scheldt. Castlereagh and Chatham, the two men most responsible for the composition of the expeditionary force, were influenced to increase the strength of the army because of the close proximity of Britain to its theater of operation. Perhaps too, they were cognizant of the criticisms leveled against previous amphibious campaigns of the Revolutionary and Napoleonic periods when the British forces committed proved too small to effect their objectives. Consequently, this expedition was planned and executed on a grand scale, and its failure was commensurate with its magnitude.

The expedition had repercussions in Holland, France, and the Iberian peninsula. Napoleon blamed his brother Louis for the partial success of the British attack, which indicated to Napoleon the need for firmer control over northern Europe, especially the coastal areas of Holland. The Dutch had been unable to defend themselves; the king had failed to raise a significant force, and those Dutch troops who did see action acquitted themselves disgracefully. Walcheren was Louis's final test, and he had failed. Now Napoleon was provided with a convenient new charge of incompetence to add to the old ones he hurled at his brother.

Consequently, as the British evacuated the Scheldt estuary, Napoleon ordered Walcheren occupied in the name of France, and he indicated that any resistance would be the ruin of Holland. In March 1810, Louis was forced to accept a treaty calling for French annexation of additional areas and for French troops and customs officials to enforce the Continental System on the Dutch coast and rivers.[16] Napoleon's verbal attacks on his brother continued throughout the spring of 1810. Completely despondent and disillusioned, Louis finally abdicated on July 1, and his kingdom was quickly incorporated into the French empire.

In Paris, the landing of the British in the Scheldt estuary had caused concern and confusion. In Napoleon's absence, the French government was in the hands of the emperor's ministers, under the presidency of the archchancellor, Jean-Jacques Cambacérès. He, along with Joseph Fouché, minister of police, and Admiral Decrès, minister of marine, were directly concerned (because of their respective portfolios) with formulating measures in response to the British landing. While Cambacérès awaited Napoleon's instructions, Fouché, on his own initiative, levied the National Guard of northern France in order to provide necessary manpower to defend the threatened areas of the empire. With some 200,000 French soldiers in the Iberian peninsula, 100,000 in Italy, and 300,000 in Germany, the coastal areas of France and Holland were indeed weakly defended. The other ministers opposed Fouché's levy of the National Guard because they feared Napoleon would never approve such a measure. The National Guard was identified with the days of the Revolution and their role had been minimized during the years of the empire. Much to everyone's surprise, Napoleon heartily approved the levy and quickly extended it on a nationwide basis.[17] With recruitment for the Grand Army falling behind and the continued possibility of a resumption of the Austrian war, the National Guard could now provide France with an additional eighty thousand men under arms. Consequently, as Britain was reducing her military strength in the marshes of Zealand, Napoleon was reorganizing his forces and incorporating these new levies of National Guardsmen into the Grand Army.[18]

The British expedition also made Napoleon more aware of the potentials of the Scheldt, and as a result, he refortified its naval establishments during 1810/11 by restoring Flushing's docks and arsenal, enlarging the dockyards at Antwerp, and increasing the size of his fleet. By 1812 the Scheldt formed a significant part of a revived French naval capability, which, had Napoleon been more patient with Russia, might have enabled him to have seriously threatened Britain again with invasion.[19]

Finally, the disastrous Scheldt expedition prompted the British government to concentrate its future efforts in the Iberian peninsula by giving full support to the operations of the duke of Wellington and his Spanish and Portuguese allies. By pumping in literally millions of pounds in arms and supplies, by training, clothing, feeding, and commanding Iberian forces, and by allowing Wellington freedom of command in the Peninsula, the British, after 1809, began to slowly see the fruits of their labors. In 1810 Napoleon ordered Prince André Massena to invade Portugal at the head of a well-seasoned army. Temporarily checked by Wellington at the Battle of Bussaco (September 17), Massena eventually pushed on to Lisbon. But here he encountered Wellington's fortified Lines of Torres Vedras stretching across the Lisbon Peninsula. Unable to breach these defenses, Massena's army, threatened by starvation after 108 days before the Lines of Torres Vedras, withdrew into western Spain.[20]

Now taking the offensive, Wellington's Anglo-Portuguese army, supported by Spanish contingents, launched a concerted drive to expel the French from the Iberian peninsula. Throughout 1811/12, Wellington's strength in the Peninsula grew, and in the spring of 1812 he marched into Spain, smashed Marshal Marmont's overextended army at Salamanca (July 21), and briefly occupied Madrid (August 12). Forced back into western Spain by superior French forces, Wellington patiently prepared for the campaign of 1813. At the head of an Anglo-Portuguese army of almost one hundred thousand men, Wellington moved into north Spain in the spring of 1813 and attempted to drive a wedge between Madrid and the French frontier. His march culminated at Vitoria, where on June 21 he soundly defeated King Joseph's French army and drove them back toward the Pyrenees.[21] Wellington's victory at Vitoria not only liberated Spain from French control, it also persuaded the hesitant Austrian emperor Francis I to join yet another coalition with England, Russia, and Prussia to bring down Napoleon's empire. By October 1813, as Napoleon was being overwhelmed at the Battle of the Nations near Leipzig, Wellington was invading southern France. Napoleon's empire was falling.

In conclusion, the British expedition to the Scheldt in 1809 accomplished very little at a great cost to Great Britain in money, men, and national reputation. The expedition will long be remembered in history more for what it might have accomplished than for its actual achievements. It was only through efforts elsewhere, especially in the Iberian Peninsula, that Britain and her allies were able to achieve the success against Napoleon that they had been seeking so earnestly in 1809.

Appendix A

THE BRITISH ARMY SENT TO THE SCHELDT IN 1809

Commander in Chief, the Earl of Chatham

	Officers	Men

ARMY OF WALCHEREN
Commanded by Lt. Gen. Sir Eyre Coote

RIGHT WING—Maj. Gen. Graham

	Officers	Men
95th Rifle Corps, detachment	1	30
68th Light Infantry (2 companies)	6	162
1st Foot, 3rd batt. (Royals)—Col. Hay	51	1027
5th Foot, 1st batt.—Maj. Emes	44	991
35th Foot, 2nd batt.—Maj. Armett	34	797
Total	136	3007

CENTRE—Lt. Gen. Lord Paget

	Officers	Men
Brig. Gen. Rottenburg's Brigade:		
95th Rifle Corps, detachment	—	120
68th Light Infantry, 2nd batt.—Lt. Col. Johnstone	37	687
85th Foot—Lt. Col. Cuxler	46	630
Total	83	1437
Brig. Gen. Brown's Brigade:		
23rd Foot, 2nd batt.—Lt. Col. Wyatt	22	434
26th Foot, 1st batt.—Lt. Col. Maxwell	45	727
32nd Foot, 1st batt.—Lt. Col. Hinde	37	625
81st Foot, 2nd batt.—Maj. Williams	39	716
Total	143	2502

RESERVE—Brig. Gen. Houston

	Officers	Men
14th Foot, 2nd batt.—Lt. Col. Nicolls	41	876

	Officers	*Men*
51st Foot, 1st batt.—Lt. Col. Mainwaring	34	679
82nd Foot, 1st batt.—Lt. Col. Grant	36	1035
Total	111	2590

LEFT WING—Lt. Gen. Fraser

Maj. Gen. Picton's Brigade:

95th Rifle Corps, detachment	—	50
71st Foot, 1st batt.—Lt. Col. Pack	42	1024
36th Foot, 1st batt.—Col. Burne	48	765
63rd Foot, 2nd batt.—Lt. Col. Gordon	30	631
77th Foot—Lt. Col. Maddison	33	599
Batt. of detachments—Lt. Col. Cochran	44	851
8th Foot, 2nd batt., 2 companies	8	210
Total	205	4130
Walcheren Army Total	595	13666

RESERVE OF THE ARMY
Lt. Gen. Sir John Hope

Brig. Gen. Disney's Brigade:

1st Foot Guards, 1st batt.—Col. Anson	54	1409
1st Foot Guards, 3rd batt.—Col. Cooke	37	1165
Flank companies of Guards:		
Lt. Col. Cock's Grenadiers	9	259
Lt. Col. Lambert's Light Infantry	9	258
Total	109	3091

Maj. Gen. Lord Dalhousie's Brigade:

4th Foot, 1st batt.—Lt. Col. Wynch	38	1056
4th Foot, 2nd batt.—Lt. Col. Espinasse	39	983
28th Foot, 1st batt.—Lt. Col. Belson	30	689
Total	107	2728

Maj. Gen. Erskine's Brigade:	Officers	Men
20th Foot—Lt. Col. Ross	49	919
92nd Foot, 1st batt.—Lt. Col. Cameron	42	1041
Total	91	1960
Reserve Total	307	7779

SECOND DIVISION
Lt. Gen. Lord Huntley

Maj. Gen. Dyott's Brigade:	Officers	Men
6th Foot, 1st batt.—Lt. Col. Murray	46	1040
50th Foot, 1st batt.—Lt. Col. Stewart	46	927
91st Foot, 1st batt.—Lt. Col. Douglas	41	695
Total	133	2662
Brig. Gen. Montresor's Brigade		
9th Foot, 1st batt.—Lt. Col. Cameron	44	1020
38th Foot, 1st batt.—Lt. Col. Greville	39	873
42nd Foot, 1st batt.—Lt. Col. Stirling	39	822
Total	122	2715
Second Division Total	255	5377

LIGHT DIVISION
Lt. Gen. the Earl of Rosslyn

Maj. Gen. Linsingen's Brigade:	Officers	Men	Horses
3rd Dragoons, 6 troops—Lt. Col. Mundy	22	550	505
12th Light Dragoons, 6 troops—Col. Brown	24	568	515
Wagon Train, Detachment—Col. Hamilton	9	172	127
9th Light Dragoons, Detachment—			
Lt. Col. Chabot	22	567	474
2nd Dragoon Guards, 6 troops—			
Lt. Col. Beresford	22	523	494
Total	99	2380	2115

	Officers	Men	Horses
Maj. Gen. Stewart's Brigade:			
43rd Foot, 2nd batt.—Lt. Col. Hull	36	665	
52nd Foot, 2nd batt.—Lt. Col. Ross	29	470	
95th Foot, 2nd batt., 8 companies—			
Lt. Col. Wade	49	858	
Total	114	1993	—
Col. Baron Alton's Brigade:			
1st Light batt., King's German Legion—			
Lt. Col. Leonhart	32	811	
2nd Light batt., King's German Legion—			
Lt. Col. Hackett	32	715	
2nd Light Dragoons, King's German Legion—			
Lt. Col. Rodewald	33	629	610
Total	97	2155	610
Light Division Total	310	6528	2725

THIRD DIVISION
Lt. Gen. Grosvenor

	Officers	Men
Maj. Gen. Leith's Brigade:		
59th Foot, 2nd batt.—Maj. McGregor	42	863
11th Foot, 2nd batt.—Lt. Col. Gubbins	45	906
79th Foot, 1st batt.—Lt. Col. Cameron	39	1052
Total	126	2821
Brig. Gen. Ackland's Brigade:		
2nd Foot, 3rd batt.—Lt. Col. Iremonger	40	888
76th Foot, 1st batt.—Col. Shaw	48	798
84th Foot, 2nd batt.—Lt. Col. Lloyd	44	840
Total	132	2526
Third Division Total	258	5347

	Officers	Men	Horses
ROYAL ARTILLERY—Brig. Gen. McLeod	106	3121	1776
ROYAL ENGINEERS—Col. Fyers	29	296	
ROYAL WAGGON TRAIN—Col. Hamilton	21	408	127
ROYAL STAFF CORPS—Capt. Read	6	138	
ROYAL VETERANS (7th batt.)—Lt. Walker	1	52	
Total	163	4015	1903
Totals of the British army	1888	42712	4501

Source: *Parliamentary Papers,* vol. 7, "Return, showing the effective strength of the army which embarked for service in the Scheldt in the month of July 1809," 12 February 1810, p. 59. This return did not include the Royal Artillery or the Royal Engineers.

Appendix B

THE BRITISH NAVAL FORCE
Commanded by Sir Richard Strachan

ARMED SHIPS

Ship of 80 guns	1
Ships of 74 guns	33
Ships of 64 guns	3
Ships of 50 guns	2
Ships of 44 guns	3
Frigates	22
Sloops	32
Bomb vessels	5
Gunbrigs (5 carrying mortars)	23
Hired cutters and luggers	17
Revenue vessels	14
Lighters from dockyards	17
Tenders	12
Gunboats	82
Total	266
Transports	352
Total of Armed Ships and Transports	618

Source: *Chatham Papers*, 30/8/260, "Abstract of Ships under the command of Sir Richard Strachan."

Appendix C

THE GARRISON OF FLUSHING, 1 AUGUST 1809
INCLUDING ALL REINFORCEMENTS
Commanded by Louis-Claude Monnet de Lorbeau

GARRISON

	Officers	Men	Total	Hospital	Effectives
1st batt. Colonials	13	712	725	144	869
Batt. returned French deserters (chasseurs)	15	940	955	134	1089
Batt. Irish	11	430	441	39	480
Regiment of Prussians:					
1st batt.	3	7	10	33	43
2nd batt.	22	780	802	27	829
3rd batt.	21	774	795	42	837
6th Veteran Regiment, 2nd batt., 1st & 2nd companies	4	46	50	2	52
Cannoneers, Coast Guard, company	2	126	128	2	130
Cannoneers, Veterans, 8th company	2	63	65	2	67
Gendarmerie			4		4
1st Regiment, Foot Artillery	1	97	98	2	100
Total Garrison, 1 August	94	3975	4073	427	4500

REINFORCEMENTS

1 AUGUST

65th Regiment, 3rd batt.   660

2 AUGUST

8th Provisional Demibrigade, 4th batt.:
    22nd Regiment, 5th batt. (2 companies)
    54th Regiment, 5th batt. (2 companies)   }   608
    45th Regiment, 5th batt. (2 companies)

72nd Regiment, detachment, and 108th Regiment, detachment   375
Cannoneers   20

4 AUGUST

48th Regiment, 4th batt. (3 companies)   320

6 AUGUST

8th Provisional Demibrigade, 3rd batt.:
   13th Light Infantry, 5th batt. (3 companies) ⎫
   27th Light Infantry, 5th batt. (3 companies) ⎬   550
                                                ⎭
48th Regiment (3 companies)   420
Prussian detachment   190

                                  Total Reinforcements   3143

            Total Garrison and Reinforcements   7643

Source: *Situations: Armée du Nord*, Carton C² 512.

Notes

CHAPTER 1

1. For a breakdown of the ships involved, see Appendix B.
2. The standard works on the Continental System are François Crouzet, *L'Economie Britannique et le blocus continental, 1806–1813*, 2 vols.; and Eli Hecksher, *The Continental System.*
3. Gabriel H. Lovett, *Napoleon and the Birth of Modern Spain*, p. 26.
4. Ibid., pp. 21–22.
5. August Fournier, *Napoleon the First*, p. 429.
6. Lovett, *Napoleon and Modern Spain*, p. 121.
7. Ibid., pp. 145–53.
8. John M. Sherwig, *Guineas and Gunpowder*, pp. 198–99.
9. Sir William Napier, *History of the War in the Peninsula*, 1: 143–45.
10. David G. Chandler, *The Campaigns of Napoleon*, pp. 656–58.
11. M. A. Thiers, *History of the Consulate and the Empire*, 10: 2. Napoleon literally dashed back to Paris, arriving at the Tuileries on the night of January 22.
12. Walter C. Langsam, *The Napoleonic Wars and German Nationalism in Austria*, pp. 52–55.
13. Fournier, *Napoleon the First*, p. 454.
14. Sherwig, *Guineas and Gunpowder*, p. 211.
15. Great Britain, *Cobbett's Parliamentary Debates*, vol. 16 (1810), "Canning's Speech," 29 March 1810, cols. 325–51. Hereinafter cited as *Parliamentary Debates.*
16. Great Britain, House of Commons, *Parliamentary Papers, Minutes of the Evidence Taken Before the House, Relating to the Expedition to the Scheldt*, vol. 7 (Session 23, January–June, 1810) Starhemberg to Canning, 18 May 1809, p. 42. Hereinafter cited as *Parliamentary Papers. See also* the *Times* (London), 21 February 1810. The *Times* published most of the documents, correspondence, and testimony relative to the expedition during the parliamentary inquiry held in 1810.
17. Piers Mackesy, *The War in the Mediterranean, 1803–1810*, p. 333. Stuart landed his troops on Ischia and Procida on June 25, but he

evacuated them to Sicily four weeks later because of the archduke John's defeat.

18. *Parliamentary Debates,* vol. 16, "Canning's Speech," 29 March 1810, cols. 328–29. Schill and the young duke of Brunswick had tried to rally the Germans early in 1809 but had met with little success. Schill was killed in May and Brunswick fled the country on an English ship. Rumors circulated that he would join the expedition to the Scheldt, but he did not.

19. Sherwig, *Guineas and Gunpowder,* p. 203.

20. *Parliamentary Papers,* vol. 8, "Testimony of William Huskisson, Secretary to the Treasury," 6 March 1810, pp. 229–33.

21. Robert Stewart, Viscount Castlereagh, *Correspondence, Despatches, and other Papers of Viscount Castlereagh,* "Letter prepared for William Pitt," 25 December 1797, 6: 303. Hereinafter cited as *Castlereagh's Correspondence.*

22. Sir Archibald Alison, *The Lives of Lord Castlereagh and Sir Charles Stewart,* 1: 287.

23. *Castlereagh's Correspondence,* "Memorandum for the consideration of the Cabinet, respecting an Expedition to Walcheren," n.d., pp. 247–56. Castlereagh's papers suggest that he had done a great deal of research into the problems inherent in such an operation.

24. For an interesting discussion of Napoleon's chances of invading Great Britain in the years after Trafalgar see Richard Glover's "The French Fleet, 1807–1814; Britain's Problem; And Madison's Opportunity," *Journal of Modern History,* 39(1967): 233–52.

25. *A Collection of Papers Relating to the Expedition to the Scheldt, Presented to Parliament in 1810,* "Intelligence from a confidential person," 8 May 1809, p. 278. Hereinafter cited as *Scheldt Papers.*

26. Pierre E. Albert Du Casse, ed., *Les rois frères de Napoléon Ier,* pp. 101–2. *See also* D. Labarre de Raillicourt, *Louis Bonaparte roi de Hollande frère et père d'empereurs,* p. 304; and Owen Connelly, *Napoleon's Satellite Kingdoms,* p. 132.

27. Louis Bonaparte, *Documens historiques et réflexions sur le gouvernement de la Hollande,* 3: 301. This edition spelled the word *Documens* rather than the usual *Documents.*

28. Du Casse, *Les rois frères,* p. 102.

29. Louis Bonaparte, *Documens historiques,* 3: 127. The remainder of the island was Dutch.

30. Labarre de Raillicourt, *Louis Bonaparte,* pp. 265–311.

31. *Scheldt Papers,* "Letter from a Secret Agent," 20 February 1809, p. 237.

32. *Parliamentary Papers*, vol. 6, Boxer to Campbell, 3 March 1809, p. 55.

33. *Parliamentary Debates*, vol. 15, "Testimony of Dundas," 2 February 1810, Appendix, col. 86.

34. Great Britain, Public Record Office, 30/8/366, *The Chatham Papers*, Castlereagh to Chatham, 18 May 1809. Castlereagh offered the command of the expedition to Chatham on this date and was already engaged in making extensive preparations for it.

35. *Scheldt Papers*, Campbell to Pole, 15 March 1809, p. 249.

CHAPTER 2

1. *Parliamentary Debates*, vol. 15, "Testimony of Dundas," 5 February 1810, Appendix, col. 86.

2. Ibid., cols. 91–92; John W. Fortescue, *A History of the British Army*, 7: 35.

3. *Castlereagh's Correspondence*, "Memorandum upon the supposed practicability of Destroying the French Ships and Vessels in the Scheldt, and in the Arsenals at Antwerp," 31 May 1809, pp. 257–61. This and the other memoranda were officially written at the request of the commander in chief, Dundas, then transmitted to Castlereagh.

4. Ibid., "Memorandum relative to the projected Expedition against Walcheren," 1 June 1809, pp. 261–65.

5. Ibid., Brownrigg to the Commander in Chief, 2 June 1809, p. 268; "Memorandum relative to the projected Expedition to the Scheldt," 3 June 1809, p. 269.

6. *Parliamentary Debates*, vol. 15, "Memorandum relative to the projected Expedition to the Scheldt," 3 June 1809, Appendix, cols. 154–56.

7. *Castlereagh's Correspondence*, Dundas to Castlereagh, 3 June 1809, pp. 270–71.

8. *Parliamentary Debates*, vol. 15, "Testimony of Castlereagh," 1 March 1810, Appendix, col. 522.

9. *Scheldt Papers*, Campbell to Pole, 15 March 1809, p. 249; Strachan to Mulgrave, 15 April 1809, p. 260; Hanchett to Mulgrave, 27 April 1809, pp. 272–73. Of John Martin Hanchett, Clowes writes, "It is believed that he was a natural son of the Prince of Wales, afterwards George IV." *See* William Laird Clowes, *The Royal Navy, a History from the Earliest Times to the Present*, 5: 271.

10. *Scheldt Papers*, "Intelligence received from a deserter from West Capelle by Sir Richard Strachan," 8 May 1809, pp. 278–79.

11. Ibid., "Intelligence from a confidential Person," 8 May 1809, pp. 279–82.

12. Ibid., "Intelligence from Holland," 1 July 1809, pp. 291–95.

13. *Parliamentary Debates,* vol. 15, "Testimony of Castlereagh," 1 March 1810, Appendix, col. 522. The Scheldt operation enabled "Great Britain to employ a larger proportion of its disposable force against the enemy than it could attempt to do in any other mode, or in any other direction." "Project of Instructions, No. 2, communicated by Visc. Castlereagh to Lt. Gen. the Earl of Chatham," June 1809, col. 428. From Castlereagh's testimony it appears that these instructions were written on June 23.

14. Fortescue, *British Army,* p. 55. Chatham's torpor was notorious. *See* Great Britain, Historical Manuscript Commission, *Dropmore Papers,* vol. 9, Grenville to Wickham, 28 July 1809, p. 312; *Morning Chronicle,* 12 July 1809: "Some hesitation has taken place as to the appointment of the Earl of Chatham. It is wished to give him certain instructions, but like the great Suvarov, he is no doubt conscious of his own powers, and says, 'If they think me fit to take the command of 40,000 men, they must give me credit for capacity to judge for myself, as to the plan of operations.' We did not suspect that the Earl of Chatham had so much vigour." *See also* Denis Gray, *Spencer Perceval; The Evangelical Prime Minister 1762–1812,* p. 279: "You might . . . just as well talk of a *coup-de-main* in the court of chancery as a surprise attack on Antwerp under Chatham."

15. Sir Thomas Picton, *Memoirs,* p. 232. "The reason for his being selected in preference to the many more able and distinguished officers was unfortunately too apparent; his fortune was embarrassed, and this lucrative command would improve it."

16. Arthur Bryant, *Years of Victory,* p. 368; Fortescue, *British Army,* p. 54. This position is not supported in Castlereagh's initial letter to Chatham offering him the command. It would appear that Castlereagh and the duke of Portland were the main supporters of Chatham. *Chatham Papers,* 30/8/366, Castlereagh to Chatham, 18 May 1809. Current gossip had Canning actually being opposed to Chatham's appointment. *See* Henry Lord Brougham, *The Life and Times of Henry Lord Brougham,* Brougham to Grey, 30 June 1809, pp. 305–6.

17. Gray, *Spencer Perceval,* p. 217; *Parliamentary Debates,* vol. 15, "Testimony of Dundas," 5 February 1810, Appendix, cols. 90–92.

18. C. Greenhill Gardyne, *The Life of a Regiment,* p. 171.

19. *Castlereagh's Correspondence,* Chatham to Castlereagh, 18 May 1809, pp. 256–57; *Scheldt Papers,* "Memorandum of the Board of Ad-

miralty," 9 June 1809, p. 313; *Parliamentary Papers*, vol. 8, "Testimony of Popham," 12 February 1810, pp. 89–95.

20. *Castlereagh's Correspondence*, Castlereagh to George III, 14 June 1809, pp. 275–76.

21. Ibid., "Landing Troops Between Sandfleet and Lillo," 19 June 1809, pp. 280–81. This document was based on the opinions of Sir Home Popham and Capt. Robert Plampin, both of whom had been at Antwerp in 1794 and were familiar with the beach in the Sandvliet area.

22. Ibid., George III to Castlereagh, 22 June 1809, p. 282; *Parliamentary Debates*, vol. 15, "Testimony of Dundas," 5 February 1810, Appendix, col. 90; *Parliamentary Papers*, vol. 7, "Return, Shewing the Effective Strength of the Army which Embarked for Service in the Scheldt in the Month of July 1809," 12 February 1810, p. 59. This return does not include the Royal Artillery or Royal Engineers. *See* Appendix A.

23. Thomas Creevey, *The Creevey Papers*, Moore to Creevey, 19 September 1809, 1: 95; William Richardson, *A Mariner of England*, p. 220.

24. *Parliamentary Debates*, vol. 15, "Testimony of Strachan," 15 February 1810, Appendix, col. 260.

25. *Chatham Papers*, 30/8/263, "Officer List," 7 July 1809. Fortescue, (*British Army*, p. 56) states that Lt. Gen. Sir John Cradock commanded a division of the expedition. Although his name does appear on the officer list of July 7, Cradock did not accompany the forces to the Scheldt.

26. Great Britain, Public Record Office, W.O. 6/27, 15 July 1809; *Parliamentary Debates*, vol. 15, "Testimony of Sir Rupert George, Chairman of the Transport Board," 8 February 1810, Appendix, col. 141; *Parliamentary Papers*, vol. 8, "Testimony of Popham," 12 February 1810, pp. 89–95. Popham had written Castlereagh a lengthy memorandum concerning the expedition on 12 June 1809, in which he suggested embarking troops at Portsmouth for this reason.

27. The *Times*, 3 July 1809. This rumor was true. Sir Rupert George, chairman of the transport board, had made such a suggestion to Castlereagh, but the latter was reluctant to force neutral ships into service. See *Parliamentary Debates*, vol. 15, "Testimony of George," 8 February 1810, Appendix, cols. 145–46.

28. Even with the arrival of the transports from Portugal, there still were not enough ships to transport all the horses to the Scheldt. Some 313 horses were embarked at Ramsgate as late as August 14—over two weeks after the expedition had sailed—and an additional thirty horses

were never embarked for lack of transport. See *Chatham Papers*, 30/8/263, "Memorandum relative to Embarkation of Ordnance, Stores, etc., for the Scheldt," 16 February 1810.

29. *Castlereagh's Correspondence*, Popham to Castlereagh, 13 June 1809, pp. 273–75.

30. Ibid., Castlereagh to George III, 15 July 1809, p. 283. It appears there were actually 266 rather than 264 ships of war, bringing the total number of ships employed to 618. *See* Appendix B.

31. *Gazette*, 12 July 1809. This embargo continued until August 2.

32. *Castlereagh's Correspondence*, George III to Chatham, 16 July 1809, p. 285.

33. Ibid., Castlereagh to Chatham, July 1809, pp. 290–93; Castlereagh testified that these instructions which he drew up for Chatham, although bearing no date, were actually given to Chatham on July 23. It is interesting to note Castlereagh's statement that the expedition was not "equipped upon a scale which would qualify it to enter immediately upon a campaign" (*Parliamentary Debates*, vol. 15, "Testimony of Castlereagh," 1 March 1810, Appendix, cols. 423–29). The number of troops, cavalry, ordnance, stores, and provisions, belie this statement. See *Chatham Papers*, 30/8/263, for details of the expedition's strength and equipment.

34. *Castlereagh's Correspondence*, Castlereagh to Chatham, [23] July 1809, pp. 292–93.

35. *Scheldt Papers*, The Lords of the Admiralty to Strachan, 17 July 1809, pp. 341–47.

36. *Castlereagh's Correspondence*, Popham to Castlereagh, 13 June 1809, p. 274; Chatham to Castlereagh, n.d., p. 275. This letter appears to have been written also on June 13.

37. The principal problem in preparing the expedition to sail seems to have been the lack of a sufficient number of transports. See *Parliamentary Debates*, vol. 15, "Testimony of Sir Rupert George," 8 February 1810, Appendix, cols. 141–47.

38. *Morning Chronicle*, 1 August 1809; *Times*, 17 July 1809; *Hull Packet*, 24 July 1809.

39. *Times*, 18 July 1809; *The Annual Register* (1809), p. 224; "Gaily dressed ladies crowded the beach . . . all was enthusiasm, excitement and expectation" (Gardyne, *Life of a Regiment*, p. 173).

40. *Chatham Papers*, 30/8/365, Bathurst to Canning, 29 July 1809. Benjamin Bathurst was the British envoy to Austria. Bathurst wrote that although an armistice had been signed, "I have the strongest reason to believe the war will be continued with great activity."

41. The disappointing news of Wagram, coupled with what the press considered "inexcusable delay" in launching the expedition, prompted several biting editorials. "But what can be expected from a set of Ministers, who, instead of being at their posts attending to their business, are running like a number of children to see the fine sight of a large fleet setting sail" (*Morning Chronicle*, 24 July 1809). See also *Times*, 22 July 1809.

42. Christopher Lloyd, *The Nation and the Navy*, p. 195; Fortescue, *British Army*, p. 56.

CHAPTER 3

1. Louis Bonaparte, *Napoléon Ier et le roi Louis*, Louis to Napoleon, 18 May 1809, p. 199.

2. Louis Bonaparte, *Louis Bonaparte en Hollande*, pp. 28–29.

3. Louis Bonaparte, *Napoléon Ier*, p. lxxxiv.

4. Napoléon Ier, *Correspondance de Napoléon Ier*, Napoleon to Clarke, 11 January 1809, vol. 18, no. 14679, p. 228. Hereinafter cited as *Correspondance de Napoléon Ier*. Henri Jacques Guillaume Clarke, comte d'Hunebourg, duc de Feltre, was French minister of war from 1807 to 1814. Monnet was not relieved of his command.

5. Ibid., Napoleon to Louis, 22 February 1809, no. 14801, p. 331.

6. Louis Bonaparte, *Napoléon Ier*, Louis to Napoleon, 26 February 1809, pp. 194–95.

7. Ibid., Napoleon to Louis, 11 March 1809, p. 195.

8. *Correspondance de Napoléon Ier*, "Orders," 13 March 1809, no. 14892, pp. 403–6.

9. Louis Bonaparte, *Napoléon Ier*, Napoleon to Louis, 21 March 1809, pp. 196–97.

10. A fleet sailed from Portsmouth on April 15 carrying Sir Arthur Wellesley, two regiments of heavy dragoons, and horse artillery. Arthur Wellesley, duke of Wellington, *The Dispatches of Field Marshal and Duke Wellington*, Wellesley to Beresford, 23 April 1809, 4: 265.

11. Louis Bonaparte, *Napoléon Ier*, Louis to Napoleon, 4 April 1809, pp. 197–98. Louis also reported that English ships were reconnoitering his shores and taking soundings off the coast.

12. Edward Pelham Brenton, *The Naval History of Great Britain from the Year 1783 to 1822*, 4: 283.

13. Louis Bonaparte, *Napoléon Ier*, Louis to Napoleon, 26 April 1809, p. 198. Denis, comte Decrès, was Napoleon's minister of the navy.

14. Napoleon I, *Unpublished Correspondence of Napoleon I Pre-*

served in the War Archives, Napoleon to Clarke, 4 April 1809, 3: 7–9. Hereinafter cited as *Unpublished Correspondence of Napoleon.*

15. Ibid., Napoleon to Clarke, 5 April 1809, pp. 10–11.

16. *Parliamentary Papers,* vol. 8, "Testimony of Strachan," 15 February 1810, pp. 97–110.

17. Louis Bonaparte, *Napoléon Ier,* Louis to Napoleon, 6 May 1809, p. 199.

18. Ibid., Louis to Napoleon, 18 May 1809, p. 199.

19. Ibid. Louis cautioned his brother that Admiral Missiessy's plan for the defense of the fleet was "the same idea which Admiral Brueys had at Aboukir." Brueys's fleet had been destroyed in 1798 by Adm. Horatio Nelson at the Battle of the Nile.

20. Ibid.

21. Louis Bonaparte, *Documens historiques,* 3: 125.

22. *Le Moniteur universel,* 12 June 1809. An extract containing the article appeared in this Paris paper.

23. Louis Bonaparte, *Napoléon Ier,* Louis to Napoleon, 16 June 1809, p. 201.

24. Ibid., Louis to Napoleon, 1 July 1809, pp. 201–3. These accusations appeared in *Le publiciste* on 18 June 1809. Another attack appeared on June 18 in the *Journal de l'empire.* See D. Labarre de Raillicourt, *Louis Bonaparte,* p. 284.

25. Louis Bonaparte, *Napoléon Ier,* Napoleon to Louis, 17 July 1809, p. 204. Napoleon demanded that France and Holland have the same policy: "Do not make me occupy your ports to collect my customs."

26. *Correspondance de Napoléon Ier,* Napoleon to Louis, 17 July 1809, vol. 19, no. 14433, p. 307.

27. Napoleon I, *New Letters of Napoleon I,* Napoleon to Fouché, 26 July 1809: "For the last two months, the Continent has been kept in a fright about the great English expedition" (p. 139).

28. *Le Moniteur universel,* 13 July 1809; 20 July 1809; 2 August 1809. This extract from an Amsterdam paper was dated 21 July 1809.

29. *Unpublished Correspondence of Napoleon,* Napoleon to Clarke, 21 July 1809, 3: 135.

30. A.L.R., Comte de Martel, *Walkeren, d'après les documents inédits,* p. 359; Albert Jean Michel de Rocca, *La campagne de Walcheren et d'Anvers,* p. 89.

31. France, Ministère de la Guerre, Archives Historiques, *Correspondance: Armées du Nord,* Carton C² 103, "Précis des dispositions faites précédemment pour la sûreté des côtes qui se trouvaient menacées par la Grand Expedition Anglaise, et des mesures prises par le Ministre de

la Guerre pour la défense de l'Escaut, au premier bruit de l'apparition de l'Ennemi sur ce point," 31 August 1809.

32. *Unpublished Correspondence of Napoleon,* Napoleon to Clarke, 21 July 1809, 3: 135.

33. Martel, *Walkeren,* p. 278.

34. *Correspondance: Armées du Nord,* Carton C² 101, Rousseau to Clarke, 25 July 1809.

35. Ibid., Sainte-Suzanne to Clarke, 29 July 1809.

36. Louis Bonaparte, *Documens historiques,* 3: 126–27.

37. Anthanase Garnier, *La cour de Hollande sous le règne de Louis Bonaparte,* p. 197.

CHAPTER 4

1. These smaller islands included St. Joostland, between Walcheren and South Beveland; Wolversdyle, south of North Beveland; Toleland, the island extension northwest of Bergen-op-Zoom; and Duiverland, southeast of Schouwen. Often not even named on the maps of the day, these islands will appear only occasionally in this narrative.

2. *Hull Packet,* 29 August 1809.

3. Ibid.

4. Francis Duncan, *History of the Royal Regiment of Artillery,* 2: 224.

5. The British authorities were familiar with Sir John Pringle's book describing the types of diseases which often appeared among armies in the low areas of Holland and the methods of preventing their occurrences. However, extra health precautions were not considered necessary for a short campaign. Pringle's book and related medical problems will be discussed later.

6. The British had more complete information on the West Scheldt; however, some of the naval officers considered the East Scheldt the better route. See *Parliamentary Debates,* vol. 15, "Testimony of Sir Richard Keats," 19 February 1810, Appendix, col. 270.

7. *Parliamentary Papers,* vol. 6, "Proposed Disposition for the Attack of the Island of Walcheren," p. 335.

8. Ibid., p. 332. The number of troops cited throughout the text, unless otherwise indicated, includes the rank and file only. For a complete total see Appendix A.

9. Ibid., p. 330. The memorandum was dated 24 July 1809.

10. *Scheldt Papers,* Strachan to Seymour, 24 July 1809, pp. 396–98.

11. *Parliamentary Papers,* vol. 6, p. 329.

12. *Scheldt Papers,* Strachan to Seymour, 24 July 1809, pp. 397–98.

13. Ibid., Strachan to Keats, 24 July 1809, p. 382. The Reserve was composed of a brigade of guards under Gen. Sir Moore Disney and the brigades of Maj. Gen. George Ramsay, earl of Dalhousie and Sir William Erskine, totaling 7,261. *See* Appendix A.

14. *Parliamentary Debates,* vol. 15, "Testimony of Sir John Hope," 21 February 1810, Appendix, col. 322.

15. Ibid., "Orders of the Marquis of Huntley," 25 July 1809, col. 286.

16. National Maritime Museum, *Owen Papers,* 52/061, Strachan to Owen, 21 July 1809. Hereinafter cited as *Owen Papers.*

17. *Scheldt Papers,* Strachan to Barton, 22 July 1809, p. 390. The Light Division included 4,043, while the Third had a strength of 5,012. *See* Appendix A.

18. Ibid., Strachan to Keats, 24 July 1809, p. 387. Barton's new orders were contained in this dispatch.

19. *Parliamentary Papers,* vol. 8, "Memorandum: being the result of a Conversation between Admiral Sir Richard Strachan, Captain Sir Home Popham, Lt. General Sir John Hope, and Lt. General Brownrigg," 24 July 1809, p. 330.

20. Ibid. The primary reason for this alteration was that Hope's troops were embarked in men of war. These large ships could not proceed up the East Scheldt closer than fifteen miles to the landing point. It was calculated that the boats would require two days to carry the men the remaining distance, whereas the Veere Gat was deep enough for men of war. Once in the Scheldt, however, reversion was made to the original plan because of circumstances which later developed.

21. *Scheldt Papers,* Bolton to Strachan, 23 July 1809, pp. 309–10.

22. *Chatham Papers,* 30/8/260, "Journal of the Proceedings of the Army under the Command of Lieutenant General the Earl of Chatham." Hereinafter cited as "Journal of the Army." This journal is also found in *Parliamentary Papers,* vol. 6.

23. *Scheldt Papers,* Strachan to Otway, 26 July 1809, p. 402.

24. Ibid., Foster to Pole, 29 July 1809. Mathew Foster received the telegraphic dispatch from Gardner and forwarded it to Pole at the admiralty.

25. The army was composed nominally of six divisions; however, these are not to be confused with the five divisions or units into which the expedition, both naval and military, was divided.

26. The Stone Deep and the East Capelle Roads were different names for the same anchorage. The British suffered their first casualty on the 28th when a seaman on the *Venerable,* John Llyons, fell from

the main yard and was killed. Great Britain, Public Record Office, *Admiralty Papers*, 53/1474, Ship's Log, *Venerable*, 28 July 1809, p. 165.

27. Ibid., 29 July 1809. The Ship's Log for the evening of the 29th reads, "Strong winds, cloudy; rain."

28. *Scheldt Papers*, Strachan to Pole, 4 August 1809, pp. 408–11.

29. *Parliamentary Debates*, vol. 15, "Testimony of Rosslyn," 20 February 1810, Appendix, col. 342. The original plans called for these divisions to hold an anchorage which would enable them to proceed up the West Scheldt as soon as a safe entrance to the river was secured.

30. *Parliamentary Debates*, vol. 15, "Testimony of Strachan," 15 February 1810, Appendix, cols. 264–65.

31. *Scheldt Papers*, Bolton to Strachan, 7 July 1809, p. 299.

32. Ibid., Strachan to Owen, 21 July 1809, p. 294.

33. Ibid., Strachan to Gardner, 16 July 1809, p. 388. Gardner was instructed to pass up the West Scheldt after Cadsand was taken and to take a position southeast of Flushing; *Parliamentary Papers*, vol. 6, Strachan to Gardner, 20 July 1809, p. 115.

34. *Scheldt Papers*, Strachan to Gardner, 24 July 1809, p. 472.

35. *Parliamentary Debates*, vol. 15, "Testimony of Gardner," 20 February 1810, Appendix, col. 266.

36. Ibid., "Orders of the Marquis of Huntley," 25 July 1809, col. 286; "Testimony of Huntley," 20 February 1810, col. 287.

37. Ibid. While the expedition was forming in the Downs, the commanding officers remained on shore, usually at Deal or Ramsgate. Brownrigg and Chatham had returned to Deal on the twenty-sixth.

38. *Owen Papers*, Strachan to Owen, 26 July 1809.

39. *Parliamentary Debates*, vol. 15, "Testimony of Huntley," 20 February 1810, Appendix, col. 288; *Parliamentary Papers*, vol. 6, Brownrigg to Huntley, 30 July 1809, p. 340.

40. Ibid., Huntley to Chatham, 8 August 1809. Huntley based his estimates of the French force upon the number of troops seen marching upon the dykes and the varying types of uniforms which indicated distinct military groups. The actual French force upon Cadsand is noted hereafter.

41. *Parliamentary Debates*, vol. 15, "Testimony of Huntley," 20 February 1810, Appendix, col. 289.

42. *Parliamentary Papers*, vol. 6, Strachan to Gardner, 29 July 1809, p. 115.

43. *Parliamentary Debates*, vol. 15, "Testimony of Gardner," 20 February 1810, Appendix, col. 267.

44. Ibid. "The distance of Commodore Owen's squadron from me was

12 miles in a direct line, the approach circuitous by boats, owing to shoals, the winds as I shall read from the *Blake's* Log, 'Fresh breezes and cloudy.'"

45. *Parliamentary Papers,* vol. 6, Strachan to Gardner, 2 August 1809, p. 117. This statement is in apparent contradiction to some of his later correspondence and to his testimony before the parliamentary committee in 1810.

46. *Parliamentary Debates,* vol. 15, "Testimony of Huntley," 20 February 1810, Appendix, col. 289; *Parliamentary Papers,* vol. 6, Huntley to Chatham, 8 August 1809, p. 342. In this report Huntley detailed his activities from July 29 to August 3. Ibid., Strachan to Gardner, 3 August 1809, p. 342. Gardner forwarded this order to Huntley.

47. Brownrigg did write Huntley on July 29 and again on the thirtieth; the second letter assured Huntley that he would have the use of Gardner's boats.

48. *Parliamentary Debates,* vol. 15, "Testimony of Strachan," 15 February 1810, col. 264. All the divisions had difficulty in procuring enough pilots to direct the ships of the expedition.

49. Ibid. "The weather was so very bad that we were obliged to go into the Roompot, from the apprehension that many of our transports would drive on shore, and that great part of our flotilla if not the whole might be sunk."

50. Ibid. "We should still have found difficulty in getting the transports out of the East Scheldt into the West Scheldt, on account of the wind blowing in and generally blowing very fresh."

51. Normally this would pose no problem for the superior naval force which the British had in the Scheldt. The strong wind from the south, however, prevented the blockade from becoming totally effective until after Flushing had been reinforced several times.

52. *Parliamentary Debates,* vol. 15, "Testimony of Huntley," 20 February 1810, col. 293.

53. *Correspondance: Armées du Nord,* Carton C^2 101, Sainte-Suzanne to Clarke, 28 July 1809. This telegraphic dispatch was sent late on the 28th, and with the initial sighting troops began to reinforce Cadsand, while the entire coast from Boulogne to Flushing was alerted.

54. *Parliamentary Debates,* vol. 15, "Testimony of Gardner," 20 February 1810, Appendix, col. 268. "I suppose the whole of the boats of the squadron I had the honor to command might have carried from 400 to 500 men."

55. *Correspondance: Armées du Nord,* Carton C^2 101, Rousseau to Clarke, 25 July 1809. French troops were continually arriving during

the 30th, making it difficult to determine the exact number at any one time.

56. *Parliamentary Debates,* vol. 15, "Testimony of Lord Huntley," 20 February 1810, Appendix, col. 293.

57. Ibid., vol. 16, Appendix, cols. 1112–30. In the "Letters of Proceedings" of Sir Richard Strachan and Lord Chatham, both agreed that since Rosslyn's and Grosvenor's divisions had been forced into the Roompot, Cadsand was no longer necessary.

58. See *Chatham Papers,* 30/8/260, "Journal of the Army," p. 1; *See also* Strachan's testimony before the parliamentary committee on 15 February 1810 in *Parliamentary Debates,* vol. 15, col. 264.

CHAPTER 5

1. *Correspondance: Armées du Nord,* Carton C^2 101, Monnet to Clarke, 26 July 1809; see also *Le Moniteur universel,* 23 August 1809. This Parisian paper, like the *Times* of London, published many of the documents and correspondence relative to the expedition.

2. *Correspondance: Armées du Nord,* Carton C^2 103, "Rapport des événements qui ont eu lieu pendant le siège de Flessingue jusqu'à la capitulation de la dite ville depuis le 29 juillet jusqu'au 17 août 1809" 17 August 1809, p. 1. Cited hereinafter as "Lammens's Journal." Lammens, mayor of the city and territory of Flushing, wrote this account at Ghent on 5 October 1809, as part of his official report to the French minister of war.

3. Ibid., Carton C^2 102, "Rapport fait par le général de brigade Osten à son Excellence Monseigneur le Ministre de la Guerre," 15 August 1809, p. 1. Cited hereinafter as "Osten's Journal." Osten's account of the siege of Flushing, although included with the documents of August 15, actually was written at the request of General Clarke on 30 August 1810. Osten had just returned from England where he had been held a prisoner of war since the surrender of Flushing.

4. Ibid., "Tableau de la situation des troupes qui composaient la garrison de Flessingue au 30 juillet, et renforts qui ont été dirigés sur cette place jusqu'au 6 août inclusivement," 6 August 1809. *See* Appendix C.

5. Ibid., Louis to Clarke, 9 August 1809. The Dutch troops numbered fewer than 1,000. General Stewart Bruce is not to be confused with the more popular and successful General David-Hendrikius Bruce.

6. Ibid., "Osten's Journal," pp. 1–2.

7. Ibid., p. 6.

8. *Chatham Papers,* 30/8/260, "Journal of the Army," p. 2.

9. Ibid. This division consisted of Captain Marsh's light brigade of artillery, with three ammunition carriages; Gen. Franz Rottenburgh's brigade (2,479 men); and Gen. Gore Brown's brigade (1,695 men).

10. William Wheeler, *The Letters of Private Wheeler*, p. 28.

11. *Correspondance: Armées du Nord*, Carton C² 102, "Osten's Journal," p. 7.

12. *Chatham Papers*, 30/8/260, "Journal of the Army," p. 2.

13. N. Ludlow Beamish, *History of the King's German Legion*, 1: 221.

14. *Chatham Papers*, 30/8/260, "Journal of the Army," p. 3. Sir John Cradock, although initially appointed to command a division of the army to the Scheldt, was later ordered to remain in the Peninsula. Gen. Thomas Graham assumed Cradock's command on the expedition. Graham's brigade consisted of 4,000 men; Picton's, 2,494; and the remaining detachments of Houston's brigade totaled 1,481.

15. Richard D. Henegan, *Seven Years' Campaigning in the Peninsula and the Netherlands from 1808 to 1815*, 1: 121.

16. Harry Ross-Lewin, *With the Thirty-Second in the Peninsula and Other Campaigns*, p. 126. The Seventy-first suffered twenty-five casualties in this encounter.

17. *Scheldt Papers*, Strachan to Pole, 4 August 1809, p. 410.

18. *Parliamentary Debates*, vol. 15, "Copy of the Terms of Capitulation of Ter Veere," 1 August 1809, Appendix, col. 27; *see also* Richardson, *A Mariner of England*, p. 264.

19. *Chatham Papers*, 30/8/262, Chatham to Castlereagh, 2 August 1809.

20. *Correspondance: Armées du Nord*, Carton C² 102, "Osten's Journal," pp. 8–9.

21. *Chatham Papers*, 30/8/260, "Journal of the Army," pp. 3–4. *See* Appendix A.

22. *Correspondance: Armées du Nord*, Carton C² 102, "Osten's Journal," p. 10.

23. John Green, *The Vicissitudes of a Soldier's Life*, pp. 29–33.

24. Henry William Paget, *One Leg, the Life and Letters of Henry William Paget*, p. 105.

25. Ibid., p. 106.

26. *Chatham Papers*, 30/8/260, "Journal of the Army," p. 5.

27. *Correspondance: Armées du Nord*, Carton C² 102, "Osten's Journal," p. 9.

28. William Wheater, *A Record of the Services of the 51st*, p. 72.

29. *Correspondance: Armées du Nord,* Carton C² 102, "Osten's Journal," p. 11.

30. Ibid.

31. Paget, *Life and Letters,* p. 106. Paget estimated his losses to be "four officers wounded, and about 90 men killed and wounded." *See also* the *Scheldt Papers,* 2 August 1809, pp. 79–80. The official English returns indicate that the English losses from the landing on Walcheren until August 2 totaled 46 killed, 213 wounded, and 34 missing. The French casualties for the same period numbered 500 (*Correspondance: Armées du Nord,* Carton C² 102, Clarke to Napoleon, 4 August 1809.)

32. *Scheldt Papers,* Strachan to Pole, 5 August 1809, p. 411.

33. *Chatham Papers,* 30/8/260, "Journal of the Siege of Flushing, 1809," p. 2. This journal was prepared by Col. William Fyers, commander of the engineers of Chatham's army besieging Flushing (hereinafter cited as "Fyers's Journal"). This account was later edited and published. *See* "Journal of the Siege of Flushing, 1809," *Journal of the Society for Army Historical Research,* 13(1934): 145–58.

34. *Chatham Papers,* 30/8/260, "Journal of the Army," p. 5.

35. F. Brodigan, ed., *Historical Records of the Twenty-Eighth North Gloucestershire Regiment,* p. 55.

36. *Scheldt Papers,* Keats to Strachan, 1 August 1809, p. 411.

37. *Chatham Papers,* 30/8/260, "Journal of the Army," p. 6.

38. *Correspondance: Armées du Nord,* Carton C² 102, Louis to Clarke, 9 August 1809. In addition to these troops, Admiral Missiessy landed 250 marines to support Bruce.

39. Desertion evidently took a heavy toll among the Dutch troops. Labarre de Raillicourt, *Louis Bonaparte,* p. 291, places the total at only 397; while Admiral Keats estimated about 600. See *Scheldt Papers,* Keats to Strachan, 3 August 1809, p. 413.

40. Louis Bonaparte, *Documens historiques,* p. 128.

41. Du Casse, *Les rois frères,* p. 413; *See also* Labarre de Raillicourt, *Louis Bonaparte,* p. 292; Louis Bonaparte, *Documens historiques,* p. 130. Bruce was restored to his former rank following the restoration of the House of Orange in 1814.

CHAPTER 6

1. *Correspondance: Armées du Nord,* Carton C² 103, "Précis des dispositions," 31 August 1809, p. 4. See also *Situations: Armées du Nord,* Carton C² 512.

2. *Correspondance: Armées du Nord,* Carton C² 102, Clarke to Napoleon, 1 August 1809.

3. Ibid., Carton C² 101, Chambarlhac to Clarke, 31 July 1809.

4. Ibid., Carton C² 103, "Précis des dispositions," 31 August 1809, p. 5; *See also* Martel, *Walkeren,* pp. 292–98.

5. *Correspondance: Armées du Nord,* Carton C² 101, Chambarlhac to Clarke, 31 July 1809.

6. Ibid., Carton C² 103, "Précis des dispositions," 31 August 1809, p. 6.

7. Ibid., Carton C² 101, Lamorlière to Clarke, 30 July 1809; Carton C² 102, Clarke to Sainte-Suzanne, 2 August 1809; Clarke to Rampon, 5 August 1809.

8. Ibid., Clarke to Napoleon, 1 August 1809.

9. Ibid., Clarke to Olivier, 2 August 1809.

10. Ibid., "Extrait des registres des actes de la préfecture, du 31 juillet 1809."

11. *Correspondance de Napoléon Ier,* vol. 19, no. 15630, Napoleon to Clarke, 9 August 1809, pp. 377–82.

12. *Correspondance: Armées du Nord,* Carton C² 102, Clarke to Saint-Laurent, 1 August 1809; Moncey to Clarke, 3 August 1809. Marshal Bon-Adrien-Jannot de Moncey, duc de Conegliano, was the inspector general of the Imperial Gendarmerie.

13. Louis Bonaparte, *Napoléon Ier,* Louis to Napoleon, 2 August 1809, p. 205; *Correspondance: Armées du Nord,* Carton C² 102, Louis to Fauconnet, 2 August 1809; Louis Bonaparte, *Documens historiques,* Louis to Chambarlhac, 1 August 1809, p. 127; Louis Bonaparte, *Napoléon Ier,* Louis to Napoleon, 2 August 1809, p. 205.

14. *Correspondance: Armées du Nord,* Carton C² 102, Tarayre to Fauconnet, 3 August 1809. General Tarayre at Bergen-op-Zoom had been supporting Bruce from his position opposite Batz on the Continent. "I had sent him munitions and provisions, and at the moment when he evacuated Batz, I had 100 men prepared to reinforce him."

15. Martel, *Walkeren,* p. 305; *See also Le Moniteur universel,* 23 August 1809, Missiessy to Decrès, 3 August 1809. When Missiessy learned that Batz was being evacuated, he sent a landing party which arrived at Batz between the time of Bruce's departure and the arrival of Disney's troops. Realizing that the spiked guns could soon be made serviceable again, Missiessy's sailors succeeded in pushing nineteen of the twenty-four guns into the moat before being forced to flee.

16. *Correspondance: Armées du Nord,* Carton C² 102, Clarke to Chambarlhac, 2 August 1809. Lillo was chiefly garrisoned by refractory

conscripts; customs agents and forest rangers were also pressed into service.

17. Ibid., Chambarlhac to Clarke, 3 August 1809.

18. Ibid., Fauconnet to Clarke, 3 August 1809; Rampon to Clarke, 3 August 1809; Clarke to Rampon, 4 August 1809. Louis Charbonnier was the military commandant at Maestrecht.

19. Ibid., Carton C² 102, Clarke to Rampon, 5 August 1809; Clarke to Sainte-Suzanne, 5 August 1809; Clarke to Rampon, 5 August 1809.

20. Ibid., Clark to Rampon, 5 August 1809.

21. Ibid., Carton C² 103, "Précis des dispositions," 31 August 1809, p. 9.

22. Ibid., Carton C² 102, Clarke to Napoleon, 7 August 1809.

23. Louis Bonaparte, *Louis Bonaparte en Hollande*, Louis to Rampon, 5 August 1809, pp. 330–31.

24. *Correspondance: Armées du Nord*, Carton C² 102, Rampon to Clarke, 7 August 1809.

25. Ibid.

26. Ibid., Olivier to Clarke, 7 August 1809; Clarke to Dejean, 7 August 1809; Carton C² 103, "Précis des dispositions," 31 August 1809, pp. 10–14.

27. *Correspondance de Napoléon Ier*, vol. 19, no. 15619, Napoleon to Clarke, 6 August 1809, p. 365.

28. Louis Bonaparte, *Louis Bonaparte en Hollande*, Louis to Cambacérès, 2 August 1809, pp. 323–24.

29. *Correspondance: Armées du Nord*, Carton C² 102, Louis to Clarke, 7 August 1809. Doboscq, who edited *Louis Bonaparte en Hollande*, incorrectly dated this letter August 8 and states that it was on this day that Louis received orders to take command of the troops in the Scheldt.

30. Louis Bonaparte, *Napoléon Ier*, Louis to Napoleon, 9 August 1809, pp. 206–9.

31. *Correspondance: Armées du Nord*, Carton C² 102, Louis to Clarke, 7 August 1809.

32. Ibid., Louis to Clarke, 7 August 1809.

33. Louis Bonaparte, *Napoléon Ier*, Louis to Napoleon, 9 August 1809, pp. 206–9.

34. Ibid.

35. *Correspondance: Armées du Nord*, Carton C² 102, Rampon to Clarke, 10 August 1809. "I will temporarily obey the orders of the King of Holland until I receive instructions on this matter." Napoleon was outraged when he learned that Clarke and Cambacérès had offered

temporary command of the forces to Louis partially because of Louis's honorary title of High Constable of the Empire. "Order the ministers to be assembled and make it known that the minister of war, because of his absolute ignorance of our constitution, has thought that the dignity of High Constable carried with it the right to command my armies; that is an error six hundred years old." More importantly, Napoleon was concerned about Louis's lack of experience. *Correspondance de Napoléon Ier*, vol. 19, no. 15665, Napoleon to Cambacérès, 16 August 1809, p. 409.

36. *Correspondance: Armées du Nord*, Carton C² 102, Rampon to Sainte-Suzanne, 8 August 1809; Louis to Clarke, 9 August 1809.

37. Ibid., Saint-Laurent to Clarke, 11 August 1809.

38. Ibid., Garnier to Saint-Laurent, 11 August 1809. Pierre Dominique Garnier was commandant of the Fourth Reserve Division at Ghent.

39. Ibid., Saint-Laurent to Clarke, 11 August 1809.

40. Louis, upon taking command of the forces in the Scheldt, announced that his command was to be called the Army of the Brabant. General Clarke occasionally referred to the force as the Corps of Observation of the Scheldt. These designations were changed again when Bernadotte assumed command.

41. *Correspondance: Armées du Nord*, Carton C² 102, Clarke to Sainte-Suzanne, 11 August 1809.

42. Ibid., Saint-Laurent to Clarke, 13 August 1809; Rampon to Clarke, 12 August 1809.

43. Rocca, *La Campagne de Walcheren*, p. 99. This measure also would have made Antwerp ineffective as a naval port until the river could be cleared. Fortunately for the French, Louis's proposal was never executed.

44. Louis Bonaparte, *Louis Bonaparte en Hollande*, Louis to Clarke, 12 August 1809, p. 341.

45. *Correspondance: Armées du Nord*, Carton C² 102, Clarke to Sainte-Suzanne, 13 August 1809. Bernadotte had incurred Napoleon's ire because of his performance during the Wagram campaign and had been sent back to Paris in disgrace. He was the only marshal immediately available to take the command at Antwerp. Bernadotte later (1810) became the crown prince of Sweden and ruled as King Charles XIV from 1818 to 1844. His descendants still rule Sweden today.

46. *Correspondance de Napoléon Ier*, vol. 19, no. 15619, Napoleon to Clarke, 6 August 1809, p. 365. Jean-Francois Dejean, in addition to

being inspector general of the engineers, also held the ministerial post of director of the administration of war in the French empire.

47. Ibid., no. 15624, Napoleon to Clarke, 7 August 1809, p. 370.

48. Ibid., Napoleon to Kellermann, 7 August 1809.

49. *Correspondance: Armées du Nord*, Carton C² 103, "Précis des dispositions," 31 August 1809, p. 9; Carton C² 102, Olivier to Sainte-Suzanne, 8 August 1809; Louis to Clarke, 9 August 1809; Clarke to Napoleon, 14 August 1809.

CHAPTER 7

1. *Chatham Papers*, 30/8/262, Chatham to Castlereagh, 2 August 1809; *Scheldt Papers*, Strachan to Pole, 4 August 1809, p. 407.

2. *Parliamentary Debates*, vol. 16, "Sir Richard Strachan's Observations on the Earl of Chatham's Statement of his proceedings," 5 March 1810, Appendix, cols. 118–24.

3. *Chatham Papers*, 30/8/260, "The Earl of Chatham's Statement of Proceedings," 15 October 1809.

4. Ibid., 30/8/262, Chatham to Castlereagh, 4 August 1809.

5. *Scheldt Papers*, Strachan to Pole, 4 August 1809, p. 407.

6. *Parliamentary Debates*, vol. 15, "Testimony of Owen," 9 February 1810, Appendix, col. 630.

7. *Correspondance: Armées du Nord*, Carton C² 103, "Précis des dispositions," 31 August 1809.

8. *Scheldt Papers*, Hanchett to Owen, 4 August 1809, p. 421. The *Raven*'s hull was damaged, two guns were dismounted, the top mast was destroyed, and the sails and rigging were shot through. Hanchett and eight of his men were wounded.

9. *Parliamentary Papers*, vol. 8, Gardner to Strachan, 3 August 1809, p. 123.

10. *Correspondance: Armées du Nord*, Carton C² 102, Rousseau to Clarke, 7 August 1809; *see also* Louis to Clarke, 9 August 1809. Louis had ordered General Rousseau and 4,000 National Guardsmen to reinforce Flushing, but the British blockade prevented it.

11. Henegan, *Seven Years' Campaigning*, p. 123.

12. *Parliamentary Debates*, vol. 15, Richardson to Otway, 16 August 1809, Appendix, col. 106.

13. Ibid., "Testimony of Fyers," 14 March 1810, col. 565.

14. Whitworth Porter, *History of the Corps of Royal Engineers*, 1: 249–50.

15. *Chatham Papers*, 30/8/260, "Fyers's Journal," p. 4. *See* map, p.

87. This map accompanies the "Journal," and the letter designations of the batteries are his own.

16. Ibid., p. 7.

17. Ibid., "Journal of the Army," p. 14.

18. Ibid., pp. 2–4. The collective British force on Walcheren, including Grosvenor's troops and the German light brigade, was 21,654.

19. *Correspondance: Armées du Nord,* Carton C² 102, "Osten's Journal," p. 12.

20. Ibid., p. 13.

21. Ibid., Carton C² 103, "Lammens's Journal," p. 6. The troops which retired into Flushing were causing some disorder. Lammens complained to General Monnet about these irregularities and used some of the bourgeois guard to aid the regular police in patrolling the town.

22. *Chatham Papers,* 30/8/260, "Fyers's Journal," p. 2.

23. Ibid., "Journal of the Army," p. 19. Osten does not record this in any of his papers.

24. Ibid., p. 15. For an excellent contemporary account of the British occupation of South Beveland, see Frederick William Trench's manuscript "Journal of the Walcheren Expedition," National Army Museum, London.

25. *Scheldt Papers,* p. 413.

26. *Chatham Papers,* 30/8/260, Strachan to Chatham, 3 August 1809.

27. Duncan, *Royal Regiment of Artillery,* p. 230; *Chatham Papers,* 30/8/260, "Journal of the Army," p. 18.

28. *Chatham Papers,* 30/8/260, "Journal of the Army," p. 19; *see also* John T. Jones, *Journal of Sieges,* 3: 262.

29. *Chatham Papers,* 30/8/369, Strachan to Chatham, 3 August 1809; Chatham to Strachan, 4 August 1809.

30. National Maritime Museum, *Keats Papers,* [Kea/11] 15, Strachan to Keats, 5 August 1809.

31. *Chatham Papers,* 30/8/368, "Popham's Memorandum," 5 August 1809. Popham suggested that they might want to attack Williamstadt or other Dutch ports farther to the north.

32. Popham, of course, had been consulted on several occasions during the planning of the expedition, but in his will, dated 18 July 1809, he stated that it was his design. See Richard A. Waite, Jr., "Sir Home Riggs Popham" (Ph.D. diss., Harvard University, 1942).

33. *Chatham Papers,* 30/8/368, Popham to Chatham, 29 July 1809. This letter must have influenced both Strachan and Chatham for in it Popham states, "possibly this operation may save the necessity of Cadsand, as the anchorage is better here than I expected, and instead of

mooring one hundred ships, I will now moor two hundred." Popham wrote this immediately after returning from reconnoitering the Roompot anchorage.

34. Ibid., 30/8/366, Castlereagh to Chatham, 8 August 1809. An excerpt from this letter praising the success of British army was read to the forces besieging Flushing on August 11. *See* "Trench's Journal," p. 57.

35. See Fortescue, *British Army*, p. 75.

36. *Chatham Papers*, 30/8/369, Strachan to Chatham, 31 July 1809. "I was very much mortified to find your Lordship was gone before I had the honor of seeing you . . . and I would make any sacrifice of time to have the honor of an interview, more especially as I cannot approve of the manner in which the Naval Force has been applied this morning to the great waste of ammunition and stores without effecting one good purpose. . . . I hope whenever your Lordship wishes to have the Navy employed in a particular way, that you would be pleased to signify your wishes to me."

37. Ibid., Strachan to Chatham, 2 August 1809.

38. Ibid., 30/8/260, "Strachan's Observations," 5 March 1810; see also *Parliamentary Debates*, vol. 16, Appendix, col. 1126.

39. *Chatham Papers*, 30/8/260, "Chatham's Statement of Proceedings," 15 October 1809. Compare this account with "Strachan's Observations," 5 March 1810. *See also* Chatham's marginal notes on his personal copy of "Strachan's Observations" for the extent of their differences. These will be discussed later.

40. Ibid., "Journal of the Army," pp. 23–24.

41. Ibid., p. 52.

42. *Correspondance: Armées du Nord*, Carton C² 102, "Osten's Journal," pp. 15–16.

43. Richard Cannon, ed., *Historical Record of the First or Royal Regiment of Foot*, p. 179.

44. *Chatham Papers*, 30/8/260, "Journal of the Army," pp. 25–26.

45. *Correspondance: Armées du Nord*, Carton C² 102, "Osten's Journal," p. 16.

46. Ibid., p. 17. The number of casualties seems rather high, especially the losses sustained by Serier's Forty-eighth. There may be some truth to the statement made by a soldier of the Seventy-first Regiment that the "French troops were so drunk they could not cry for mercy." See "Journal of a Soldier of the 71st Regiment, From 1806–1815," *Memorials of the Late War*, volume 27 of *Constable's Miscellany*, p. 71. The high losses may be more properly attributed to the poor quality

of the troops involved. Osten supports this position throughout his journal.

47. *Chatham Papers*, 30/8/260, "Journal of the Army," p. 33.

48. *Scheldt Papers*, Keats to Strachan, 12 August 1809, pp. 430–31.

49. *Parliamentary Papers*, vol. 8, Strachan to Gardner, 3 August 1809, p. 118.

50. Ibid., Strachan to Gardner, 5 August 1809, p. 121.

51. Ibid., Gardner to Strachan, 8 August 1809, p. 125. Gardner states in this letter that he was making the necessary arrangements to send the frigates up the river in consequence of receiving Strachan's orders of the 6th and 7th. Strachan subsequently testified that he had ordered the frigates up on the 6th, but his actual order of the 6th does not appear in the papers relating to the expedition.

52. *Chatham Papers*, 30/8/369, Strachan to Chatham, 8 August 1809.

53. *Parliamentary Papers*, vol. 8, Strachan to Gardner, 8 August 1809, p. 125. Strachan's information concerning the batteries was erroneous. The bombardment did not begin until the 13th.

54. The other ships were the *Pearlen, Amethyst, Rota, L'Aigle, Dryad, Euryalus, Nymphen, Statira,* and *Heroine.* See *Parliamentary Papers*, vol. 8, Owen to Gardner, 11 August 1809, pp. 127–28.

55. *Correspondance: Armées du Nord,* Carton C² 102, "Osten's Journal," p. 20; See also *Situations: Armées du Nord,* Carton C² 512.

56. *Scheldt Papers*, Strachan to Pole, 12 August 1809, p. 426.

57. Ibid., Strachan to Pole, 17 August 1809, p. 432.

58. *Correspondance: Armées du Nord,* Carton C² 102, Monnet to Clarke, 4 August 1809.

59. *Correspondance de Napoléon Ier,* vol. 19, no. 15619, Napoleon to Clarke, 6 August 1809, p. 365. "I have given the order, which you will repeat to him, to cut the dykes if that were necessary."

60. *Correspondance: Armées du Nord,* Carton C² 102, Osten to Clarke, 30 August 1810.

61. Ibid., Carton C² 103, "Lammens's Journal," p. 6; *See also* Porter, *Royal Engineers*, p. 252.

62. *Chatham Papers*, 30/8/260, "Fyers's Journal," p. 15; Porter, *Royal Engineers*, p. 253. The Dutch citizens of Walcheren were motivated in their attempt to assist the British not only because of their desire to save their own farm land, but also because the presence of the British army opened traffic in restricted goods from Britain normally denied them during wartime.

63. *Parliamentary Debates*, vol. 15, "Testimony of Fyers," 14 March 1810, Appendix, col. 565. This appears to be a natural appointment

since Fyers was the commanding engineer on the expedition. The engineers on Walcheren prior to August 8 were commanded by Colonel D'Arcy, whose placement of the batteries during the first days of the siege was criticized by Gen. Sir Thomas Picton in his *Memoirs*, p. 233: "The batteries and trenches were formed one after another without method or arrangement; and much confusion existed in consequence of neither the officers nor soldiers attached to the engineer department knowing their proper situations, by which the works were carried on very slowly."

64. *Correspondance: Armées du Nord*, Carton C² 102, "Osten's Journal," p. 14.

65. Ibid., p. 19. The Colonials returned to their posts when Osten assured them that the water would drain in a direction away from Flushing.

66. *Chatham Papers*, 30/8/260, "Journal of the Army," p. 43.

67. Ibid., "Fyers's Journal," pp. 15–16.

68. *Parliamentary Debates*, vol. 15, Richardson to Otway, 16 August 1809, Appendix, col. 106.

69. *Chatham Papers*, 30/8/260, "Journal of the Army," p. 48.

70. *Scheldt Papers*, Strachan to Pole, 17 August 1809, p. 434.

71. *Correspondance: Armées du Nord*, Carton C² 102, "Osten's Journal," p. 24.

72. *Chatham Papers*, 30/8/260, "Journal of the Army," p. 55.

73. *Correspondance: Armées du Nord*, Carton C² 102, "Osten's Journal," p. 22; *Chatham Papers*, 30/8/260, "Journal of the Army," p. 19.

74. H. O'Donnell, ed., *Historical Records of the 14th Regiment of Foot*, p. 89.

75. *Correspondance: Armées du Nord*, Carton C² 102, "Osten's Journal," p. 23; *Chatham Papers*, 30/8/260, "Journal of the Army," p. 55.

76. *Chatham Papers*, 30/8/263, Pasley to Fyers, 14 August 1809. Capt. William Pasley of the Royal Engineers was wounded on the night of August 14 while participating in Colonel Pack's attack on the French outpost on the east dyke.

77. *Scheldt Papers*, Strachan to Pole, 17 August 1809, pp. 432–36.

78. *Correspondance: Armées du Nord*, Carton C² 102, "Osten's Journal," p. 24.

79. Ibid., Carton C² 103, "Lammens's Journal," pp. 14–15.

80. *Chatham Papers*, 30/8/260, "Fyers's Journal," p. 23.

81. Ibid., Coote to Monnet, 14 August 1809. "The General Commanding is induced by the feelings of Humanity to Summon you to surrender, with your Garrison, Prisoners of War. . . ."

82. Richard Cannon, ed., *Historical Record of the 36th, or the Herefordshire Regiment of Foot*, p. 76.

83. *Correspondance: Armées du Nord*, Carton C² 102, "Osten's Journal," p. 25; *Chatham Papers*, 30/8/260, "Fyers's Journal," p. 28. It is interesting to note that Pack's assault was the first attempt made by the British to gain possession of this significant position.

84. *Correspondance: Armées du Nord*, Carton C² 102, "Osten's Journal," p. 25. Monnet to Coote, 15 August 1809; *Chatham Papers*, 30/8/260, Coote to Monnet, 15 August 1809.

85. *Correspondance: Armées du Nord*, Carton C² 103, "Lammens's Journal," pp. 13–16.

86. Ibid., Carton C² 102, Osten to Clarke, 30 August 1810; Carton C² 103, "Lammens's Journal," p. 17. In his letter to Clarke, Osten relates that General Monnet, while a prisoner in England, attempted to falsify documents so that they would show that a council had been called and had agreed to surrender the town on the morning of August 15.

87. *Chatham Papers*, 30/8/261, Chatham to Castlereagh, 16 August 1809.

88. Ibid., 30/8/260, "Journal of the Army," p. 61. Monnet informed General Coote that it would be noon before the garrison would be prepared to leave Flushing. However, since the prisoners would have to march some ten miles to the embarkation point at Ter Haak and since there would not be enough daylight hours to effect the operation, it was delayed until the morning of the 18th.

89. Jones, *Sieges*, p. 287. Jones gave the number killed among the inhabitants of Flushing at 335 and indicated a larger number injured. Other sources make no attempt to give a definite figure for killed and wounded inhabitants. Neither Lammens nor Osten considered the subject in their reports.

90. Dyott, *Dyott's Diary*, p. 282. *See also* George Hargrove, Jr., *An Account of the Islands of Walcheren and South Beveland Against Which the British Expedition Proceeded in 1809*, pp. 23–32.

91. *Chatham Papers*, 30/8/261, Chatham to Castlereagh, 16 August 1809; *Parliamentary Debates*, vol. 15, Strachan to Pole, 17 August 1809, Appendix, cols. 106–11. The British losses on Walcheren from July 30 to August 15, including army and navy, totaled 127 killed and 636 wounded.

92. *Chatham Papers*, 30/8/261, Chatham to Castlereagh, 16 August 1809. Chatham stated the number to be more than 1,000, which probably is substantially correct.

93. *Correspondance: Armées du Nord*, Carton C² 102, 7 August 1809,

"Tableau de la situation des troupes qui composaient la garrison de Flessingue." Osten, in his journal, lists the number of troops in the garrison at 6,733. See "Osten's Journal," p. 28.

94. *Chatham Papers*, 30/8/261, Chatham to Castlereagh, 16 August 1809. The return listing the prisoners and deserters was included in this letter.

95. Ibid., "Situation des troupes de la place de Flessingue, à l'Epoque de 17 août 1809." This paper was prepared by Monnet's chief of staff, Petrizoli. A return of the garrison on 13 August 1809, signed by General Monnet, listed its strength at 4,379. A close inspection, however, reveals an error in addition, making the correct total 5,370. Ibid., Chatham to Castlereagh, 16 August 1809. This return was enclosed in the above letter. General Osten states that Flushing's garrison upon surrender amounted to only 3,773, excluding 489 sick and wounded in the hospitals of Flushing. *Correspondance: Armées du Nord*, Carton C² 102, "Osten's Journal," p. 28.

96. *Correspondance, Napoléon Ier*, vol. 19, no. 15699, Napoleon to Decrès, 22 August 1809, p. 450.

97. Napoleon I, *Napoleon Self-Revealed*, p. 245.

98. *Le Moniteur universel*, 9 December 1809; *See also* "Trench's Journal," p. 73. "General Monnet ought to be hanged for not surrendering before the town was ruined; and for surrendering afterwards with such an army as he had and such a store of provisions . . . a supply for 5,000 men for 1½ years."

99. *Castlereagh's Correspondence*, Henry Vernon to Castlereagh, 1 February 1810, p. 328. Mr. Vernon talked to Monnet while he was a prisoner in England and quoted the French general as saying "his garrison was composed of men of all nations, who would not obey his orders, and who had fired on him and his officers." General Osten, in his journal, indicated that the troops, especially the French ex-deserter battalion, were of poor quality but said nothing of their insubordination.

100. *Chatham Papers*, 30/8/260, "Chatham's Statement of Proceedings," 15 October 1809.

CHAPTER 8

1. Louis Bonaparte, *Louis Bonaparte en Hollande*, Louis to Clarke, 14 August 1809, p. 345; Rocca, *La campagne de Walcheren*, p. 102. "It would not take less than one of the best leaders of France to organize

our army, or rather armed rabble, in such desperate circumstances and in such inextricable chaos as we found ourselves."

2. Dunbar P. Barton, *Bernadotte and Napoleon, 1763–1810*, p. 239.

3. *Correspondance: Armées du Nord*, Carton C² 102, Rampon to Clarke, 15 August 1809.

4. Rocca, *La campagne de Walcheren*, pp. 102–3.

5. Louis Bonaparte, *Napoléon Ier*, Louis to Napoleon, 16 August 1809, p. 211. Louis stated that the current situation in Holland was critical since most of his troops were on the Scheldt. "I wish, Sire, that you would order my troops in Germany and Spain to return."

6. *Correspondance: Armées du Nord*, Carton C² 103, Dejean to Clarke, 16 August 1809. Also on the 16th, the bulletins from Breskens announced the apparent capitulation of Flushing.

7. Ibid., Clarke to Moncey, 14 August 1809.

8. Ibid., Clarke to Bernadotte, 15 August 1809. These reinforcements were composed of three detachments from the Twenty-sixth, Sixty-sixth, and Eighty-second Regiments of Light Infantry, totaling 1,500 men. The remainder of the reinforcements included detachments from the Eighth Demibrigade at Strasbourg, dragoons from the First Military Division in Paris, Twenty-eighth Light Cavalry, and finally, troops of the Twenty-sixth Light Cavalry.

9. *Correspondance de Napoléon Ier*, vol. 19, no. 15620, Napoleon to Clarke, 7 August 1809, p. 367.

10. *Correspondance: Armées du Nord*, Carton C² 103, "Report of the Departments called to raise National Guard," 16 August 1809. The twenty-one departments were: Escaut, Nord, Pas de Calais, Lys, Meuse, Somme, Marne, Moselle, Meurthe-et-Moselle, Vosges, Seine-et-Oise, Seine, Aisne, Loire, Eure, Aube, Haute-Marne, Yonne, Loiret, Ardennes, and Deux Nethes.

11. Ibid. Colaud was named governor of Antwerp on August 17. See Clarke to Bernadotte, 17 August 1809.

12. *Correspondance: Armées du Nord*, Carton C² 102, Clarke to Napoleon, 14 August 1809; Clarke to Bernadotte, 15 August 1809. Garnier's 8,000 National Guardsmen at Ghent were available, but were held in reserve until the 30,000 National Guard ordered out on August 15 were formed.

13. Ibid., Dejean to Clarke, 16 August 1809. Marshal Dumonceau had 4,000 Dutch troops at Bergen-op-Zoom to support the Army of the North.

14. Ibid., Clarke to Moncey, 16 August 1809.

15. Ibid., Bernadotte to Clarke, 17 August 1809; Clarke to Napoleon, 24 August 1809. The front line of defense, including Yzendyke, Sas de Gand, Antwerp, and the forts between Antwerp and Bergen-op-Zoom, was provisioned for periods from ten days for the small forts to six months for the 12,500 men at Antwerp. The second line of defense, including Ostend, Ghent, Lille and Nieuport, was provisioned for up to a year.

16. Ibid., Bernadotte to Clarke, 18 August 1809.

17. *Chatham Papers*, 30/8/260, "Journal of the Army," p. 68. Fraser's command consisted of the brigades under General Picton and General Brown and the light infantry of the Seventy-first Regiment.

18. *Parliamentary Debates*, vol. 16, "Strachan's Narrative," 5 March 1810, Appendix, col. 1125.

19. *Parliamentary Papers*, vol. 8, "Testimony of Huskisson," 6 March 1810, pp. 229–33; *see also* Fortescue, *British Army*, p. 85.

20. "Trench's Journal," pp. 65–66.

21. *Correspondance: Armées du Nord*, Carton C² 102, Rampon to Clarke, 9 August 1809.

22. Ibid., Carton C² 103, Bernadotte to Clarke, 18 August 1809.

23. *Correspondance: Armées du Nord*, Carton C² 103, de Caux to Clarke, letters of 17, 19, and 25 August 1809.

24. Ibid., Bernadotte to Clarke, 20 August 1809. The narrowness of the river and its numerous bends contributed to the effectiveness of these defensive measures.

25. *Correspondance de Napoléon Ier*, vol. 19, no. 15681, Napoleon to Decrès, 22 August 1809, pp. 424–26.

26. *Correspondance: Armées du Nord*, Carton C² 103, Clarke to Moncey, 20 August 1809. This area on the left bank remained under Bernadotte's command since it formed an approach to Antwerp. Napoleon had actually wanted this army to be called the Corps of Tête de Flandre, but Clarke misunderstood his letter.

27. Ibid., Bernadotte to Clarke, 21 August 1809.

28. Ibid., Clarke to Napoleon, 22 August 1809. These detachments came from more than twenty different regiments.

29. Ibid., Bernadotte to Clarke, 22 August 1809.

30. Ibid., Moncey to Bernadotte, 23 August 1809.

31. Ibid., Dejean to Clarke, 23 August 1809.

32. Ibid., Bernadotte to Clarke, 23 August 1809.

33. Ibid., Bernadotte to Clarke, 24 August 1809. Napoleon had reached the same conclusion and consequently had ordered Moncey to

establish his headquarters at Tête de Flandre if Antwerp were menaced. *Correspondance de Napoléon Ier*, vol. 19, no. 15709, Napoleon to Bernadotte, 24 August 1809, p. 460.

34. Ibid., Moncey to Bernadotte, 24 August 1809. Moncey had already sent a few detachments of mounted gendarmes to Hulst prior to the 24th, and on August 25 he was able to dispatch Gen. Gabriel-Joseph Clement with several more detachments of infantry in consequence of the arrival of reinforcements on the left bank.

35. Ibid., Moncey to Bernadotte, 25 August 1809.

36. Ibid., Clarke to Napoleon, 26 August 1809.

37. *Correspondance de Napoléon Ier*, vol. 19, no. 15698, Napoleon to Clarke, 22 August 1809, p. 449.

38. *Correspondance: Armées du Nord*, Carton C^2 103, Clarke to Napoleon, 26 August 1809.

39. Louis Bonaparte, *Louis Bonaparte en Hollande*, Louis to Dumonceau, 24 August 1809, pp. 348–49; Louis to Bernadotte, 24 August 1809.

40. *Correspondance: Armées du Nord*, Carton C^2 103, Bernadotte to Clarke, 25 August 1809. General Charbonnier had 1,500 troops on the left bank between Doel and Tête de Flandre.

41. Ibid., Bernadotte to Clarke, 27 August 1809.

42. Ibid., Clarke to Bernadotte, 28 August 1809; *Correspondance de Napoléon Ier*, vol. 19, no. 15698, Napoleon to Clarke, 22 August 1809, pp. 447–50. Clarke's letter to Bernadotte included Napoleon's orders for the defense of Antwerp.

43. Ibid.

44. *Chatham Papers*, 30/8/260, "Journal of the Army," pp. 74–75.

45. Chatham also had requested Sir John Hope to prepare a memorandum concerning possible methods of attacking Antwerp. Hope's paper, written on August 23, was almost identical to Brownrigg's memorandum. *Parliamentary Debates*, vol. 15, "Confidential Memorandum," 23 August 1809, Appendix, cols. 376–81.

46. Ibid., "Copy of a Paper, submitted by Lieutenant General Brownrigg, Quartermaster General, to the Lieutenant Generals of the Army assembled at Fort Batz," 27 August 1809, cols. 314–18.

47. *Chatham Papers*, 30/8/260, "Journal of the Army," p. 76.

48. Ibid., 30/8/263, "General Monthly Return," 25 August 1809. Brownrigg seems to have underestimated the strength of the army. This monthly return indicates over 38,000 effectives. *See* Appendix A.

49. *Parliamentary Debates*, vol. 15, Brownrigg's paper, Appendix, cols. 315–16.

50. Ibid.; see also *Correspondance de Napoléon Ier*, vol. 19, no.

15666, Napoleon to Fouché, 16 August 1809, pp. 409–11. "It would take the English a siege of six months and 60,000 to capture Antwerp."

51. *Correspondance de Napoléon Ier*, no. 15698, Napoleon to Clarke, 22 August 1809, p. 449. Napoleon foresaw this possibility and ordered Moncey to establish his headquarters at Tête de Flandre if Antwerp were attacked.

52. *Parliamentary Debates*, vol. 15, Brownrigg's paper, Appendix, col. 317.

53. Ibid., "Opinions of the Lieutenant Generals of the Army," 27 August 1809, cols. 318–20. The lieutenant generals were Coote, Rosslyn, Huntley, Grosvenor, Hope, Paget, and Brownrigg.

54. *Scheldt Papers*, "Strachan's Narrative," pp. 783–85.

55. *Parliamentary Debates*, vol. 15, "Opinions of the Lieutenant Generals of the Army," 27 August 1809, Appendix, col. 320.

56. *Chatham Papers*, 30/8/261, Chatham to Castlereagh, 29 August 1809.

57. *Scheldt Papers*, Keats to Rosslyn, 17 August 1809, p. 462.

58. *Chatham Papers*, 30/8/369, Strachan to Chatham, 26 August 1809.

59. *Owen Papers*, Strachan to Owen, 27 August 1809; See also *Scheldt Papers*, Strachan to W. W. Pole, 27 August 1809, pp. 463–67. The reference to shortage of provisions and water stemmed from Strachan's having received an erroneous report which stated that there was less than a week's provision for the forces. Strachan immediately placed the naval forces on two-thirds ration.

60. *Chatham Papers*, 30/8/369, Strachan to Chatham, 29 August 1809.

61. Ibid., Chatham to Strachan, 29 August 1809.

62. Ibid., Strachan to Chatham, 31 August 1809.

63. *Correspondance: Armées du Nord*, Carton C² 103, Clement to Bernadotte, 30 August 1809.

64. *Chatham Papers*, 30/8/368, Popham to Chatham, 1 September 1809.

CHAPTER 9

1. *Parliamentary Debates*, vol. 15, Chatham to Castlereagh, 29 August 1809, Appendix, col. 42.

2. *Chatham Papers*, 30/8/260, "Journal of the Army," p. 76. Chatham evidently had not seen the latest return of the sick when he dispatched his letter to Castlereagh.

3. Ibid., pp. 77–78.

4. *Scheldt Papers*, Webbe to Cary, 11 September 1809, pp. 39–41; *Chatham Papers*, 30/8/260, "Journal of the Army," p. 82.

5. John Harris, *Recollections of Rifleman Harris*, pp. 173–74.

6. William Dyott, *Dyott's Diary*, p. 285.

7. *Chatham Papers*, 30/8/260, "Journal of the Army," p. 81.

8. Ibid., p. 84.

9. *Scheldt Papers*, Coote to Castlereagh, 31 August 1809, p. 32.

10. *Parliamentary Papers*, vol. 6, Strachan to Gardner, 2 September 1809, p. 130. This order applied to the seven ships of the line in Gardner's division.

11. Ibid., Otway to Gardner, 4 September 1809, p. 131.

12. *Chatham Papers*, 30/8/260, "Journal of the Army," p. 86.

13. Ibid., 30/8/261, Chatham to Castlereagh, 6 September 1809.

14. Ibid., 30/8/260, "Journal of the Army," p. 87.

15. Ibid., p. 78. The occupation forces left on Walcheren consisted of the following troops: the brigades of Dyott, Picton, Ackland, Brown, Rottenburg, Alton, and Colonel Hay (Hay's brigade was composed of all the troops of General Graham's old Right Wing, except for the detachment of the Ninety-fifth Rifle Corps and the detachment of the Sixty-eighth Light Infantry). In addition to the above-mentioned brigades, detachments of the Ninth Light Dragoons, Royal Wagon Train, Royal Artillery, Royal Engineers, and Royal Staff Corps remained on Walcheren. The rank and file totaled 16,766; but including officers of all the services, the total number of men remaining on Walcheren amounted to approximately 19,000.

16. Ibid., p. 87; see also *Scheldt Papers*, p. 715.

17. *Correspondance: Armées du Nord*, Carton C² 103, Bernadotte to Clarke, 30 August 1809.

18. Ibid., Moncey to Clarke, 29 August 1809.

19. Ibid., Moncey to Clarke, 31 August 1809. Moncey now reported that he had 30,000 troops organized under arms.

20. Louis Bonaparte, *Documens historiques*, p. 144.

21. Arthur Fischer, *Napoléon et Anvers*, "Ordre du jour," 1 September 1809, p. 171.

22. *Correspondance de Napoléon Ier*, vol. 19, no. 15785, Napoleon to Clarke, 11 September 1809, p. 530.

23. Ibid., no. 15788, "Decret," 11 September 1809, p. 532; no. 15792, Napoleon to Clarke, 12 September 1809, p. 535. "Those who remain in the island of Cadsand, in the swamps of Bergen-op-Zoom, in South Beveland, are lost troops; they will all be in the hospitals."

24. *Castlereagh's Correspondence*, Castlereagh to Coote, 18 September 1809, p. 323.

25. *Parliamentary Debates*, vol. 15, Coote to Chatham, 9 September 1809, Appendix, col. 47.

26. *Scheldt Papers*, Coote to Castlereagh, 17 September 1809, p. 138. In addition to the increasing sickness, Coote reported that 498 men had died during the preceding two weeks.

27. Ibid., Coote to Castlereagh, 23 September 1809, pp. 146–50.

28. *Parliamentary Debates*, vol. 15, "Testimony of Sir Lucas Pepys, Physician General to the Forces," 23 February 1809, Appendix, col. 110.

29. *Scheldt Papers*, Coote to Castlereagh, 23 September 1809, pp. 146–50.

30. *Castlereagh's Correspondence*, Castlereagh to Coote, 24 September 1809, p. 327.

31. *Scheldt Papers*, Liverpool to Coote, 12 October 1809, p. 44. Coote employed over four hundred inhabitants in the hospitals while he was in command on Walcheren.

32. Dyott, *Dyott's Diary*, p. 287.

33. *Scheldt Papers*, Burrows to Coote, 18 September 1809, p. 143. Francis Burrows was the deputy inspector of hospitals and senior medical officer on Walcheren.

34. Brougham, *Life and Times*, p. 307; *Parliamentary Debates*, vol. 15, "Testimony of William Lidderdale, Surgeon to the Forces," 15 March 1810, Appendix, col. 635.

35. John Pringle, *Observations on the Diseases of the Army*, as quoted by Hargrove, *Walcheren and South Beveland*, pp. 66–67. See also *Parliamentary Debates*, vol. 15, "Testimony of Pepys," 2 February 1810, Appendix, col. 110; and also Lord Grey's speech published in the *Morning Chronicle*, 26 January 1810.

36. *Parliamentary Debates*, vol. 15, "Testimony of Dundas," 2 February 1810, Appendix, cols. 84–90.

37. *Scheldt Papers*, Webbe to Cary, 11 September 1809, pp. 39–41. A week later Francis Burrows reported that many of the cases had deteriorated into typhus fever and that "we have now, therefore, the effects of contagion, in addition to climate, to contend with" (Burrows to Coote, 18 September 1809, pp. 141–44). *See also* Sir James McGrigor, *The Autobiography and Services of Sir James McGrigor*, p. 239.

38. *Wellington's Dispatches*, Wellington to Liverpool, 15 December 1810, 7: 50. "I am concerned to add . . . an increased degree of sickness has appeared in the 3rd Batt. of the Royals the 4th and 9th regiments, all of which had been in Walcheren."

39. *Castlereagh's Correspondence*, Renny to Castlereagh, 3 March 1810, pp. 337–46.

40. For an excellent study of the medical literature of the physicians who actually treated the soldiers, see Robert M. Feibel, "What Happened at Walcheren: The Primary Sources," *Bulletin of the History of Medicine*, 42(1968): 62–79.

41. Hargrove, *Walcheren and South Beveland*, p. 70.

42. Feibel, "What Happened at Walcheren," pp. 64–65. "In view of the periodicity of the fever, the splenomegaly, the frequent relapses, and the value of bark in simple cases, it seems clear that endemic malaria formed a substantial substrate of disease. . . . Further, it is unlikely on epidemiologic grounds that malaria could infect so many soldiers in such a short time. The common findings of ulcerated intestines indicate typhoid fever or dysentery. The overcrowding of the sick . . . and the filth consequent upon the lack of medical attention would predispose to typhoid and dysentery as well as to typhus."

43. *Scheldt Papers*, Hope to Castlereagh, 24 September 1809, pp. 38–39. Hospitals were established at Harwich, Ipswich, and Yarmouth to accommodate a total of 1,932; at Deal for 1,250; and at Portsmouth for 1,700. These facilities were expanded as more sick troops were evacuated from Walcheren.

44. Ibid., Coote to Castlereagh, 6 October 1809, pp. 160–65.

45. *Parliamentary Papers,* vol. 7, Bathurst to Canning, 20 September 1809, p. 43. Benjamin Bathurst, the British agent in Vienna, had evidence that Austria might renounce the armistice and continue the war against Napoleon. When this information proved false and a peace treaty was signed, Bathurst was forced to leave Vienna. While making his way back to London, he was killed by either brigands or French agents. See Sherwig, *Guineas and Gunpowder*, p. 213.

46. John Steven Watson, *The Reign of George III, 1760–1815*, p. 143.

47. *Parliamentary Debates*, vol. 15, Coote to Castlereagh, 14 October 1809, Appendix, col. 61. There were premature celebrations on the Continent before the treaty was actually signed on October 14.

48. *Scheldt Papers*, "Liverpool to the officer commanding his Majesty's troops in Walcheren," 24 October 1809, p. 47. This letter was written during the transition period between Don's arrival and Coote's departure from Walcheren; consequently, it was addressed to neither Don nor Coote.

49. Ibid., Liverpool to Don, 27 October 1809, pp. 48–49. Verification came the following day, Saturday, October 28, when the terms of the treaty of Schoenbrunn were received in London.

50. Ibid., Don to Liverpool, 27 October 1809, pp. 185–87.

51. *Correspondance de Napoléon Ier*, vol. 19, no. 15917, Napoleon to Bessières, 8 October 1809, pp. 654–55.

52. Louis Bonaparte, *Napoléon Ier*, Napoleon to Champagny, 11 October 1809, pp. 217–18. L. A. Champagny, duke of Cadore, was minister of foreign affairs. *Correspondance de Napoléon Ier*, vol. 20, no. 15967, Napoleon to Clarke, 21 October 1809, pp. 11–13.

53. Ibid., no. 15994, Napoleon to Clarke, 2 November 1809, p. 30.

54. Napoleon I, *Lettres inédits de Napoléon Ier*, Napoleon to Bessières, 20 November 1809, pp. 377–78.

55. *Scheldt Papers*, Don to Liverpool, 29 October 1809, pp. 187–91.

56. Ibid., Liverpool to Don, 9 November 1809, pp. 53–54; and Liverpool to Don, 13 November 1809, pp. 55–57.

57. Ibid., Liverpool to Don, 4 November 1809, pp. 51–52.

58. *Parliamentary Debates*, vol. 15, Don to Liverpool, 27 November 1809, Appendix, col. 79. Before Walcheren was finally evacuated near the end of December, however, another 381 men had been stricken with the fever. The following is the number (by months) of sick and wounded sent to England from Walcheren: August, 200; September, 1,953; October, 5,516; November, 4,813; December, 381. The total number evacuated was 12,863, of which 533 were wounded men. *Chatham Papers*, 30/8/261, "Return of the Sick and Wounded sent to England from Walcheren at different Times." The total number of troops who died from the fever was 3,960. See *Scheldt Papers*, "Return," 1 February 1810, p. 63.

59. Richardson, pp. 273–74.

60. *Parliamentary Debates*, vol. 15, Pilkington to Don, 11 December 1809, Appendix, col. 83; Don to Liverpool, 23 December 1809, col. 81.

61. Ibid.; *Unpublished Correspondence of Napoleon I*, Napoleon to Clarke, 13 December 1809, 3: 359. Clarke was ordered to instruct Bessières to occupy Walcheren in the name of the emperor rather than the king of Holland. *See* Louis Bonaparte, *Napoléon Ier*, Napoleon to Martin Gaudin, minister of finance, 3 January 1810, p. 218. "I have united the island of Walcheren to France." The annexation of Walcheren was just the first step in the eventual incorporation of Holland into the French empire in July 1810.

CHAPTER 10

1. *Times*, 5 and 12 August 1809. Throughout August and September the British press was filled with information and editorials on the ex-

pedition. See *Morning Chronicle* (London), *London Gazette, Hull Packet, Shrewsbury Chronicle, Dublin Journal,* and other contemporary newspapers for their coverage.

2. Charles Grenville, duke of Buckingham and Chandos, *Memoirs of the Court and Cabinets of George the Third from the Original Family Documents,* 4: 48–49.

3. Brougham, *Life and Times,* p. 310.

4. *Morning Chronicle,* 14 August 1809.

5. *Times,* 2 September 1809.

6. Ibid., 4 September 1809.

7. *Morning Chronicle,* 5 September 1809; *The Naval Miscellany,* 2: 390–91. In a letter dated 25 August 1809, C. W. Boys, a naval officer on the expedition, wrote: "When the commander-in-chief arrived here he brought with him on a cart, I should think built for the purpose, two turtles. . . . When I met Colonel Hay . . . and asked him where the General was, his reply, [was] more expressive than I can make by the manner in which it was given, but he said, 'I don't know; somewhere in the rear. . . . Everything goes on at headquarters as if they were at the Horse Guards; . . . you must call between certain hours, send up your name and wait your turn.'"

8. Théo Fleischman, *L'Expédition Anglaise sur le Continent en 1809,* p. 70.

9. *Times,* 11 September 1809. Although there is doubtless some truth to these accusations, it should be observed in fairness to Lord Chatham that most of these remarks emanated from naval personnel.

10. Ibid., 13 September 1809; *Morning Chronicle,* 12 September 1809.

11. Ibid., 29 September 1809.

12. John W. Fortescue, *British Statesmen of the Great War, 1793–1814,* p. 233. The prime minister, the duke of Portland, Castlereagh, Canning, and Lord Granville Leveson-Gower all resigned their positions in the cabinet. The press at first speculated that the failure of the expedition was the cause of the dissolution of the cabinet.

13. *Times,* 22 September 1809. The *Times* stated erroneously that the duel was prompted by Canning's criticism of Castlereagh, blaming him for the failure of the expedition: "He is said to have charged the Noble Lord with the whole blame of the defects in the plan of the Expedition, and of whatever there was of misconduct in carrying it into execution." The actual reason for the duel appears to have been Canning's secret maneuver in attempting to remove Castlereagh from the cabinet. Castlereagh learned what had been transpiring behind his back for

several months and demanded satisfaction from Canning, who obliged and, on the second exchange on Putney Heath, received a bullet in his right thigh.

14. Ibid., 11 October 1809. This particular reprint from *Le Moniteur universel* stated that the expedition failed because it had no chance of success. "It would have failed, because, in fact, fools only could attempt a similar expedition . . . where fevers carry off half of the army."

15. Ibid., 25 November 1809.

16. Ibid., 21 December 1809.

17. Ibid., 7 December 1809.

18. *Scheldt Papers,* "Speech of the Lords Commissioners to both Houses of Parliament," 26 January 1810, pp. 3–4.

19. George III, *The Later Correspondence of George III,* 5: 500. Castlereagh voted in favor of the inquiry, Canning against.

20. *Parliamentary Debates,* vol. 15, "Testimony of Huskisson," 6 March 1810, Appendix, col. 430; See also *Parliamentary Papers,* vol. 8, for the minutes of evidence relating to the expedition.

21. *Parliamentary Debates,* vol. 15, cols. 434–37. Huskisson testified that the government had the equivalent of £125 thousand sterling in Dutch specie.

22. Ibid., "Testimony of Warton," 13 March 1810, col. 514. Lord Porchester, in his opening speech on the expedition, (27 January, col. 165 had accused the government of spending £5 million on the Scheldt enterprise.

23. Ibid., "Testimony of George," 8 February 1810, cols. 141–47.

24. Ibid., "Testimony of Castlereagh," 13 March 1810, cols. 514–45.

25. *Chatham Papers,* 30/8/263, "Abstract of Ordnance, Ammunition, and Stores embarked on the Expedition."

26. *Parliamentary Papers,* vol. 8, "Testimony of Castlereagh," 13 March 1810, pp. 285–93. *See also* the testimony of Gen. Sir Thomas Trigge, Lieutenant General of Ordnance, 8 February 1810, pp. 37–39.

27. Ibid., "Testimony of Brownrigg," 15 March 1810, pp. 327–66.

28. The medical board consisted of Sir Lucas Pepys, physician general; Thomas Keate, surgeon general; and Francis Knight, inspector general of the army hospitals. Several weaknesses were revealed in the composition of the medical board, not the least of which was lack of cooperation among its three current members (Sir James McGrigor, *Autobiography,* p. 253). The reform of the medical board in 1810 was not the direct result of the Walcheren disaster, as has often been stated. *See* Kate Elizabeth Crowe, "The Walcheren Expedition and the New Army Medical Board," *English Historical Review,* 88(1973): 770–85.

29. Bark, or quinine, the extraction of cinchona bark, was used to treat various kinds of fever, especially in the Indies; and it was thought that it would cure the Walcheren fever. It was found to be successful in many cases and was used almost exclusively for the treatment of the troops.

30. *Parliamentary Debates,* vol. 15, "Testimony of Keate," 6 February 1810, Appendix, col. 455.

31. Ibid. Keate testified that he received a request for bark on September 18, delivered the request to the storekeeper general on September 27, and had it shipped to Walcheren on the 30th, where it arrived in store on October 15. He gave no excuse for his leisurely action; "Testimony of McGrigor," 6 March 1810, col. 482.

32. McGrigor, *Autobiography,* p. 241.

33. *Parliamentary Debates,* vol. 15, "Testimony of Lidderdale," 13 March 1810, Appendix, col. 635. Two hospital ships, the *Asia* and the *Aurora,* 480 tons each, accompanied the expedition. *See* "Testimony of George," 8 February 1810, col. 147.

34. See T. H. McGuffie, "The Walcheren Expedition and the Walcheren Fever," *English Historical Review,* 62(1947): 191–202.

35. *Parliamentary Debates,* vol. 15, "Testimony of Pepys," 5 February and 8 March 1810, Appendix, col. 110 and col. 483. *See also* Dr. Robert Renny's report on the causes of the fever in *Castlereagh's Correspondence,* pp. 337–46.

36. *Parliamentary Papers,* vol. 8, "Testimony of Owen," 9 February 1810, pp. 73–81; *Parliamentary Debates,* vol. 15, "Testimony of Huntley," 20 February 1810, Appendix, col. 293; "Testimony of Gardner," 15 February 1810, col. 267.

37. Huntley presented his instructions from Brownrigg, dated 25 July 1809 (ibid., "Testimony of Huntley," 20 February 1810, cols. 284–87); "Testimony of Strachan," 15 February 1810, col. 242.

38. Ibid., "Testimony of Gardner," 15 February 1810, cols. 266–67.

39. Ibid., "Testimony of Coote," 27 February 1810, col. 406; ibid., "Testimony of Don," 8 March 1810, col. 487.

40. *Parliamentary Debates,* vol. 15, "Testimony of Chatham," 22 February 1810, Appendix, col. 350. The narrative had been completed on 15 October 1809. For his "unconstitutional" action, Chatham was censured by the House of Commons, and subsequently resigned his cabinet position as master general of the ordnance.

41. Ibid. Chatham explained his behavior in his papers, stating that "a special report of the transactions in the Scheldt was *called* for by His

Majesty, and none was ever asked of me, by the Secretary of State" (*Chatham Papers*, 30/8/260, "Memorandum by Chatham," n.d.).

42. *Parliamentary Papers*, vol. 8, "Testimony of Strachan," 12 March 1810, pp. 293–303.

43. *Parliamentary Debates*, vol. 16, "Rear Admiral Sir Richard Strachan's Observations on the Earl of Chatham's Statement of his Proceedings dated October 15, 1809, presented to the King February 14, 1810," Appendix, cols. 1117–25.

44. *Chatham Papers*, 30/8/260, "The Earl of Chatham's Statement of his Proceedings, dated October 15, 1809, presented to the King February 14, 1810."

45. Ibid.

46. *Parliamentary Debates*, vol. 16, "Strachan's Observations," Appendix, cols. 117–20.

47. Ibid., vol. 15, "Testimony of Strachan," 12 March 1810, Appendix, col. 535.

48. Ibid., "Chatham's Narrative," cols. 1109–10.

49. Ibid., "Strachan's Observations," cols. 1124–29.

50. Ibid., vol. 15, "Testimony of Strachan," 12 March 1810, Appendix, cols. 531–33; ibid., vol. 16, "Strachan's Observations," Appendix, cols. 1127–28; see also *Chatham Papers*, 30/8/260, Chatham's marginal notes on "Strachan's Observations." Chatham, in his testimony before the committee investigating the expedition, was not questioned concerning Strachan's interpretation of their meeting on August 1. In his papers, however, Chatham accused Strachan of inventing the story that Chatham had agreed to proceed by South Beveland. "He could not have understood this . . . the whole of this has been suggested to him since." He added, "a journal of the proceedings of the Fleet would have been more useful than this paper of Strachan's."

51. *Parliamentary Debates*, vol. 16, "Strachan's Observations," Appendix, col. 1126.

52. *Chatham Papers*, 30/8/260, Chatham's marginal notes on "Strachan's Observations."

53. Ibid., vol. 15, "Testimony of Chatham," 27 February 1810, Appendix, col. 390. Chatham also testified that although there were captured guns and ammunition on South Beveland, the guns were not on traveling carriages; and sufficient horses were not available to drag them.

54. Strachan solicited the opinions of Capt. Richard Davies, commander of a division of gunboats in the Slough during the expedition,

and Capt. Richard Jones, who was in charge of the navigation of the Slough and responsible for landing the troops on South Beveland. Both of these naval officers supported Strachan's assertions. However, the testimonies of General Brownrigg, Lord Rosslyn, and Sir John Hope were in complete agreement with Chatham.

55. Ibid., vol. 16, "Chatham's Narrative," Appendix, col. 1113.

56. Ibid., vol. 15, "Testimony of Strachan," 15 February 1810, Appendix, col. 255.

57. Ibid., vol. 16, "Chatham's Narrative," Appendix, col. 1114.

58. Ibid., vol. 15, "Testimony of Strachan," 15 February 1810, Appendix, col. 246.

59. Ibid., vol. 16, "Chatham's Narrative," Appendix, col. 1109; ibid., "Strachan's Observations," col. 1127. Strachan commented in his observations that "Lord Chatham seemed to think it necessary that all the men of war and transports should assemble in the Upper Scheldt at Batz." Chatham countered that it was not his opinion, but part of the original plan (*Chatham Papers*, 30/8/260, marginal notes on "Strachan's Observations").

60. *Parliamentary Debates*, vol. 15, "Testimony of Strachan," 15 February 1810, Appendix, col. 259. "From the bad weather we experienced in the beginning of the Expedition, the delay in proceeding up the Scheldt arose."

61. Ibid., vol. 16, "Strachan's Observations," Appendix, col. 1129. Speaking of Chatham's decision not to proceed via South Beveland, Strachan declared: "With him alone was there an option between a march of 36 hours and a voyage of an indefinite length." Chatham observed, however, in his marginal notes on Strachan's paper in the *Chatham Papers*, that the evidence presented during the inquiry proved that this procedure was impracticable.

62. *Chatham Papers*, 30/8/260, marginal notes on "Strachan's Observations." Strachan had concluded his "observations" by stating that Chatham seemed unaware that the adverse winds had blown the expedition into the Roompot. Chatham commented in his notes that "Lord Chatham neither was nor is aware . . . he was blown into the East Scheldt."

63. Ibid., 30/8/260, "Journal of the Army," p. 13; *Parliamentary Debates*, vol. 15, "Testimony of Brownrigg," 15 March 1810, Appendix, col. 592; "Testimony of Rosslyn," 15 March 1810, col. 578; "Testimony of Hope," 15 March 1810, col. 583.

64. *Parliamentary Debates*, vol. 16, "Porchester's Speech," 26 March 1810, cols. 46–81.

65. Ibid., "Castlereagh's Speech," 26 March 1810, cols. 81–134.

66. Ibid., "Craufurd's Speech," 27 March 1810, cols. 203–54. General Charles Craufurd was the elder brother of Robert, who served under Wellington in Spain.

67. The debate had continued early into the morning of March 31. Sir Home Popham was speaking, attempting to clarify some of the statements made by Sir Richard Strachan concerning the navigation of the Scheldt. When Popham used the Dutch word *Roompot* in an unfortunate connection, the Commons broke into laughter and shouted Popham down. It was in this mood that the House of Commons voted on the resolutions.

68. Ibid., col. 429.

69. *Times*, 5 April 1810.

70. *Parliamentary Debates,* vol. 16, "Speech of Lord Darnley in the House of Lords," 5 April 1810, col. 452.

CHAPTER 11

1. Joseph Fouché, *Memoirs*, p. 283. "But in the interval the English appeared in the Escaut with a formidable expedition, which, had it been more ably conducted, might have brought back success to our enemies, and given Austria time to rally."

2. *Castlereagh's Correspondence,* "The King's Instructions to the Earl of Chatham," 16 July 1809, p. 285.

3. *Correspondance de Napoléon Ier*, vol. 20, no. 16019, Napoleon to Eugene, 22 November 1809, p. 49. This estimate was made by Napoleon a month prior to the British evacuation of Flushing.

4. As quoted in Louis Madelin, *Histoire du consulat et de l'empire,* 8:238.

5. *Chatham Papers*, 30/8/365, Bathurst to Canning, 29 July 1809, p. 83. Several dispatches from the Austrian government requesting continued British efforts in the Scheldt were made public during the parliamentary inquiry.

6. *Parliamentary Debates,* vol. 15, "Testimony of Castlereagh," 13 March 1810, Appendix, cols. 536–47.

7. *Correspondance de Napoléon Ier*, vol. 19, no. 15620, Napoleon to Clarke, 7 August 1809, pp. 367–69; "The negotiations continue at Altenburg, but they move slowly, waiting on the results of the events in the Scheldt" (no. 15714, Napoleon to Clarke, 26 August 1809, pp. 465–67).

8. Ibid., no. 15778, Napoleon to Champagny, 10 September 1809, pp. 522–25.

9. A. F. Fremantle, *England in the Nineteenth Century*, 2: 289. John W. Fortescue is one of the few historians who have given detailed study to the expedition and he concluded that it had very little chance of success. However, Fortescue based his remarks concerning the French-Dutch forces in the Scheldt on Martel (*Walkeren*), and he did not take into account the caliber of these troops, their poor leadership and equipment, and the state of the defenses along the Scheldt and at Antwerp. See Fortescue, *British Army*, p. 96.

10. *Parliamentary Debates*, vol. 15, "Testimony of Chatham," 27 February 1810, Appendix, col. 351. This was the general opinion of the commanding officers on the expedition, including Hope, Brownrigg, and Strachan.

11. *Correspondance: Armées du Nord*, Carton C² 103, "Précis des disposition," 31 August 1809, p. 5; *See also* Carton C² 102, Rampon to Sainte-Suzanne, 8 August 1809.

12. Ibid., Fauconnet to Clarke, 8 August 1809. These two forts were rapidly being strengthened, but they were the only serious obstacles confronting the British between Batz and Antwerp.

13. *Correspondance: Armées du Nord*, Carton C² 103, Dejean to Clarke, 23 August 1809. Dejean, inspector general of the engineers, stated that if the English "had been a little audacious and attacked by land and sea, they could have forced the imperfect and incomplete defenses we had here . . . and could have burned the city and docks of Antwerp."

14. Napoleon devoted over one hundred letters and orders to the expedition, and in many of these he indicated a great deal of anxiety, especially for his fleet and the docks and arsenal at Antwerp.

15. Barry E. O'Meara, *Napoleon in Exile*, 1:157.

16. Louis Bonaparte, *Documens historiques*, pp. 227–31. The area given to France included Zealand, Brabant, and part of Gelderland.

17. *Correspondance de Napoléon Ier*, vol. 19, no. 15749, Napoleon to comte de Cessac, director of military conscription, 4 September 1809, pp. 492–94; *see also* no. 15750, Napoleon to Clarke, 5 September 1809, pp. 494–99.

18. Thiers, *Consulate and Empire*, 11:121–22.

19. Richard Glover, "French Fleet," pp. 233–52.

20. Donald D. Horward, *The Battle of Bussaco*, p. 144.

21. Napier, *War in Peninsula*, 5:115–37.

Bibliography

PRIMARY SOURCES

UNPUBLISHED MANUSCRIPTS

France. Ministère de la Guerre. Archives Historiques. *Correspondance: Armées du Nord*. Carton C² 101–6.

France. Ministère de la Guerre. Archives Historiques. *Situations: Armée du Nord*. Carton C² 512. 1809.

Great Britain. National Army Museum. Frederick William Trench's manuscript, "Journal of the Walcheren Expedition."

Great Britain. National Maritime Museum. *Keats Papers*. [Kea/11] 15.

Great Britain. National Maritime Museum. *Owen Papers* [52/061].

Great Britain. Public Record Office. Admiralty. 1/3987. *A Precis of All the Papers in the Admiralty Office Which Have Any Relation to the Expedition to the Scheldt*.

Great Britain. Public Record Office. Admiralty. 53/1474. Ship's Log: *Venerable*. 17 May 1808–30 July 1811.

Great Britain. Public Record Office. *Chatham Papers*. 30/8/260–369.

Great Britain. Public Record Office. War Office Papers. 1/190–95, 641–45, 721, 1121–26; 3/133, 595; 6/126–33.

CORRESPONDENCE, MEMOIRS, AND DOCUMENTS

Abbot, Charles, Lord Colchester. *Diary and Correspondence of Charles Abbot, Lord Colchester*. Vol. 2. London: John Murray, 1861.

The Annual Register, or a View of the History, Politics, and Literature, for the Year 1809. London: W. Otridge, 1811.

Bonaparte, Louis. *Documents [sic] historiques et réflexions sur le gouvernement de la Hollande*. Vol. 3. Paris: Chez Aillaud, 1820.

———. *Louis Bonaparte en Hollande d'après ses lettres 1806–1810*. Compiled and edited by André Duboscq. Paris: Emile-Paul, 1911.

———. *Napoléon Ier et le roi Louis d'après les documents conservés aux archives nationales*. Compiled by Félix Rocquain. Paris: Librairie de Firmin-Didot, 1875.

Brougham, Henry, Lord. *The Life and Times of Henry, Lord Brougham*. Vol. 1. New York: Harper, 1871.

Bunbury, Sir Henry. *Narratives of Some Passages in the Great War with France.* London: Peter Davies, 1927.

Cadell, Charles. *Narrative of the Campaigns of the Twenty-eighth Regiment, since Their Return from Egypt in 1802.* London: Whittaker, 1835.

Campbell, Colin, Lord Clyde. *The Life of Colin Campbell, Lord Clyde, Illustrated by Extracts from His Diary and Correspondence.* Edited by Lt. Gen. Lawrence Shadwell. Vol. 1. London: William Blackwood, 1881.

Canning, George. *The Speeches of the Right Honourable George Canning.* Edited by R. Therry. Vol. 2. London: James Ridgway, 1836.

Castlereagh, Robert Stewart, Viscount. *Correspondence, Despatches, and other Papers of Viscount Castlereagh.* Edited by William W. Vane. Vol. 6. London: William Shoberl, 1851.

Cobbett, William. *Cobbett's Political Register.* Vol. 17 (January–June 1810). London: T. C. Hansard, 1810.

A Collection of Papers Relating to the Expedition to the Scheldt Presented to Parliament in 1810. Compiled by A. Strahan. London: A. Strahan, 1811.

Constable's Miscellany of Original and Selected Publications in the Various Departments of Literature, Science, and the Arts. Vol. 27. "Journal of a Soldier of the 71st Regiment, from 1806–1815." *Memorials of the Late War.* Edinburgh: Constable, 1828.

Cooke, Captain John. *Memoirs of the Late War: Comprising a Personal Narrative of Captain Cooke of the Forty-third Regiment of Light Infantry.* Vol. 1. London: Henry Colburn & Richard Bentley, 1831.

Creevey, Thomas. *The Creevey Papers: A Selection from the Correspondence and Diaries of the Late Thomas Creevey, M. P.* Edited by Sir Hubert Maxwell. Vol. 1. London: John Murray, 1904.

Du Casse, Baron Pierre E. Albert, ed. *Les rois frères de Napoléon Ier. Documents inédits relatifs au premier empire.* Paris: Librairie Germer Bailliere, 1883.

Dyott, William. *Dyott's Diary.* Edited by Reginald W. Jeffery. Vol. 1. London: Archibald Constable, 1907.

Fouché, Joseph. *Memoirs.* Vol. 1. Paris: Société des Bibliophiles, n.d.

Fyers, Colonel William. "Journal of the Siege of Flushing, 1809." *Journal of the Society for Army Historical Research.* Edited by Major Evan W. H. Fyers. 13 (1934): 145–58.

Fyler, Colonel Arthur. *The History of the Fiftieth or the Queen's Own Regiment.* London: Chapman, 1895.

George III. *The Later Correspondence of George III.* Edited by A. Aspinal. Vol. 5. Cambridge: Cambridge University Press, 1970.

Gomm, William Maynard. *Letters and Journals of Sir William Maynard Gomm.* Edited by Francis Culling Carr-Gomm. London: John Murray, 1881.

Great Britain. *Cobbett's Parliamentary Debates.* Vols. 15 and 16. London: T. C. Hansard, 1810.

Great Britain. *Historical Manuscript Commission.* Vol. 9. Dropmore MSS. London: Mackie, 1906.

Great Britain. House of Commons. *The Journals of the House of Commons.* Vol. 65: 23 January–21 August 1810.

Great Britain. House of Commons. *Parliamentary Papers.* Vols. 6–8. *Paper, Presented to the House by His Majesty's Command, Relating to the Expedition to the Scheldt.*

Green, John. *The Vicissitudes of a Soldier's Life, or a Series of Occurrences from 1806 to 1815; together with an Introductory and a Concluding Chapter: the Whole Containing, with Some Other Matters, a Concise Account of the War in the Peninsula, from Its Commencement to Its Final Close.* Louth: John Green, 1827.

Grenville, C., Duke of Buckingham and Chandos. *Memoirs of the Court and Cabinets of George the Third from the Original Family Documents.* Vol. 4. London: Hurst & Blackett, 1855.

Hargrove, George, Jr. *An Account of the Islands of Walcheren and South Beveland Against Which the British Expedition Proceeded in 1809.* Dublin: Gilber & Hodges, 1812.

Harris, John. *Recollections of Rifleman Harris.* Edited by Henry Curling. New York: Robert M. McBride, 1929.

Henegan, Sir Richard D. *Seven Years' Campaigning in the Peninsula and the Netherlands, from 1808 to 1815.* Vol. 1. London: Henry Colburn, 1846.

Holland, Lady Elizabeth. *The Journal of Elizabeth Lady Holland, 1791–1811.* Edited by Earl of Ilchester. London: Longman & Green, 1908.

Kincaid, Sir John. *Adventures in the Rifle Brigade in the Peninsula, France, and the Netherlands, from 1809 to 1815.* New York: Robert M. McBride, 1929.

———. *Random Shots from a Rifleman.* London: Maclaren, n.d.

Labédoyère, Count Charles. *Memoirs of the Public and Private Life of Napoleon Bonaparte.* Vol. 2. London: George Virtue, 1841.

Leveson-Gower, Lord Granville, First Earl Granville. *Private Corre-*

spondence, 1781–1821. Edited by Castalia Countess Granville. Vol. 2. London: John Murray, 1916.

McGrigor, Sir James. *The Autobiography and Services of Sir James McGrigor Bart, Late Director-General of the Army Medical Department, with an Appendix of Notes and Original Correspondence.* London: Longman, Green, Longman & Roberts, 1861.

Mockler-Ferryman, A. F. *The Life of a Regimental Officer during the Great War, 1793–1815.* London: William Blackwood, 1913.

Montholon, le Général Comte de. *Memoires pour servir à l'histoire de France, sous Napoléon, écrits a Sainte-Hélène, par les généraux qui ont partagé sa captivité, et publiés sur les manuscrits entièrement corrigés de la main de Napoléon.* Vols. 1 and 2. Paris: Firmin Didot, Père et Fils, 1823.

Morley, Stephen. *Memoirs of a Sergeant of the Fifth Regiment of Foot.* Ashford: J. Elliott, 1842.

Napoleon I. *Correspondance de Napoléon Ier.* Vols. 18–20. Paris: Imprimerie Impériale, 1865.

———. *Lettres inédits de Napoléon Ier.* Edited by Léon Lecestre. Vol. 1. Paris: Plon & Nourrit, 1897.

———. *Napoleon Self-Revealed.* Translated and edited by J. M. Thompson. Boston: Houghton Mifflin, 1934.

———. *New Letters of Napoleon I, Omitted from the Edition Published under the Auspices of Napoleon III.* Edited and translated by Lady Mary Loyd. London: William Heinemann, 1898.

———. *Unpublished Correspondence of Napoleon I Preserved in the War Archives.* Edited by Ernest Picard and Louis Tuetey. Translated by Louis Seymour Houghton. Vol. 3. New York: Duffield, 1913.

The Naval Chronicle for 1809: Containing a General and Biographical History of the Royal Navy of the United Kingdom. Vol. 22. London: Joyce Gold, 1809.

The Naval Miscellany. Edited by John Knox Laughton. Vol. 2. London: Naval Records Society, 1912.

O'Meara, Barry E. *Napoleon in Exile, or, a Voice from St. Helena. The Opinions and Reflections of Napoleon on the Most Important Events in His Life and Government, in His Own Words.* Vol. 1. New York: Worthington, 1890.

Paget, Henry William, First Marquess of Anglesey. *One Leg; the Life and Letters of Henry William Paget, First Marquess of Anglesey, 1768–1854.* London: Jonathan Cape, 1861.

Picton, Sir Thomas. *Memoirs.* Edited by H. B. Robinson. Vol. 1. London: Richard Bentley, 1836.

Richardson, William. *A Mariner of England: An Account of the Career of William Richardson From Cabin Boy in the Merchant Service to Warrant Officer in the Royal Navy (1780–1819) as told by Himself.* Edited by Colonel Spencer Childers. London: Conway Maritime Press, 1970.

Robertson, D. *The Journal of Sergeant D. Robertson, Late 92nd Foot: Comprising the Different Campaigns, between the Years 1798 and 1818, in Egypt, Walcheren, Denmark, Sweden, Portugal, Spain, France, and Belgium.* Perth: J. Fisher, 1842.

Rocca, Albert Jean Michel de. *La campagne de Walcheren et d'Anvers.* Bruxelles: P. J. de Mat, 1816.

Rose, George. *The Diaries and Correspondence of the Right Honourable George Rose.* Edited by Leveson V. Harcourt. Vol. 2. London: Richard Bentley, 1860.

Ross-Lewin, Harry. *With the Thirty-Second in the Peninsular and Other Campaigns.* Edited by John Wardell. London: Simpkin & Marshall, 1904.

Segur, Philippe P. *An Aide-de-Camp of Napoleon.* Translated by H. A. Patchett-Martin. New York: D. Appleton, 1895.

St. Clair, Lt. Colonel Thomas Staunton. *A Residence In the West Indies and America, with a Narrative of the Expedition to the Island of Walcheren.* 2 vols. London: Richard Bentley, 1834.

Steevens, Charles. *Reminiscences of My Military Life, from 1795 to 1818.* London, 1878.

Vassall, Henry Richard, Third Lord Holland. *Further Memoirs of the Whig Party, 1807–1821, with Some Miscellaneous Reminiscences.* London: John Murray, 1905.

Wellington, Arthur Wellesley, Duke of. *The Dispatches of Field Marshal the Duke of Wellington.* Compiled by Lt. Col. Gurwood. Vols. 7 and 8. London: John Murray, 1838.

Wheeler, William. *The Letters of Private Wheeler, 1809–1828.* Edited by B. H. Liddell Hart. London: Michael Joseph, 1951.

Windham, William. *Speeches in Parliament of the Right Honourable William Windham.* Vol. 3. London: Longmans, Hurst, 1812.

NEWSPAPERS

Dublin Journal, 1809–19.
Gazette (London), 1809–10.
Hampshire Chronicle, 1809–10.
Hull Packet, 1809–10.
Le Moniteur universel (Paris), 1809–10.

Morning Chronicle (London), 1809–10.
Shrewsbury Chronicle, 1809–10.
Times (London), 1809–10.

SECONDARY SOURCES

Aiken, John. *Annals of the Reign of George the Third.* Vols. 1 and 2. London: Longman, Hurst, Rees, Orme and Brown, 1816.

Alison, Sir Archibald. *Lives of Lord Castlereagh and Sir Charles Stewart, the Second and Third Marquesses of Londonderry, with Annals of Contemporary Events in Which They Bore a Part, from the Original Papers of the Family.* Vol. 1. Edinburgh: W. Blackwood, 1861.

Anonymous. *Flushing, Middleburg, and the Island of Walcheren.* Middleburgh: F. B. Den Boer, 1899.

Arnault, M. A. *Life and Campaigns of Napoleon Bonaparte.* Vols. 1 and 2. Boston: Phillips & Sampson, 1850.

Atteridge, A. Hilliard. *Napoleon's Brothers.* New York: Brentano's, 1909.

Aubrey-Fletcher, H. L. *A History of the Foot Guards to 1856.* London: Constable, 1927.

Bagot, Josceline. *George Canning and His Friends, Containing Hitherto Unpublished Letters, Jeux d'Esprit, . . .* Vol. 1. London: John Murray, 1909.

Barrett, Charles Raymond Booth, ed. *The 85th King's Light Infantry.* London: Spottiswoode, 1913.

Barton, Sir Dunbar P. *The Amazing Career of Bernadotte.* Boston: Houghton Mifflin, 1929.

―――. *Bernadotte and Napoleon, 1763–1810.* London: John Murray, 1921.

Beamish, N. Ludlow. *History of the King's German Legion.* Vol. 1. London: Thomas and William Boone, 1832.

Blanco, Richard L. *Wellington's Surgeon General: Sir James McGrigor.* Durham, N.C.: Duke University Press, 1974.

Brenton, Edward Pelham. *The Naval History of Great Britain.* Vol. 2. London: Henry Colburn, 1837.

―――. *The Naval History of Great Britain from the Year 1783 to 1822.* Vol. 4. London: C. Rice, 1825.

Brett-James, Antony. "The Walcheren Failure." *History Today* 13 (December 1963): 811–20.

Brodigan, F., ed. *Historical Records of the Twenty-Eighth North*

Gloucestershire Regiment. London: Blackfriars Printing and Publishing, 1884.

Bruun, Geoffery. *Europe and the French Imperium*. New York: Harper & Brother, 1938.

Bryant, Arthur. *Years of Victory*. London: The Reprint Society, 1944.

Cambridge Modern History. Edited by A. W. Ward, et al. Vol. 9. New York: Macmillan, 1906.

Cannon, Richard, ed. *Historical Record of the British Army, the First, or Royal Regiment of Foot*. London: Adjutant General's Office, Horse Guards, 1846.

――――. *Historical Record of the Thirty-Sixth, or the Herefordshire Regiment of Foot*. London: Parker, Furnivall & Parker, 1853.

Chandler, David G. *The Campaigns of Napoleon*. New York: Macmillan, 1966.

Clowes, William Laird. *The Royal Navy, a History from the Earliest Times to the Present*. Vol. 5. London: Sampson Low & Marston, 1900.

Connelly, Owen. *Napoleon's Satellite Kingdoms*. New York: Free Press, 1965.

Cross, Arthur Lynn. *A History of England and Great Britain*. New York: Macmillan, 1919.

Crouzet, François. *L'Economie britannique et le blocus continental, 1806–1813*, 2 vols. Paris: Presses universitaires de France, 1958.

Crowe, Kate Elizabeth. "The Walcheren Expedition and the New Army Medical Board: A Reconsideration." *English Historical Review* 88 (1973): 770–885.

Duncan, Francis. *History of the Royal Regiment of Artillery*. Vol. 2. London: John Murray, 1879.

Dupin, Charles. *View of the History and Actual State of the Military Force of Great Britain*. Translated by an officer. London: John Murray, 1822.

Edmundson, Georges. *The History of Holland*. Cambridge: University Press, 1922.

Feibel, Robert M. "What Happened at Walcheren: The Primary Sources." *Bulletin of the History of Medicine* 42 (1968): 62–79.

――――. "Major-General Thomas Staunton St. Clair." *Journal of the Society for Army Historical Research* 48 (Spring 1970): 29–34.

Fiéffé, Eugène. *Histoire des troupes étrangères au service de France, depuis leur origine jusqu'à nos jours, et de tous les régiments levés dans les pays conquis sous la premier république et sous l'empire*. Vol. 2. Paris: Librairie Militaire, 1854.

Fischer, Arthur. *Napoléon et Anvers*. Anvers: Librairie Loosbergh, 1933.

Fleischman, Théo. *L'Expédition Anglaise sur le Continent en 1809*. Brussels: La Renaissance du Livre, 1973.

Fortescue, John W. *British Statesmen of the Great War*. Oxford: Clarendon Press, 1911.

————. *A History of the British Army*. Vol. 7. London: Macmillan, 1912.

Fournier, August. *Napoleon the First*. Edited by Edward Gaylord Bourne. Translated by M. B. Corwin and A. D. Bissell. New York: Henry Holt, 1903.

Fremantle, A. F. *England in the Nineteenth Century*. Vol. 2. London: George Allen & Unwin, 1930.

Gardyne, C. Greenhill. *The Life of a Regiment. The History of the Gordon Highlanders from Its Formation in 1794 to 1816*. London: The Medici Society, 1929.

Garnier, Athanase. *La cour de Hollande sous le règne de Louis Bonaparte*. Paris: Chez Persan, 1823.

Glover, Richard. *Britain at Bay Defence against Bonaparte, 1803–14*. London: George Allen & Unwin, 1973.

————. "The French Fleet, 1807–1814: Britain's Problem: And Madison's Opportunity." *Journal of Modern History* 39 (1967): 233–52.

————. *Peninsular Preparation; The Reform of the British Army 1795–1809*. Cambridge: Cambridge University Press, 1963.

Gray, Denis. *Spencer Perceval; The Evangelical Prime Minister 1762–1812*. London: University of Manchester Press, 1963.

Hecksher, Eli Filip. *The Continental System: An Economic Interpretation*. Edited by Harold Westergaard. Gloucester, Mass.: Peter Smith, 1964.

Horward, Donald D. *The Battle of Bussaco: Massena vs. Wellington*. Tallahassee, Fla.: Florida State University Studies No. 44, 1965.

Innes, A. D. *A History of England*. New York: G. P. Putnam's Sons, 1912.

James, William. *The Naval History of Great Britain*. Vol. 4. London: Macmillan, 1902.

Jones, Major General Sir John T. *Journal of Sieges Carried on by the Army under the Duke of Wellington in Spain*. Vol. 3. London: John Weale, 1846.

Labarre de Raillicourt, D. *Louis Bonaparte roi de Hollande frère et père d' empereurs*. Paris: J. Peyronnet, 1963.

Lanfrey, Pierre. *The History of Napoleon the First.* Vol. 3. London: Macmillan, 1876.

Langsam, Walter C. *The Napoleonic Wars and German Nationalism in Austria.* New York: Columbia University Press, 1930.

Lecene, Paul. *Les marins de la république et de l'empire, 1793–1815.* Paris: Librairie Centrale des Publications Populaires, 1884.

Lefebvre, Georges. *Napoléon.* Paris: Presses Universitaires de France, 1941.

Lever, Sir Tresham. *The House of Pitt, A Family Chronicle.* London: John Murray, 1947.

Lloyd, Christopher. *The Nation and the Navy.* London: Cresset Press, 1954.

Lovett, Gabriel H. *Napoleon and the Birth of Modern Spain.* 2 vols. New York: New York University Press, 1965.

Mackenzie, T. A. et al., eds. *Historical Records of the Seventy-ninth Queen's Own Cameron Highlanders.* London: Hamilton, Adams, 1887.

Mackesy, Piers. *Statesmen at War: The Strategy of Overthrow, 1798–1799.* London: Longmans, 1974.

———. *The War in the Mediterranean, 1803–1810.* New York: Longmans, Green, 1957.

Madelin, Louis. *Histoire du consulat et de l'empire.* Vol. 8. Paris: Librairie Hachette, 1945.

Marcus, G. J. *The Age of Nelson The Royal Navy 1793–1815.* New York: Viking Press, 1971.

Martel, A.L.R., Comte de. *Walkeren, d'après les documents inédits.* Paris: E. Dentu, 1883.

McGuffie, T. H. "The Walcheren Expedition and the Walcheren Fever." *English Historical Review* 62 (1947): 191–202.

Nabonne, Bernard. *Bernadotte.* Paris: La Nouvelle Edition, 1946.

Napier, William. *History of the War in the Peninsula and in the South of France From the Year 1807 to the Year 1814.* 6 vols. London: Frederick Warne, 1892.

Norie, J. W. *The Naval Gazetteer.* London: J. W. Norie, 1827.

O'Donnell, H., ed. *Historical Records of the Fourteenth Regiment.* Debonport: A. H. Swiss, 1893.

Oman, Charles W. C. *A History of the Peninsular War.* Vol. 1. Oxford: Clarendon Press, 1902.

Parker, Harry. *Naval Battles.* London: T. H. Parker, 1911.

Pingaud, Leonce. *Bernadotte, Napoléon et les Bourbons.* Paris: Plon-Nourrit, 1901.

Porter, Whitworth. *History of the Corps of Royal Engineers.* Vol. 1. London: Longman & Green, 1889.

Rose, John H. *The Life of Napoleon I.* Vols. 1 and 2. New York: Brace, 1924.

Sherwig, John M. *Guineas and Gunpowder; British Foreign Aid in the Wars with France 1793–1815.* Cambridge, Mass.: Harvard University Press, 1969.

Six, Georges. *Dictionnaire biographique des généraux et amiraux Français de la Révolution et de l'Empire.* 2 vols. Paris: G. Saffroy, 1934.

Sloane, William M. *Life of Napoleon Bonaparte.* Vol. 3. New York: Century, 1896.

Sorel, Albert. *L'Europe et la révolution française.* Vol. 7. Paris: Plon-Nourrit, 1907.

Thomazi, Auguste. *Napoléon et ses marins.* Paris: Editions Berger-Levrault, 1950.

Waite, Richard A., Jr. "Sir Home Riggs Popham, Rear Admiral of the Red Squadron." Ph.D. diss., Harvard, 1942.

Walpole, Spencer. *The Life of the Right Honourable Spencer Perceval.* Vol. 2. London: Hurst & Blackett, 1874.

Watson, John Steven. *The Reign of George III, 1760–1815.* Oxford: Clarendon Press, 1960.

Wheater, W. A. *Record of the Services of the Fifty-first, the King's Own Light Infantry Regiment.* London: Longmans & Green, 1870.

Whyte, Frederick, and Atteridge, A. Hilliard. *A History of the Queen's Bays, the Second Dragoon Guards, 1685–1929.* London: Jonathan Cape, 1930.

Wilberforce, Robert Isaac, and Wilberforce, Samuel. *The Life of William Wilberforce.* Vol. 3. London: John Murray, 1838.

Yarrow, David. "A Journal of the Walcheren Expedition, 1809." *The Mariner's Mirror* 61 (1975): 183–89.

Index